INTERPRETING
QUALITATIVE DATA

INTERPRETING QUALITATIVE DATA

Methods for Analysing Talk, Text and Interaction

David Silverman

SAGE Publications
London • Thousand Oaks • New Delhi

SAGE Publications Ltd
6 Bonhill Street
London EC2A 4PU

SAGE Publications Inc
2455 Teller Road
Thousand Oaks, California 91320

SAGE Publications India Pvt Ltd
32, M-Block Market
Greater Kailash – I
New Delhi 110 048

British Library Cataloguing in Publication data

Silverman, David
 Interpreting Qualitative Data: Methods
 for Analysing Talk, Text and Interaction
 I. Title
 301.072

 ISBN 0–8039–8757–9
 ISBN 0–8039–8758–7 (pbk)

Library of Congress catalog card number 93–085497

Typeset by Photoprint, Torquay, Devon
Printed in Great Britain by The Cromwell Press Ltd,
Broughton Gifford, Melksham, Wiltshire

Contents

Preface and Acknowledgments

This is my second text on qualitative methodology. In 1985, when *Qualitative Methodology and Sociology* was published, I sought to address three themes:

1 The need to avoid making a choice between many of the polarities current in theory and methodology (e.g. structure or meaning, macro or micro, quantity or quality).
2 Contrary to the impression that such eclectism may create, the need to reject the assumption that, in qualitative research, 'anything goes'. So, for instance, the issue of the 'validity' or accuracy of our descriptions is vitally important, whether our methods are qualitative or quantitative.
3 The issue of the practical applicability of research has only arisen for some more theoretically oriented researchers as a result of competition for scarce research funds. In 1985, I argued that such issues need to be taken far more seriously. However, I had little time for forms of intervention which end up by imposing social 'experts' on the population, or by 're-educating the public'. Rather than being a legislator for change, I saw the researcher as someone who facilitates changes which mobilise the innovatory capacity of people.

Eight years later, I have not changed my views on these three matters. In the 1990s, just like the 1980s, false polarities and descriptions of dubious validity are still all too common. Moreover, qualitative researchers have still had limited success in convincing policy-makers of the relevance of their findings.

Like my earlier text, this present book is not a 'cookbook': it does not discuss in detail many of the practical issues involved in the research process (e.g. how to obtain access, how to present oneself to research subjects). As then, I still believe that some of these issues can only be settled by practical experience. Others involve concealed analytic issues (e.g. about the character of observation) which are discussed in this book.

As in 1985, I also develop my presentation through many detailed examples of qualitative research studies. As then, I still believe that there is little to be gained by rote learning about the advantages and disadvantages of various approaches or methods.

Mick Bloor has put this point very clearly:

> It seems something of a commonplace among research sociologists that texts on methodology are only of very limited utility in study design, certainly they

contain no templates which can be applied unproblematically for the resolution of particular research problems . . . the methodological writings which most sociological researchers seem to find most useful tend to be those which are grounded in particular research projects rather than general surveys of methodological techniques. (Bloor 1978, 545)

What, then, are the reasons for this new book? What does it seek to offer which is any different from what I had to say in 1985?

The first difference is structural. As I said at the time, the 1985 book was rather more concerned with strategy than with tactics. I felt that a lot of deadwood needed to be cleared away and this meant that I spent quite a bit of time on fairly abstract, theoretical issues. Although, following Bloor, I used many concrete examples from research studies, the overall approach was, I now feel, too compatible with a fairly passive learning experience.

However, there are better examples to choose from. In Ancient Greece, Socrates encouraged understanding by asking his students pointed questions. Much more recently, another philosopher, Ludwig Wittgenstein, filled his book *Philosophical Investigations* (1968), with hundreds of provocative questions. Interestingly enough, a period teaching in an elementary school had shown him how real learning often comes by working through particular examples.

The point has not been lost in distance-learning programmes (like those at the British Open University). Learning through doing is a wonderful way of appropriating knowledge and turning it into useful skills. Thus, in the central six chapters of this book, I provide many exercises, linked to the surrounding text.

These exercises involve the reader in gathering and/or analysing data. My aim is that the users of this book will learn some basic skills in generating researchable problems and analysing qualitative data. As I have confirmed through using these materials for assessment on an undergraduate course, the exercises also give students an ability to show the skills of their craft in a way that is not usually possible in the confines of a usual examination method.

However, although this structural feature is the most noticeable departure of the present book, it also has another aspect that I should remark on.

Any textbook writer has two options. The first option is to write a general survey of the field, covering the territory in a fairly dispassionate manner. This has the advantage of conveying to the student many competing positions without imposing the author's own view.

The second option is to structure the book around a central argument. This is likely to produce a more lively and integrated text – but at the cost of fairness and range.

On the whole, I have chosen the second option. The book has, I hope, a clear argument. However, as I trust will become clear, this argument is advanced without succumbing to two vices:

– assuming that there are particular 'right' or 'wrong' models of society or methodologies

– taking sides on the many spurious polarities which still bedevil much of social science (e.g. quality vs. quantity, structure vs. meaning, macro vs. micro).

Yet this only tells you what I am *not* doing. What, then, is my argument?

What I have to say stems from my discomfort with a fairly large proportion of the 'qualitative' research to be found in the leading contemporary academic journals. This discomfort arises from four related tendencies which, in the context of this Preface, I can only list without giving any evidence (more detail is provided in Silverman: 1989a):

1 A failure of analytic nerve in that the issues of theory-building are, at best, addressed only in the first few lines of an article, while the remainder reads like Mills' 'abstracted empiricism'. This is often allied to a stress on the 'exploratory' nature of the research undertaken as opposed to the attempt to test hypotheses deriving from the increasing body of empirical knowledge and analytical approaches.
2 The attempt to identify qualitative research with 'open-ended', 'informal' interviews. Unlike quantitative researchers, it sometimes seems, our aim is to 'empathise' with people and to turn ourselves into mirrors of other people's 'experiences'.
3 The use of data-extracts which support the researcher's argument, without any proof that contrary evidence has been reviewed. Alternatively, the attempt to downplay such issues of validity and reliability in research (as either inappropriate or politically incorrect) and to replace them with other criteria like the 'authenticity' with which we have reproduced 'experience'.
4 A belief that a particular, partisan moral or political position determines how we analyse data and what constitutes a 'good' piece of research.

As opposed to each of these arguments, I propose the following. First, social theory is not an 'add-on' extra but is the animating basis of social research. Second, while 'open-ended' interviews can be useful, we need to justify departing from the naturally occurring data that surrounds us and to be cautious about the 'romantic' impulse which identifies 'experience' with 'authenticity' (see Silverman: 1989b and Chapter 1, below).

Third, I insist on the relevance of issues of validity and reliability to field research: we cannot be satisfied merely with what I have called elsewhere (Silverman: 1989a) 'telling convincing stories'. Contrary to the assumption of many social scientists, as well as funding bodies, generalisability need not be a problem in qualitative research.

Finally, I follow Max Weber (1946) in recognising the value positions that can arise in the choice of research topics and in discussion of the relevance of research findings. Nonetheless, I totally reject 'partisanship' as a basis for assessing research findings or even as a standard for determining for others what are the most appropriate topics for investigation. Unfortunately, I am not convinced that 'political correctness' (either of the radical left or the managerial right) does not enter into the decisions of some funding bodies and editorial boards.

None of this means that the reader should expect to find that this book contains a polemic. My central aim is to show the value of a range of methodologies in social research and to equip the reader with some of the skills necessary to apply these methodologies.

It is the *craft* of social research that this book sets to convey rather than the passive ability to regurgitate appropriate answers in methodology examinations. To take textbooks too seriously or, still worse, to cluster together in 'schools' of sociology advances neither our own thought nor its contribution to the community.

In this context, we would do well to recall the words of Wittgenstein, who in closing his *Tractatus Logico-Philosophicus* tells us:

> My propositions serve as elucidations in the following way: anyone who understands me eventually recognises them as nonsensical, when he has used them – as steps – to climb up beyond them (he must, so to speak, throw away the ladder after he has climbed up it). He must transcend these propositions, and then he will see the world aright. (Wittgenstein: 1971, 6.54)

It is my hope that, for many beginning researchers, this book may serve as something like Wittgenstein's ladder, providing an initial footing for readers to go off to do their own research – charting new territories rather than restating comfortable orthodoxies.

A number of friends have contributed to this book. Among those who have helped are: Carolyn Baker, Mick Bloor, Robert Dingwall, Barry Glassner, Jay Gubrium, Sally Hunt, David Lazar, Georgia Lepper, Anssi Peräkylä and Lindsay Prior. Grateful thanks are also due to my editor at Sage, Stephen Barr, and to Greer Rafferty at Goldsmiths'. Naturally, I alone am responsible for any errors or omissions contained in this book.

PART ONE

THEORY AND METHOD IN QUALITATIVE RESEARCH

1

Beginning Research

This is a text on qualitative methodology. However, any methodology only makes sense if we understand what the research process is all about. We will, therefore, begin this chapter by exploring the nature of social research.

In doing so, we will consider the following two issues:

1   How to generate a research problem.
2   The variety of qualitative methods.

At the outset, it helps to clarify our terms. In this chapter, we shall be discussing theories, hypotheses, methods and methodologies. In Table 1.1, I set out how each term will be used.

Table 1.1:   *Basic Concepts in Research*

Concept	Meaning	Relevance
Theory	A set of explanatory concepts	Usefulness
Hypothesis	A testable proposition	Validity
Methodology	A general approach to studying research topics	Usefulness
Method	A specific research technique	Good fit with theory, hypothesis and methodology

As we see from Table 1.1, theories provide a set of explanatory concepts. These concepts offer ways of looking at the world which are essential in defining a research problem. As we shall see shortly, without a theory, there is nothing to research. In social research, examples of such theories are *functionalism* (which looks at the functions of social institutions), *behaviourism* (which defines all behaviour in terms of 'stimulus' and 'response') and *symbolic interactionism* (which focusses on how we attach symbolic meanings to interpersonal relations).

So theories provide the impetus for research. As living entities, they are also developed and modified by good research. However, as used here, theories are never disproved but only found more or less useful.

This last feature distinguishes theories from hypotheses. Unlike theories, hypotheses are tested in research. Examples of hypotheses, considered later in this book, are:

- that how we receive advice is linked to how advice is given
- that responses to an illegal drug depend upon what one learns from others
- that voting in union elections is related to non-work links between union members.

As we shall see, a feature of many qualitative research studies is that there is no specific hypothesis at the outset but that hypotheses are produced (or induced) during the early stages of research. In any event, unlike theories, hypotheses can, and should, be tested. Therefore, we assess a hypothesis by its validity or truth.

A methodology is a general approach to studying a research topic. It establishes how one will go about studying any phenomenon. In social research, examples of methodologies are *positivism* (which seeks to discover laws using quantitative methods) and, of course, *qualitative methodology* (which is often concerned with inducing hypotheses from field research). Like theories, methodologies cannot be true or false, only more or less useful.

Finally, methods are specific research techniques. These include quantitative techniques, like statistical correlations, as well as techniques like observation, interviewing and audio-recording. Once again, in themselves, techniques are not true or false. They are more or less useful, depending on their fit with the theories and methodologies being used, the hypothesis being tested and/or the research topic that is selected. So, for instance, positivists will favour quantitative methods and interactionists often prefer to gather their data by observation. But, depending upon the hypothesis being tested, positivists may sometimes use qualitative methods – for instance in the exploratory stage of research. Equally, interactionists may sometimes use simple quantitative methods, particularly when they want to find an overall pattern in their data.

Having set out some basic concepts, we can now turn to the first issue to be discussed in this chapter.

Using Theory to Generate a Research Problem

After long experience in supervising research, at both undergraduate and graduate levels, I find that beginning researchers tend to make two basic errors. First, they fail to distinguish sufficiently between research problems and problems that are discussed in the world around us. The latter kind of problems, which I shall call 'social problems', are at the heart of political debates and fill the more serious newspapers. However, although social problems, like unemployment, homelessness and racism, are important, by themselves they cannot provide a researchable topic.

The second error to which I have referred is sometimes related to the first. It arises where apprentice researchers take on an impossibly large research problem. For instance, it is important to find the causes of a social problem like homelessness, but such a problem is beyond the scope of a single researcher with limited time and resources. Moreover, by defining the problem so widely, one is usually unable to say anything in great depth about it.

As I tell my students, your aim should be to say 'a lot about a little (problem)'. This means avoiding the temptation to say 'a little about a lot'. Indeed, the latter path can be something of a 'cop-out'. Precisely because the topic is so wide-ranging, one can flit from one aspect to another without being forced to refine and test each piece of analysis.

In this part of the chapter, I shall focus on the first of these errors – the tendency to choose social problems as research topics. However, in recommending solutions to this error, I shall imply how one can narrow down a research topic.

What Is a Problem?

One has only to open a newspaper or to watch the television news to be confronted by a host of social problems. As I write, the British news media are full of references to a 'wave' of crimes committed by children – from the theft of cars to the murder of old people and other children. There are also several stories about how doctors infected by HIV have continued to work and, by implication, have endangered their patients.

The stories have this in common: both assume some sort of moral decline in which families or schools fail to discipline children and in which physicians fail to take seriously their professional responsibilities. In turn, the way each story is told implies a solution: tightening up 'discipline' in order to combat the 'moral decline'.

However, before we can consider such a 'cure', we need to consider carefully the 'diagnosis'. Has juvenile crime increased or is the apparent increase a reflection of what counts as a 'good' story? Alternatively, might the increase be an artifact of what crimes get reported?

Again, how many health care professionals have actually infected their patients with HIV? I know of only one (disputed) case – a Florida dentist. Conversely, there is considerable evidence of patients infecting the medical staff who treat them. Moreover, why focus on HIV when other conditions like hepatitis B are far more infectious? Could it be that we hear so much about HIV because it is associated with 'stigmatised' groups?

However, apparent 'social' problems are not the only problems that may clamour for the attention of the researcher. Administrators and managers point to 'problems' in their organisations and may turn to social scientists for solutions.

It is tempting to allow such people to define a research problem – particularly as there is usually a fat research grant attached to it! However, we must first look at the terms which are being used to define the problem. For instance, many managers will define problems in their organisation as problems of 'communication'. The role of the researcher is then to work out how people can communicate 'better'.

Unfortunately, talking about 'communication problems' raises many difficulties. For instance, it may deflect attention from the communication 'skills' inevitably used in interaction. It may also tend to assume that the solution to any problem is more careful listening, while ignoring power relations present inside and outside patterns of communication. Such relations may also make the characterisation of 'organisational efficiency' very problematic. Thus 'administrative' problems give no more secure basis for social research than do 'social' problems.

Of course, this is not to deny that there are any real problems in society. However, even if we agree about what these problems are, it is not clear that they provide a researchable topic, particularly for the apprentice researcher.

Take the case of the problems of people infected with HIV. Some of these problems are, quite rightly, brought to the attention of the public by the organised activities of groups of people who carry the infection. What social researchers can contribute are the particular theoretical and method-ological skills of their discipline. So economists can research how limited health care resources can be used most effectively in coping with the epidemic in the West and in the Third World. Among sociologists, survey researchers can investigate patterns of sexual behaviour in order to try to promote effective health education, while qualitative methods may be used to study what is involved in the 'negotiation' of safer sex or in counselling people about HIV and AIDS.

The Trap of Absolutism

At last, by showing what social research *can* do, we seem to be hitting a positive note. However, there is one further trap which lies in our path when we are trying to define a research problem. What I call the 'absolutist' trap arises in the temptation to accept uncritically the conven-tional wisdoms of our day. Let me list the four such 'wisdoms' I will be considering:

- 'scientism'
- 'progress'
- 'tourism'
- 'romanticism'.

The first two issues mainly relate to quantitative social scientists; the last two are more of a problem for qualitative researchers.

Scientism: This involves uncritically accepting that 'science' is both highly distinct from, and superior to, 'common sense'. For instance, the quantitative researcher might study the relationship between the 'efficiency' of an organisation and its management 'structure'. The aim might be to get a more reliable and valid picture than we might get from 'common sense'.

However, what is 'efficient' and what is the management 'structure' cannot be separated from what the participants in the organisation do themselves. So, 'efficiency' and 'structure' are not stable realities but are defined and redefined in different organisational contexts (e.g. internal meetings, labour–management negotiations, press releases, etc.). Moreover, the researchers themselves will, inevitably, use their common-sense knowledge of how organisations operate in order to define and measure these 'variables' (see Cicourel: 1968, Silverman: 1975a).

This is *not* to say that there is no difference between 'science' and 'common sense'. Of course, social science needs to study how 'common sense' works in a way which 'common sense' would not and could not follow for itself. In doing so, however, it will inevitably draw upon common-sense knowledge. Scientism's mistake is to position itself entirely apart from, and superior to, 'common sense'.

Progress: In the nineteenth century, scientists believed they could detect a path leading towards 'progress' in history (e.g. Darwin on 'the origin of species', Marx on the inevitability of the demise of 'regressive' economic systems). This belief was maintained, with some modifications after the experiences of the two world wars, well into the twentieth century.

However, an uncritical belief in 'progress' is an unacceptable basis for scientific research. For instance, it is dangerous to assume that we can identify social progress when doctors listen more to their patients (Silverman: 1987, Ch. 8), when prison inmates are offered parole or when all of us feel freer to discuss our sexuality (Foucault: 1977, 1979). In each case, if we assume 'progress', then we may fail to identify the 'double-binds' of any method of communication and/or new forms of power.

Both 'scientism' and a commitment to 'progress' have had most impact on quantitative researchers. I now turn to two traps that have had a more direct influence on qualitative research.

Tourism: I have in mind the 'up-market' tourist who travels the world in search of encounters with alien cultures. Disdaining package tours and even the label of 'tourist', such a person has an insatiable thirst for the 'new' and 'different'.

The problem is that there are worrying parallels between the qualitative researcher and this kind of tourist. Such researchers often begin without a hypothesis and, like the tourist, gaze rapaciously at social scenes for signs of activities that appear to be new and different.

The danger in all this is that 'touristic' researchers may so focus on cultural and 'sub-cultural' (or group) differences that they fail to recognise similarities between the culture to which they belong and the cultures which they study. As Moerman (1974) noted in his study of a tribe in Thailand, once you switch away from asking 'leading' questions (which assume cultural differences) to observation of what people actually are doing, then you may find certain *common* features between social patterns in the West and East (see Chapter 9, pp. 196–197).

Romanticism: Just as the nineteenth century was the age of 'progress', so it was the time in which people expected that literature, art and music would express the inner world of the artist and engage the emotions of the audience. This movement was called 'romanticism'.

As I later argue, there is a hint of this romanticism in some contemporary qualitative research (Chapter 9, pp. 197–210). This particularly applies where the researcher sets out to record faithfully the 'experiences' of some, usually disadvantaged, group (e.g. battered women, gay men, the unemployed, etc.).

As I later suggest, the romantic approach is appealing but dangerous. It may neglect how 'experience' is shaped by cultural forms of representation. For instance, what we think is most personal to us ('guilt', 'responsibility') may be simply a culturally given way of understanding the world (see my discussion of the mother of a young diabetic person in Chapter 6, pp. 121–122). So it is problematic to justify research in terms of its 'authentic' representation of 'experience' when what is 'authentic' is culturally defined.

This argument has implications for analysing interview data which I touch upon below. For the moment, I will conclude this section on generating a research problem by examining how different kinds of sensitivity can provide a solution to the twin traps of 'absolutism' and sliding into societal versions of 'social problems'.

Sensitivity and Researchable Problems

The various perspectives of social science provide a sensitivity to many issues neglected by those who define 'social' or administrative 'problems'. At the same time, it is possible to define and study any given research topic without falling into the 'absolutist' trap.

Let me distinguish four types of sensitivity:

- historical
- cultural
- political
- contextual.

I will explain and discuss each of these in turn.

Historical sensitivity: I have already implied how we can use this kind of sensitivity by looking critically at assumptions of 'progress' in society. This means that, wherever possible, we should examine the relevant historical evidence when we are setting up a topic to research. For instance, in the 1950s and 1960s it was assumed that the 'nuclear family' (parents and children) had replaced the 'extended family' (many generations living together in the same household) of pre-industrial societies. Researchers simply seemed to have forgotten that lower life-expectancy may have made the 'extended family' pattern relatively rare in the past.

Again, historical sensitivity helps us to understand how we are governed. For instance, until the eighteenth century, the majority of the population were treated as a threatening 'mob' to be controlled, where necessary, by the use of force. Today, we are seen as individuals with 'needs' and 'rights' which must be understood and protected by society (see Foucault: 1977). But, although oppressive force may be used only rarely, we may be controlled in more subtle ways. Think of the knowledge about each of us contained in computerised data-banks and the pervasive video-cameras which record movements in many city streets. Historical sensitivity thus offers us multiple research topics which evade the 'absolutist' trap.

Cultural sensitivity: This form of sensitivity is a healthy antidote to the 'romantic' impulse. The latter impulse directs our attention to the unique experiences of individuals. Cultural sensitivity reveals how such experiences are shaped by given forms of representation.

For instance, in a study to which I shall return in greater detail (Chapter 4, pp. 73–75), Propp (1968) shows how all narratives may have a common structure deriving from the fairy story. Equally, Baruch (1982) reveals how mothers of handicapped children tell stories which appeal to their 'responsibility' in the face of adversity (Chapter 5, pp. 108–114). In both cases, we are provided with a way of turning our studies of texts or interviews into highly researchable topics.

Political sensitivity: Allowing the current media 'scares' to determine our research topics is just as fallible as designing research in accordance with administrative or managerial interests. In neither case do we use political sensitivity to detect the vested interests behind this way of formulating a problem. The media, after all, need to attract an audience. Administrators need to be seen to be working efficiently.

So political sensitivity seeks to grasp the politics behind defining topics in particular ways. In turn, it helps in suggesting that we research how 'social problems' arise. For instance, Barbara Nelson (1984) looked at how 'child abuse' became defined as a recognisable problem in the late 1960s. She shows how the findings of a doctor about 'the battered baby syndrome' were adopted by the conservative Nixon administration through linking social problems to parental 'maladjustment' rather than to the failures of social programmes.

Political sensitivity does not mean that social scientists argue that there are no 'real' problems in society. Instead, it suggests that social science can make an important contribution to society by querying how 'official' definitions of problems arise. To be truthful, however, we should also recognise how social scientists often need to accept tacitly such definitions in order to attract research grants.

Contextual sensitivity: This is the least self-explanatory and most contentious category in the present list. By 'contextual' sensitivity, I mean two things: (a) the recognition that apparently uniform institutions like 'the family', 'a tribe' or 'science' take on a variety of meanings in different contexts; (b) the understanding that participants in social life actively produce a context for what they do and that social researchers should not simply import their own assumptions about what context is relevant in any situation.

Point (a) above is reflected most obviously in Gubrium's (1992) work on the family and Gilbert and Mulkay's (1983) study of scientists (see Chapter 3, pp. 56–58, and Chapter 9, pp. 200–202). In both cases, fruitful research topics are suggested in regard to how apparently unitary institutions assume a variable meaning according to the participants' practical purposes (e.g. social workers or lawyers discussing 'family life'; scientists discussing science in published papers or in casual conversation).

Point (b) implies that we must carefully inspect what people do and say to see how, if at all, participants organise their activities in terms of particular categories or institutions (see Schegloff: 1991). Once again, it is highly suggestive in generating possible research topics. For instance, it suggests that we reformulate questions about the *impact* of context on behaviour into questions about how participants actively produce contexts for what they are doing together.

Both points are contentious because so much social science, like common sense, takes for granted the existence of stable institutions ('the family') and identities (gender, ethnicity etc.). This is most clearly seen in quantitative studies which correlate identity-based variables (e.g. the relationship between gender and occupation). However, it is also present in qualitative studies that demand that we interpret their observations in terms of assumed social contexts.

One final point in this section. The four kinds of sensitivity we have been considering offer different, sometimes contradictory, ways of generating research topics. I am not suggesting that all should be used at the beginning of any research study. However, if we are not sensitive to *any* of these issues, then we run the danger of lapsing into a 'social-problem'-based way of defining our research topics.

The Variety of Qualitative Methods

There are four major methods used by qualitative researchers:

Observation
Analysing texts and documents

Interviews
Recording and transcribing.

These methods are often combined. For instance, **many case-studies** combine observation with interviewing. Moreover, each method can be used in either qualitative or quantitative research studies. As Table 1.2 shows, the overall nature of the research methodology shapes how each method is used.

Table 1.2: *Different Uses for Four Methods*

Method	Methodology	
	Quantitative research	Qualitative research
Observation	Preliminary work, e.g. prior to framing questionnaire	Fundamental to understanding another culture
Textual analysis	Content analysis, i.e. counting in terms of researchers' categories	Understanding participants' categories
Interviews	'Survey research': mainly fixed-choice questions to random samples	'Open-ended' questions to small samples
Transcripts	Used infrequently to check the accuracy of interview records	Used to understand how participants organise their talk

Table 1.2 underlines the point made in Table 1.1: methods are techniques which take on a specific meaning according to the methodology in which they are used.

So, in quantitative research, observation is not generally seen as a very important method of data collection. This is because it is difficult to conduct observational studies on large samples. Quantitative researchers also argue that observation is not a very 'reliable' data-collection method because different observers may record different observations. If used at all, observation is held to be only appropriate at a preliminary or 'exploratory' stage of research.

Conversely, observational studies have been fundamental to much qualitative research. Beginning with the pioneering case-studies of non-Western societies by early anthropologists (Malinowski: 1922, Radcliffe-Brown: 1948) and continuing with the work by sociologists in Chicago prior to the Second World War (Thomas and Znaniecki: 1927), the observational method has often been the chosen method to understand another culture.

These contrasts are also apparent in the treatment of texts and documents. Quantitative researchers try to analyse written material in a way which will produce reliable evidence about a large sample. Their favoured method is 'content analysis' in which the researchers establish a set of categories and then count the number of instances that fall into each category. The crucial requirement is that the categories are sufficiently precise to enable different coders to arrive at the same results when the same body of material (e.g. newspaper headlines) are examined (see Berelson: 1952).

In qualitative research, small numbers of texts and documents may be analysed for a very different purpose. The aim is to understand the participants' categories and to see how these are used in concrete activities like telling stories (Propp: 1968, Sacks: 1974), assembling files (Cicourel: 1968, Gubrium and Buckholdt: 1982) or describing 'family life' (Gubrium: 1992). The reliability of the analysis is less frequently addressed. Instead, qualitative researchers make claims about their ability to reveal the local practices through which given 'end-products' (stories, files, descriptions) are assembled.

Interviews are commonly used in both methodologies. Quantitative researchers administer interviews or questionnaires to random samples of the population; this is referred to as 'survey research'. 'Fixed-choice' questions (e.g. 'yes' or 'no') are usually preferred because the answers they produce lend themselves to simple tabulation, unlike 'open-ended' questions which produce answers which need to be subsequently coded. A central methodological issue for quantitative researchers is the reliability of the interview schedule and the representativeness of the sample.

For instance, after surveys of voting intention did not coincide with the result of the British General Election of 1992, survey researchers looked again at their methodology. Assuming that some respondents in the past may have lied to interviewers about their voting intentions, some companies now provide a ballot box into which respondents put mock ballot slips – thereby eliminating the need to reveal one's preferences to the interviewer. Attention is also being given to assembling a more representative sample to interview, bearing in mind the expense of a completely random sample of the whole British population.

'Authenticity' rather than reliability is often the issue in qualitative research. The aim is usually to gather an 'authentic' understanding of people's experiences and it is believed that 'open-ended' questions are the most effective route towards this end. So, for instance, in gathering life histories or in interviewing parents of handicapped children (Baruch: 1982), people may simply be asked: 'tell me your story'. Qualitative interview studies are often conducted with small samples and the interviewer–interviewee relationship may be defined in political rather than scientific terms (e.g Finch: 1984).

Finally, transcripts of audio-recordings are rarely used in quantitative research, probably because of the assumption that they are difficult to quantify. Conversely, as we shall see (Chapter 6), audio-recordings are an increasingly important part of qualitative research. Transcripts of such recordings, based on standardised conventions, provide an excellent record of 'naturally occurring' interaction. Compared to fieldnotes of observational data, recordings and transcripts can offer a highly reliable record to which researchers can return as they develop new hypotheses.

This rather abstract presentation can now be made more concrete by examining a number of qualitative studies using each method. I will take the example of research on social aspects of AIDS because it is a highly discussed, contemporary topic and an area in which I have worked. For each study presented, I will show how different theoretical and methodological imperatives shaped the choice and use of the method concerned.

Observation

In 1987, I began sitting in at a weekly clinic held at the Genito-Urinary Department of an English inner-city hospital (Silverman: 1989c). The clinic's purpose was to monitor the progress of HIV-positive patients who were taking the drug AZT (Retrovir). AZT then seemed able to slow down the rate at which the virus reproduces itself.

Like any observational study, the aim was to gather first-hand information about social processes in a 'naturally occurring' context. No attempt was made to interview the individuals concerned because the focus was upon what they actually did in the clinic rather than upon what they thought about what they did. The researcher was present in the consulting-room at a side-angle to both doctors and patient.

Patients' consent for the researcher's presence was obtained by the senior doctor. Given the presumed sensitivity of the occasion, tape-recording was not attempted. Instead, detailed handwritten notes were kept, using a separate sheet for each consultation.

The sample was small (fifteen male patients seen in thirty-seven consultations over seven clinic sessions) and no claims were made about its representativeness. Because observational methods were rare in this area, the study was essentially exploratory. However, as we shall see, an attempt was made to link the findings to other social research about doctor–patient relations.

As Sontag (1979) has noted, illness is often taken as a moral or psychological metaphor. The major finding of the study was the moral baggage attached to being HIV-positive. For instance, many patients used a buzzer to remind them to take their medication during the night. As one commented (P = Patient):

P: It's a dead giveaway. Everybody knows what you've got.

However, despite the social climate in which HIV infection is viewed, there was considerable variation in how people presented themselves to the medical team. Four styles of 'self-presentation' (Goffman: 1959) were identified. Each style is briefly noted below:

'*Cool*': Here even worrying medical statements were treated with an air of politeness and acceptance rather than concern or apparent anxiety. For example, one patient generally answered all questions in monosyllables.

His only sustained intervention was when he asked about the name of a doctor he would be seeing at another hospital for his skin infection. He made no comment when a doctor observed that AZT was keeping him alive.

'Anxiety':   At the other extreme, some patients treated even apparent greetings as an oppotunity to display 'anxiety'. For instance:

> Dr: How are you?
> P: Heh. Pretty weak. Something I can't put my finger on. Not right. Don't know.

'Objective':   As has been noted in other studies (see Baruch: 1982, discussed in Chapter 5, pp. 108–114), health professionals commonly present themselves to doctors as bundles of objective symptoms. One such professional, who was a patient in this clinic, behaved in exactly this way. For instance:

> P: I was wondering whether Acyclovir in connection with the AZT might cause neutropenia . . . (describing his herpes symptoms). It was interesting. So you'd suggest it four times a day. Because normally they recommend five times a day.

'Theatrical':   One way of responding to questions about one's physical condition was to downplay them in order to make observations about social situations, acknowledging the listening audience. For instance:

> Dr: How are you feeling physically?
> P: Fine. The other thing was . . . (account of doctor who didn't wave to him in the street). He's just a bloody quack like you. No offence.
> [to researcher and medical student]
> I'm a bad case by the way so don't take no notice of me.

Three important points need to be made about this discussion. First, there was no simple correspondence between each patient and a particular 'style' of self-presentation. Rather, each way of presenting oneself was available to each patient within any one consultation, where it might have a particular social function. So the focus was on social processes rather than on psychological states. Second, I have only been to able to offer brief extracts to support my argument. As we shall see in Chapter 7, such use of evidence has led to doubts about the validity or accuracy of qualitative research.

My third point is that these findings reflect only part of the study. We also discovered how the ethos of 'positive thinking' was central to many patients' accounts and how doctors systematically concentrated on the 'bodies' rather than the 'minds' of their patients – we get a sense of this in the extract immediately above where the patient resists an attempt by the doctor to get him to talk more about his physical condition. This led on to some practical questions about the division of labour between doctors and counsellors.

Textual Analysis

Kitzinger and Miller (1992) have looked at the relation between media reporting of AIDS and the audience's understanding. Their analysis of British television news bulletins provides a good example of how textual analysis may be used in qualitative research on social aspects of AIDS. It also shows how qualitative researchers try to avoid questions deriving from 'social problem' perspectives, while recognising that phenomena are always socially defined. Kitzinger and Miller's concern with the social definition of phenomena is shown by the inverted commas they place around concepts like 'AIDS', 'Africa' and what is 'really' the case. As the authors explain:

> This chapter focusses on audiences and the role of the media in changing, reinforcing or contributing to ideas about AIDS, Africa and race. It does not argue that HIV either does or not originate in Africa . . . Here we are not directly addressing questions about where the virus 'really' came from or the actual distribution of infection. Instead we are focussing on how different *answers* to these questions are produced, framed and sustained, what these tell us about the construction of 'AIDS' and 'Africa' and what socio-political consequences they carry with them. (Kitzinger and Miller: 1992, 28, my emphasis)

Over three years of television news reports were examined. In one such report, statistics on HIV infection were given for the whole of Africa and a map of Africa was shown with the word 'AIDS' fixed across the continent. The map was also stamped with the words '3 Million Sufferers'.

In the three-year period, the only country to be distinguished as different from the rest of Africa was South Africa. Indeed, on one occasion, South Africa was described as 'holding the line' against an HIV invasion from black Africa. By contrast, images of black Africans with AIDS were used in all the news reports studied. Moreover, the spread of the epidemic was related to 'traditional sexual values' or, more generally, to 'African culture'.

To see how these media images impacted upon their audience, many discussion groups were established among people with particular occupations (e.g. nurses, police, teachers), perceived 'high involvement' in the issue (e.g. gay men, prisoners) and 'low involvement' (e.g. retired people, students).

Although members of all groups were sceptical about media coverage of news issues, they nonetheless accepted the general assumption that AIDS came from Africa and is prevalent there. White people usually began from the assumption that Africa is a hotbed of sexually transmitted diseases. This was based on the belief that sexual intercourse typically begins at an early age and that sexual diseases are spread through polygamy.

However, not all individuals shared these beliefs. Kitzinger and Miller refer to several factors which led people to doubt the media treatment. Among these were the following: personal contact with alternative information from trusted individuals or organisations, personal experience of being 'scapegoated', personal experience of conditions in Africa and being black yourself.

The authors conclude:

> Our research shows both the power of the media and the pervasiveness of stock white cultural images of black Africa; it is easy to believe that Africa is a reservoir of HIV infection because 'it fits'. Journalists draw on these cultural assumptions when they produce reports on AIDS and Africa. But, in so doing, they are helping to reproduce and legitimise them. (*ibid*, 49)

Kitzinger and Miller's study has a much bigger data-base than my study of one medical clinic. However, it shares two features in common. First, in both studies, the researchers began without a hypothesis. Instead, as in much qualitative research, they sought to induce and then test hypotheses during their data-analyses. Second, both studies were theoretically driven by the assumption that social phenomena derive their meaning from how they are defined by participants. Both these features are found in the remaining two studies we shall consider.

Interviews

Weatherburn *et al* (1992) note that many studies assert that there is an association between alcohol and drug 'misuse' and 'risky' sexual behaviour. Conversely, Weatherburn *et al* suggest the following: 'the link is asserted but not proven; that the evidence is at best contradictory and that this assertion is informed by a puritanical moral agenda' (119).

In their own research, we find two assumptions which are absent from these earlier, generally quantitative, research studies:

1 No assumption is made about a strong interrelation between alcohol use and engagement in unsafe sex.
2 Psychological traits (like defects of character or weakness of resolve under the influence of alcohol) are held to be an inadequate explanation of enduring unsafe sexual practices (*ibid*, 122–123).

Weatherburn *et al*'s research is part of Project SIGMA which is a British longitudinal study of a non-clinic-based cohort of over one thousand gay men. Like other qualitative researchers, they distrusted explanations of behaviour which reduced social life to a response to particular 'stimuli' or 'variables'. Consequently, they favoured 'open-ended' questions to try to understand the meanings attached to alcohol use by their sample. For instance:

> The first question asked respondents: 'Would you say alcohol plays a significant role in your sex life?' Those respondents who said 'yes' were probed in detail about its exact nature. Respondents were also asked whether alcohol had *ever* influenced them to engage in unsafe sexual behaviours. (*ibid*, 123)

Typically, in an open-ended interview study, respondents were encouraged to offer their own definitions of particular activities, 'unsafe sex' for example.

The findings of the study reflect the complexity of the attempt to explain the 'causes' of social behaviour. The effects of alcohol were found to depend upon 'the context of the sexual encounter and the other party involved in the sexual negotiation' (129). Only in a minority of reports was alcohol treated as the 'cause' of unsafe behaviour. In the majority of cases, although people might report themselves as 'fairly drunk', they described their sexual activities as the outcome of conscious deliberation.

However, the authors raise a crucial issue about the meaning we should attach to such descriptions, given that people may recall those features that depict their behaviour as socially desirable: 'it is recognized that asking people retrospective questions about alcohol use may well be problematic, both because of social desirability phenomena and because alcohol itself impairs recall' (123).

As we shall see in Chapter 5, this observation goes to the heart of an unresolved debate about the status of interview accounts, namely are such accounts:

- true or false representations of such features as attitudes and behaviour?
- simply 'accounts', whose main interest lies in how they are constructed rather than their accuracy?

This interview study highlights the advantages of qualitative research in offering an apparently 'deeper' picture than the variable-based correlations of quantitative studies. However, it also implies why it can be difficult to get funding or acceptance for qualitative research. However questionable are the assumptions behind some quantitative research, it tends to deliver apparently reliable and valid correlations between 'variables' that appear to be self-evident. Moreover, these correlations usually lead in clear-cut policy directions.

However, some qualitative research can combine sensitivity to participants' definitions with correlations carrying direct policy implications. We shall see this in our final research study.

Transcripts

Silverman *et al*'s (1992) study was based on audio-tapes of HIV/AIDS counselling from ten different medical centres in Britain, the U.S.A. and Trinidad. The focus was on advice (both how advice was given and how it was received). The interest in advice derived from three sources:

1 The research was part-funded by the English Health Education Authority: this meant that analysis of advice sequences would be appropriate to its interest in health promotion.
2 Early work on the project had identified two basic 'communication

formats' through which such counselling was conducted; the analysis of 'information delivery' and interview formats provided a crucial resource for the analysis of how advice-giving worked (see Peräkylä and Silverman: 1991a).

3 A recent study by Heritage and Sefi (1992) of health visitors and mothers had provided important findings about the relationship between different forms of advice-giving and their uptake by the client.

As I show in Chapter 7 (p. 167), we were able to tabulate the relationship between the form in which advice was given and how it was received in fifty advice sequences. Broadly speaking, personalised advice, offered after clients had been asked to specify their concerns, was associated with a 'marked acknowledgment' (e.g. a comment on the advice or a further question from the client). Conversely, counsellors who gave generalised advice, without first getting their clients to specify a particular problem, generally received only 'unmarked acknowledgments' (e.g. 'mm', 'right', 'yes').

However, the availability of detailed transcripts meant that we could go beyond this predictable finding. In particular, we sought to address the functions of counsellors' behaviour – particularly given the fact that, if asked, many of them would have recognised that generalised advice-giving is likely to be ineffective. We hoped, thereby, to make a constructive input into policy debates by examining the *functions* of communication sequences in a particular institutional context.

Let us look at a relevant data extract. The transcription symbols are provided in Chapter 6, p. 118:

Extract 1.1
(C = Counsellor; P = Patient)

```
 1 C: .hhhh Now when someo:ne er is tested (.) and they
 2     ha:ve a negative test result .hh it's obviously
 3     idealuh:m that (.) they then look after themselves to
 4     prevent [any further risk of=
 5 P:          [Mm hm
 6 C: =infection. .hhhh I mean obviously this is only
 7     possible up to a point because if .hhh you get into
 8     a sort of serious relationship with someone that's
 9     long ter:m .hh you can't obviously continue to use
10     condoms forever. .hh Uh:m and a point has to come
11     where you make a sort of decision (.4) uh:m if you
12     are settling down about families and things that you
13     know (.6) you'd- not to continue safer sex.
14     [.hhhh Uh:m but obviously: (1.0) you=
15 P: [Mm:
16 C: =nee:d to be (.) uh:m (.) take precautions uhm (0.3)
17     and keep to the safer practices .hhh if: obviously
18     you want to prevent infection in the future.
19 P: [Mm hm
20 C: [.hhhh The problem at the moment is we've got it
21     here in {names City} in particular (.) right across
```

22   the boar:d you know from all walks of life.
23 P: Mm hm
24 C: Uh::m from you know (.) the sort of established high
25   r- risk groups (.) now we're getting heterosexual
26   (.) [transmission as well. .hh Uhm=
27 P: [Mm hm
28 C: =so obviously everyone really needs to careful. .hhh
29   Now whe- when someone gets a *positive* test result
30   er: then obviously they're going to ke- think very
31   carefully about things. .hhhh *B*eing HIV positive
32   doesn't necessarily mean that that person is going
33   to develop ai:ds (.) later on.
34   (.)
35 P: Mm hm

We can make three observations about this extract. First, C delivers advice without having elicited from P a perceived problem. Reasons of space do not allow us to include what immediately precedes this extract but it involves another topic (the meaning of a positive test result) and no attempt is made to question P about his possible response to this topic, i.e. how he might change his behaviour after a negative test result. Moreover, within this extract, C introduces fresh topics (what to do in a 'serious' relationship in lines 6–13; the spread of HIV in the city in lines 20–22) without attempting to elicit P's own perspectives.

Second, predictably, P only produces variations on 'mm hmm' in response to C's advice. While these may indicate that P is listening, they do not show P uptake and might be taken as a sign of passive resistance to the advice (see Heritage and Sefi: 1992).

Third, C does not personalise her advice. Instead of using a personal pronoun or the patient's name, she refers to 'someone' and 'they' (lines 1–4) and 'everyone' (line 28).

Advice sequences like these are very common at three out of the five counselling centres we have examined. So we have to ask ourselves why counsellors should use a format which is likely to generate so little patient uptake. Since our preference was not to criticise professionals but to understand the logic of their work, we need to look at the *functions* as well as the dysfunctions of this way of proceeding.

A part of the answer seems to lie in the content of the advice given. Note how in Extract 1.1 the counsellor is giving advice about what she tells patients *after* a particular test result. But the patient here does not yet have his result – indeed he has not yet even consented to the test. This leaves it open to the patient to treat what he is being told not as advice but as information delivery (about the advice C would give if P turned out to be seropositive or seronegative). Moreover, throughout C avoids personalising her advice. Rather than saying what she advises P to do, she uses the non-specific term 'someone'.

All the available research suggest that behaviour change rarely occurs on the basis of information alone. Why, therefore, would counsellors want to package their advice in a way which makes patient uptake less likely?

A part of the answer to this question lies in the *dysfunctions* of recipient-designed advice. Throughout our corpus of interviews, counsellors exit quickly from *personalised* advice when patients offer only minimal responses like 'mm mm's. It seems that, if someone is giving you personalised advice, if you don't show more uptake than 'mm mm', this will be problematic to the advice-giver. Conversely, if you are merely giving somebody general information, then occasional 'mm mm's are all that is required for the speaker to continue in this format. Moreover, truncated, non-personalised advice sequences are also usually far shorter – an important consideration for hard-pressed counsellors.

Another function of offering advice in this way is that it neatly handles many of the issues of delicacy that can arise in discussing sexual behaviour. First, the counsellor can be heard as making reference to what she tells 'anyone' so that this particular patient need not feel singled out for attention about his private life. Second, because there is no step-by-step method of questioning, patients are not required to expand on their sexual practices with the kinds of hesitations we have found elsewhere in our research (Silverman and Peräkylä: 1990). Third, setting up advice sequences that can be heard as information delivery shields the counsellor from some of the interactional difficulties of appearing to tell strangers what they should be doing in the most intimate aspects of their behaviour. Finally, predictably, information-oriented counselling produces very little conflict. So in Extract 1.1, there is no *active* resistance from P. Indeed, topic follows topic with a remarkable degree of smoothness and at great speed.

So the character of HIV counselling as a focussed conversation on mostly delicate topics explains why truncated advice sequences (like that seen in Extract 1.1) predominate in our transcripts.

Clearly, such sequences are functional for *both* local and institutional contexts. This underlines the need to locate 'communication problems' in a broader structural context. Our research had much to say about how counsellors can organise their talk in order to maximise patient uptake. However, without organisational change, the impact of such communication techniques alone might be minimal or even harmful. For instance, encouraging patient uptake will usually involve longer counselling sessions. Experienced counsellors will tell you that, if they take so long with one client that the waiting period for others increases, some clients will simply walk out – and hence may continue their risky behaviour without learning their HIV-status.

Undoubtedly, then, there are gains for the counsellor in setting up advice-packages which are truncated and non-personalised. Obviously, however, there are concomitant losses of proceeding this way. As we have shown, such advice packages produce far less patient uptake and, therefore, their function in creating an environment in which people might re-examine their own sexual behaviour is distinctly problematic.

Two possible solutions suggest themselves from the data analysed by this study. First, avoiding necessarily 'delicate' and unstable advice sequences but encouraging patients to draw their own conclusions from a particular line of questioning. Second, since both this method and step-by-step advice-giving take considerable time, finding ways of making more time available for more effective counselling. I take up these matters in greater detail in Chapter 8.

Having set out four different qualitative methods, I want to make two general observations. First, as I have emphasised, no research method stands on its own. So far, I have sought to show the link between methods and methodologies in social research. However, there is a broader, societal context in which methods are located and deployed. As a crude example, texts depended upon the invention of the printing press or, in the case of television or audio-recordings, upon modern communication technologies.

Moreover, such activities as observation and interviewing are not unique to social researchers. For instance, as Foucault (1977) has noted, the observation of the prisoner has been at the heart of modern prison reform, while the method of questioning used in the interview reproduces many of the features of the Catholic confessional or the psycho-analytic consultation. Its pervasiveness is reflected by the centrality of the interview study in so much contemporary social research. In the two collections of papers from which the research studies above have been selected, for example, fourteen out of nineteen empirical studies are based on interview data. One possible reason for this may not derive from methodological considerations. Think, for instance, of how much interviews are a central (and popular) feature of mass media products, from 'talk shows' to 'celebrity' interviews. Perhaps, we all live in what might be called an 'interview society' in which interviews seem central to making sense of our lives.

All this means that we need to resist treating research methods as mere *techniques*. This is reflected in the attention paid in this book to the *analysis* of data rather than to methods of data-*collection*.

Conclusion

By focussing on the topics of HIV and AIDS, I have tried to show how four different research methods can be used in qualitative research. Despite the different kinds of data which they generate, they lead to a distinctive form of analysis which is centrally concerned with avoiding a 'social problem' perspective by asking how participants attach meaning to their activities and 'problems'.

Part Two of this book sets out each research method in greater detail and Part Three returns to issues of validity and relevance which are touched upon in this chapter. However, before we deal with these detailed issues, it will be helpful, in the light of the studies discussed here, to review what other writers have said about the distinctive properties of qualitative research. This is the topic of Chapter 2.

2
The Logic of Qualitative Methodology

In traditional, quantitatively oriented texts, qualitative research is often treated as a relatively minor methodology to be used, if at all, at early or exploratory stages of a study. Viewed from this perspective, qualitative research can be used to familiarise oneself with a setting before the serious sampling and counting begins.

This view is expressed in the extract below from an early text. Note how the authors refer to 'nonquantified data' – implying that quantitative data is the standard form:

> The inspection of *nonquantified* data may be particularly helpful if it is done periodically throughout a study rather than postponed to the end of the statistical analysis. Frequently, a single incident noted by a perceptive observer contains the clue to an understanding of a phenomenon. If the social scientist becomes aware of this implication at a moment when he can still add to his material or exploit further the data he has already collected, he may considerably enrich the quality of his conclusions. (Selltiz *et al*: 1964, 435, my emphasis)

Despite these authors' 'friendly' view of the uses of 'nonquantified' data, they assume that 'statistical analysis' is the bedrock of research.

A similar focus is to be found, a quarter of century later, in another mainly quantitative text: 'Field research is essentially a matter of immersing oneself in a naturally occurring . . . set of events in order to gain firsthand knowledge of the situation' (Singleton *et al*: 1988, 11).

Note the emphasis on 'immersion' and its implicit contrast with later, more focussed research. This is underlined in the authors' subsequent identification of qualitative or field research with 'exploration' and 'description' (296) and their approval of the use of field research 'when one knows relatively little about the subject under investigation' (298–299).

In turn, the critique of purely quantitative research has a long history beginning in the 1950s. C. Wright Mills (1953) criticises the atheoretical character of much quantitative research which he calls 'abstracted empiricism'. Blumer (1968) notes how the attempt to establish correlations between variables depends upon a lack of attention to how these variables are defined by the people being studied. Finally, Cicourel (1964), influenced by Schutz and Garfinkel, draws attention to how the choice of a purely mathematical logic can neglect the common-sense reasoning used by *both* participants and researchers.

Discussion of 'the theoretical basis' of research and what it is 'meaningful' to measure has been central to the debate about different research methodologies. So one way to discover what might be the distinctive character of qualitative research would be to explore different 'schools' of social science.

'Schools' of Social Science

Much play has been made distinguishing two 'schools' of social science (e.g. Halfpenny: 1979, Silverman: 1985, Bryman: 1988). These 'schools' are associated with very different versions of research: positivism (which seeks to test correlations between variables) and interpretive social science (which is more concerned with observation and description and, at best, generating hypotheses). This picture is set out in Table 2.1.

Table 2.1: *Two 'Schools' of Social Science*

Approach	Concepts	Methods
Positivism	Social structure, social facts	Quantitative hypothesis-testing
Interpretive social science	Social construction, meanings	Qualitative hypothesis-generation

In the 1970s, it was common to criticise what was called 'positivism' (see Filmer *et al*: 1972). However, it became increasingly clear that 'positivists' were made of straw since very few researchers could be found who equated the social and natural worlds or believed that research was properly theory-free. Nonetheless, a problem remained because purely quantitative researchers may neglect the social and cultural construction of the 'variables' which they seek to correlate. As Kirk and Miller (1986) argue, 'attitudes', for instance, do not simply attach to the inside of people's heads and researching them depends on making a whole series of analytical assumptions. They conclude:

> The survey researcher who discusses is not wrong to do so. Rather, the researcher is wrong if he or she fails to acknowledge the theoretical basis on which it is meaningful to make measurements of such entities and to do so with survey questions addressed to a probability sample of voters. (1986, 15)

As we shall see in later chapters, there is undoubtedly a tradition of interpretive social science with a set of different emphases to more quantitatively oriented work. Instead of attending to the social construction of meaning, positivist research is shown to use a set of *ad hoc* procedures to define, count and analyse its variables (Blumer: 1956, Cicourel: 1964, Silverman: 1975a). Understandably, most qualitative research has preferred, instead, to describe and illuminate the meaningful social world as prescribed by the interpretivist paradigm.

Unfortunately, these 'schools' have sometimes been defined as polar opposites. The first motive behind this chapter is to undermine the assumption that these two paradigms are incommensurable or, indeed, that they offer any worthwhile description of the major alternative directions of sociological research. This does *not* mean that I shall be arguing that positivism is *superior* to interpretivism.

All this means that one of the least fruitful questions one can ask a sociologist is: 'To what school of social science do you belong?' For instance, although it would be easy to interpret this book as a defence of 'qualitative methodology', this would be misleading. For, of course, there are no principled grounds to be either qualitative or quantitative in approach. It all depends upon what you are trying to do. Indeed, often one will want to combine both approaches. For instance, in Chapter 7 I discuss how we have tested a hypothesis by using simple tabulations on fifty-odd examples of HIV counselling 'advice packages' whose form can readily be identified and counted.

In this book, I will discuss the logic behind field research, while recognising its points of continuity, as well as difference, with more quantitative or 'positivistic' studies. The presentation follows in the tradition of many sociologists who have argued about the need to avoid reducing methodological issues to ones of technique (for instance, Mills: 1953, Cicourel: 1964).

Analytical issues are central to methodological discussion. The main question, at least in case-study research, is the quality of the analysis rather than the recruitment of the sample or, say, the format of the interview (see Mitchell: 1983).

Further, such analytical issues cannot be resolved by choosing sides from spurious polarities (e.g. structure and meaning; quality and quantity). For instance, it is sometimes maintained that, while positivists are concerned with 'society', interpretive social science focusses on the 'individual'. But rather than choose one side of this polarity, we might look at how the individual/society opposition is actually used in everyday life.

We can find a striking example of how we all rely on the distinction between 'objective' and 'subjective' realities in Sacks' (1992) account of children's socialisation. Sacks suggests that adults offer two kinds of rules to children: Class 1 rules – where, for adults, the consequences flow naturally from the act (e.g. 'don't stick your hand on the stove') Class 2 rules – where, unless your behaviour is seen and somebody does something, no negative consequences follow (e.g. 'honour thy father and mother', 'don't tell lies').

Sacks points out that children recurrently have to decide whether what they are dealing with is a Class 1 (or 'objective') rule or Class 2 ('subjective'). Hence they may experiment (e.g. stick their finger into an electrical point and see if they still get a shock even when nobody is around or tell lies to see if God notices and punishes them). Since parents may try to buttress the weaker Class 2 rules by appeals to the 'long-term' consequences of evading them, they may still seem very powerful and breaking them may mean the long term experience of guilt.

Sacks shows that participants search for underlying 'social structures' and try to understand the meaning of 'experiences'. What, then, is the status of social science research which itself chooses to focus on one or other of these realities?

However, it is easier to criticise than to define a coherent alternative. Qualitative research can cover a vast range of research styles and can even be co-opted back into the positivist tradition. For instance, in British market research circles, I gather that 'qualitative' research is the latest fashion. It is seen to provide 'in-depth' material which is believed to be absent from survey research data. Above all, it is relatively cheap. However, all that is meant by qualitative research is open-ended interviews or 'panel' studies lacking a clear, analytical basis in social theory.

The polarities around which the qualitative/quantitative distinction have been based need (to use the fashionable term) to be deconstructed. Why should we assume, for instance, that we have to choose between qualitative and quantitative methods? Why can we focus on only 'meanings' but not 'structure' or on 'micro' but not 'macro' processes? Why should case-study researchers assume that there is something intrinsically purer in 'naturally occurring' data? This was the point I developed in a recent text on methodology (Silverman: 1985). The new generation of social scientists, I feel, need to be rather less smug about the rectitude of their affirmed belief in a non-positivistic research programme. Programmes are no substitute for lateral thinking *and* rigour.

What Is Qualitative Research?

There is no standard approach among qualitative researchers. For instance, Marshall and Rossman (1989) list six different qualitative research traditions, including ethnography, cognitive anthropology and symbolic interactionism. These all share a commitment to naturally-occurring data: 'Each assumes that systematic inquiry must occur in a natural setting rather than an artificially constrained one such as an experiment' (10).

However, they recognise a wide variation between various approaches:

> the approaches vary, depending on how intrusive the researcher is required to be in the gathering of data, whether these data document nonverbal or verbal behaviour or both, whether it is appropriate to question the participants as to how they view their worlds, and how the data can be fruitfully analysed. (10–11)

Some years before, Burgess (1980, 1) had used a model drawn from just one of these approaches – social anthropology. He wrote: 'It would appear that field research involves observing and analysing real-life situations, of

studying actions and activities as they occur. The field researcher, therefore, relies upon learning firsthand about a people and a culture.'

More recently, Burgess' position is supported by Agar (1986), who
comments:

> The social research style that emphasises encountering alien worlds and making
> sense of them is called *ethnography*, or 'folk description'. Ethnographers set out
> to show how social action in one world makes sense from the point of view of
> another. (12)

Both Burgess and Agar do catch field researchers' preference for
naturally occurring data. But the links to anthropology are somewhat
tenuous in much contemporary field research. Moreover, Burgess' concentration on observation and interview methods and his exclusion of
audio-recording from his list of field research methods (1980, 2) are
somewhat problematic.

More recently, Bryman (1988) has attempted to characterise qualitative
research according to six criteria. These criteria are set out in Table 2.2.

Table 2.2:   *One Version of Qualitative Research*

1   'Seeing through the eyes of . . .' or taking the subject's perspective
2   Describing the mundane detail of everyday settings
3   Understanding actions and meanings in their social context
4   Emphasising time and process
5   Favouring open and relatively unstructured research designs
6   Avoiding concepts and theories at an early stage

Source: adapted from Bryman: 1988, 61–69

However, Bryman's characterisation of qualitative research runs up
against the difficulty of over-generalising a variety of different theoretical
and research orientations. This means that there are difficulties with some
of his criteria.

'Seeing through the eyes of' (criterion 1) involves a 'subjective' perspective which derives from anthropology's distinction between *etic* analysis
(using an imposed frame of reference) and *emic* analysis (working within
the conceptual framework of those studied) (see Fielding and Fielding:
1986, 21). This can involve a failure to analyse (thereby making the
researcher redundant) and ignores practices rather than perceptions. As
Bryman asserts: 'There can be little doubt that the commitment to
explicating the *subject's interpretation of social reality* is a (one might even
say *the*) sine qua non of qualitative research' (1988, 72, my emphasis).

Similarly, criteria 5 and 6 are out of tune with the greater sophistication
of contemporary field research design, born out of accumulated knowledge
of interaction and greater concern with issues of validity and reliability.

Hammersley (1990) offers a definition of ethnography rather than
'qualitative research'. Nonetheless, it shares some properties in common

Table 2.3:   *A Second Version of Qualitative Research*

1   The use of everyday contexts rather than experimental conditions
2   A range of sources of data collection (the main ones are observation and 'informal conversations')
3   A preference for 'unstructured' data collection (no prior hypotheses, no prior definitions)
4   A concern with the 'micro' features of social life ('a single setting or group')
5   A concern with the meaning and function of social action
6   The assumption that quantification plays a subordinate role

Source: adapted from Hammersley: 1990, 1–2

with Bryman's. It is set out in Table 2.3. Once again, the criteria used in Table 2.3 are problematic, as follows:

Criterion 1: Most non-ethnographic research does not use experimental research designs (e.g. the analysis of official statistics or the use of surveys); the experimental method is only typical in psychology.

Criterion 2: Non-ethnographic research also uses a range of sources; Hammersley ignores audio- and video-tapes, as well as official documents, as sources of ethnographic data.

Criterion 3: This may have been true in the past, but increasingly ethnography begins with prior hypotheses and/or prior definitions (e.g. Dingwall and Murray 1983, Silverman, 1984).

Criterion 4: This is generally true but qualitative research is increasingly comparative (Strong: 1979a, Silverman *et al*: 1992). Moreover, as we shall see in Chapter 8, such research can claim to tell us about 'macro' structures, using the analysis of 'micro' interaction as a first step.

Criterion 5: 'Meaning' is a term which is contested between different field researchers – for instance, feminist sociologists like Stanley and Wise (1983) would point to the gendered nature of meaning, while ethno-methodologists like Garfinkel (1967) would stress everyday practices rather than meanings. However, Hammersley rightly stresses that 'func-tion' should be central to the analysis of actions. This has been neglected until recently (see my discussion of the analysis of advice sequences in Chapter 1, pp. 16–19).

Criterion 6: This is generally true but there is an increasing use of tabulations in field research (see Chapter 7, pp. 162–169).

This leaves us with very little that is non-problematic from Table 2.3. We do not say very much about field research or ethnography if we say only that it tends to be small-scale and non-quantitative.

In a more recent work, Hammersley (1992a) underlines the problematic character of any attempt to distinguish the defining characteristics of ethnography. According to Hammersley, most definitions of ethnography turn 'on a critique of quantitative, notably survey and experimental, research' (11).

This should be an easier path since it is usually simpler to say what something is *not* than to define what it *is*. However, as Hammersley himself shows, each of the claims of advocates of 'qualitative research' turns out to be problematic. I will omit from Table 2.4 the philosophical issues that Hammersley raises (e.g. idealism vs. realism, nomothetic vs. idiographic approaches). However, unlike Tables 2.2 and 2.3, I will incorporate criticisms of each criterion.

Table 2.4: *A Third Version of Qualitative Research*

---

1 A preference for qualitative data – use of words rather than numbers. However, in principal, there is no reason to prefer any form of data:

> We are not faced, then, with a stark choice between words and numbers, or even between precise and imprecise data; but rather with a range from more to less precise data. Furthermore, our decisions about what level of precision is appropriate in relation to any particular claim should depend on the nature of what we are trying to describe, on the likely accuracy of our descriptions, on our purposes, and on the resources available to us; not on ideological commitment to one methodological paradigm or another. (Hammersley: 1992a, 163)

2 A preference for naturally-occurring data – observation rather than experiment, unstructured versus structured interviews. However, this falls because, as Hammersley says, even observation can affect a setting, while choosing 'a natural setting can be unrepresentative because it differs in important ways from other cases in that category' (164). Also no research is untouched by human hands (cf. Hammersley and Atkinson: 1983 and the critique of 'naturalism').

3 A preference for meanings rather than behaviour – attempting 'to document the world from the point of view of the people studied' (165). However, as Hammersley rightly points out, this is a cop-out since respondents can do this for themselves; ultimately, the social scientist must analyse rather than simply let the participants speak for themselves (see Gilbert and Mulkay: 1983).

4 A rejection of natural science as a model. However, there are many different kinds of natural science (from botany to theoretical physics). Also qualitative research has a very problematic status if it totally fails to address the validity of its findings or reduces validity to participants' agreement with a set of findings (see Chapter 7).

5 A preference for inductive, hypothesis-generating research rather than hypothesis-testing (cf. Glaser and Strauss: 1967). However, hypotheses must *at some point* be tested, otherwise we are limited to mere speculation. As Hammersley writes: 'which of these approaches is most appropriate should depend on our purposes, and the stage that our research has reached, not on paradigmatic commitments' (169).

Source: adapted from Hammersley: 1992a, 160–172

Ultimately, Hammersley finds no grounds for distinguishing a separate basis for ethnographic research which would differentiate it from other social science approaches. Instead, he argues that: 'the process of inquiry in science is the same whatever method is used, and . . . the retreat into paradigms effectively stultifies debate and hampers progress' (1992a, 182).

I entirely agree with this observation of Hammersley's. As I have argued here, sociology has been bedevilled by the adoption of misleading polarities. Instead, if we wish to establish criteria for distinguishing field research, we will need to understand the similar issues faced by any systematic attempt at description and explanation, whether quantitative or qualitative.

Some of Hammersley's (1992a) critique of the pretensions of ethnography derives from Hammersley and Atkinson's (1983) argument about the problematic status of ethnographers' attempts to contrast their 'naturalism' with the 'positivism' of other social scientists. The former involves the following three elements set out in Table 2.5.

Table 2.5:   *A Fourth Version of Qualitative Research*

1   A preference for 'natural' settings as the primary source of data
2   A fidelity to the phenomena under study – this requires a cultural description of the meanings of phenomena to participants
3   The use of an inductivist methodology which avoids the premature testing of hypotheses

Source: adapted from Hammersley and Atkinson: 1983, 6–9

However, as Hammersley and Atkinson themselves point out, the version set out in Table 2.5 depends upon a preference for 'naturalism' which presents the following problems:

1   'Artificial' and 'natural' settings are both 'part of society' (11); no data or its analysis is ever asocial or untouched by human hands (see Cicourel's: 1964 critique of apparently neutral interviewing 'techniques').
2   Drawing data from 'natural' settings is no guarantee that one's findings are valid in other settings or in the same setting at other times.
3   'Naturalism' limits social research to cultural description, allowing no claims to validity other than understanding people's experiences.

Instead, Hammersley and Atkinson (1983) rightly argue that we might emphasise the similarities betweeen social science and natural science and their common differences from, say, journalism, e.g. the development and testing of theories (19).

Some Defining Characteristics of Qualitative Research

What, then, remains that is distinctive to qualitative or field research? Hammersley and Atkinson (1983) offer a helpful set of relevant characteristics:

1   Field research can provide a broader version of theory than simply a relationship between variables: 'a theory must include reference to mechanisms or processes by which the relationship among the variables identified is generated' (20). This point relates to Mills' (1953) early critique of the atheoretical nature of much quantitative research – what Mills referred to as its 'abstracted empiricism'.

2 The flexibility of field research 'allows theory development to be pursued in a highly effective and economical manner' (24). It is difficult to demonstrate this point succinctly. However, the reader is referred to Chapter 3 where I discuss how the concept of 'frame' (Goffman: 1974) has been used to unite a range of ethnographic studies.

3 Such studies do not 'regard theorising as restricted to social scientists' (20). This point lies at the heart of field research, whether we are simply trying to report how people 'see' things or, in a more sophisticated manner, trying to understand the social organisation of 'description' (see Chapter 4, pp. 80–89).

So we can learn from Hammersley and Atkinson's account. Moreover, unlike other research which usually shares a common model, as I show throughout this book, field research depends on a *variety* of theoretical positions with very different implications.

However, we also need to recognise that, by the 1990s, field research has had considerable time to develop and to build cumulative bodies ofknowledge – therefore, for instance, hypothesis-testing based upon agreed concepts is not only practical but often desirable.

I conclude this short chapter by offering my own account of qualitative research in Table 2.6. As the reader will note, my use of 'should' in point 1 indicates that this list is normative rather than descriptive. It is, therefore, offered as a prescription rather than a description.

Like any such list, Table 2.6 contains simplifications which can easily be criticised. In the pages that follow, a more substantial model of qualitative research is offered.

Part Two sets out in this direction. In it, we will examine, in turn, how we might analyse the four main kinds of data used in qualitative research: observation, texts, interviews and transcripts.

Table 2.6:   *A Prescriptive Model of Qualitative Research*

1   Field research should be theoretically driven rather than determined by technical considerations (what can be measured, what can be sampled). This relates to Cicourel's observations, almost thirty years ago but still largely true, on interview research:

> there has been considerable work done in calling to the researcher's attention the pitfalls and remedies in this method. But, in spite of improvement in interview techniques, little has been done to integrate social science theory with methodology. The subtleties which methodologists introduce to the novice interviewer can be read as properties to be found in the interaction between members of a society. Thus, the principles of 'good and bad interviewing' can be read as basic features of social interaction which the social scientist is presumably seeking to study. (Cicourel: 1964, 67–68)

2   Following both Cicourel and Hammersley and Atkinson, members of society also routinely employ theories about social order. This involves a methodological step which encourages us to examine social phenomena as *procedural* affairs, replacing the questions 'why do people do X in the first place?' and 'what keeps people doing X' with 'what do people *have to do* to be (routinely, unremarkably, but recognisably and readily so) doing X'. (Sharrock and Watson: 1988)

3   Field research should attempt to make problematic the common-sense reasoning used in definitions of variables (for instance, what constitutes 'suicide' or an 'organisation') and in the establishment of basic research problems (e.g. the identification of 'family' with the 'household' – see Chapter 3, pp. 56–58, and Gubrium: 1992). Ultimately, this means we must attend to common-sense assumptions about what constitutes 'the field' (see Turner: 1989).

4   While the attempt to erect a polarity between 'natural' and 'artificial' settings is spurious, it does give rise to a legitimate methodological preference. Field researchers need to be convinced that non-naturally-occurring data should be turned to in the first instance (interactionism) or at all (ethnomethodology). Following Kirk and Miller, 'qualitative research is a particular tradition in social science that fundamentally depends on watching people in their own territory' (1986, 9).

PART TWO

METHODS

3

Observation

Michael Agar (1986) has described a 'received view' of science which approaches any research project with these kinds of questions: 'What's your hypothesis?' 'How do you measure that?' 'How large is your sample?' 'Did you pre-test the instrument?'

Agar argues that it does not always make sense to ask such questions about every piece of social science research:

> For some research styles, especially those that emphasize the *scientific testing* role, those questions make sense. But for other styles – when the social researcher assumes a *learning role* – the questions don't work. When you stand on the edge of a village and watch the noise and motion, you wonder, 'Who are the people and what are they doing?' When you read a news story about the discontent of young lawyers with their profession, you wonder, 'What is going on here?' Hypotheses, measurement, samples, and instruments are the wrong guidelines. Instead, you need to learn about a world you understand by encountering it firsthand and making some sense out of it. (Agar: 1986, 12)

Although I would dispute Agar's apparent dismissal of the relevance of issues of validity and reliability to qualitative research (see Chapter 7), his examples give us an initial hold on the questions that can animate observational studies.

However, perhaps there is a simpler way of expressing Agar's question 'what is going on here?'. Let me use the example of police movies. If you go to the cinema primarily in order to see 'action' (car chases, hold-ups, etc.), then it is unlikely that you will find it easy to become a good observer. On the other hand, if you are intrigued by the *details* of policework and of criminal activity, you are very much on the right lines.

This is because social science observation is fundamentally about understanding the routine rather than what appears to be exciting. Indeed, the good observer finds excitement in the most everyday, mundane kinds of activities. For example, how police do their paperwork and assemble their files may tell us more about their activities than the occasional 'shoot-out'. For a sociological focus on this, see Cicourel (1968) (discussed in Chapter 4, p. 67). For a recent movie along these lines, see Bertrand

Tavernier's *L627*, concerned with a Paris police drug-squad. Tavernier shows us how much police time is taken up with assembling files that tell the 'right' kind of story (e.g. emphasising 'clear-up' rates on crimes).

Elsewhere, Bryman (1988, 61–66) has provided a useful list of the principal characteristics of much observational research, as follows:

1 'Seeing through the eyes of': 'viewing events, actions, norms, values, etc. from the perspective of the people being studied'.
2 Description: 'attending to mundane detail . . . to help us to understand what is going on in a particular context and to provide clues and pointers to other layers of reality'.
3 'Contextualism': 'the basic message that qualitative researchers convey is that whatever the sphere in which the data are being collected, we can understand events only when they are situated in the wider social and historical context'.
4 Process: 'viewing social life as involving interlocking series of events'.
5 Flexible research designs: 'qualitative researchers' adherence to viewing social phenomena through the eyes of their subjects has led to a wariness regarding the imposition of prior and possibly inappropriate frames of reference on the people they study'. This leads to a preference for an open and unstructured research design which increases the possibility of coming across unexpected issues.
6 Avoiding early use of theories and concepts: rejecting premature attempts to impose theories and concepts which may 'exhibit a poor fit with participants' perspectives'.

Bryman's list provides a useful orientation for the novice. However, the reader should proceed with caution. As I suggested in Chapter 2, any attempt to base observation on an understanding of how people 'see' things (item 1) can speedily degenerate into a commonsensical or psychologistic perspective. Indeed, the last third of this chapter is devoted to approaches which eschew the pursuit of 'meanings' in favour of the study of 'practices'.

The Ethnographic Tradition: From Observation to Gender

Just as, according to Bryman, the qualitative researcher seeks to see things in context, so the student needs some basic knowledge of the historical tradition from which observational studies arose. For: 'Qualitative research is an empirical, socially located phenomenon, defined by its own history, not simply a residual grab-bag comprising all things that are "not quantitative"' (Kirk and Miller: 1986, 10).

The initial thrust in favour of observational work was anthropological. Anthropologists argue that, if one is really to understand a group of people, one must engage in an extended period of observation. Anthropological fieldwork routinely involves immersion in a culture over a period

---

Exercise 3.1

An instructor begins an introductory sociology course with the following statement:

> The problem with everyday talk is that it is so imprecise. For instance, sometimes we say: 'too many cooks spoil the broth'. On other occasions, we say: 'many hands make light work'. On this course, based on scientific research, I will demonstrate which of these proverbs is more accurate.

The instructor now reports on laboratory data from an experiment where students have been assigned tasks and then work either in teams or on their own. This experiment seems to show that, all things being equal, teamwork is more efficient. Therefore, the instructor claims, we can have more confidence in the validity of the proverb: 'many hands make light work'.

Using Agar's criticisms of the 'received view' of science (p. 30), answer the following questions:

1 Are you convinced by the instructor's claim (e.g. what assumptions does the experiment make? Can proverbs be equally appropriate in different contexts?)?
2 Outline how you might do *observational* work on people's use of such proverbs (e.g. what settings would you look at? What sort of things would you be looking for?).
3 Examine *either* newspaper advertisements *or* advertisements on radio or television. Make a note when proverbs are used. What *functions* do these proverbs seem to have? Do they make the advertisement more convincing? Why?

---

of years, based on learning the language and participating in social events with them.

In an earlier text (Silverman: 1985), I discussed cognitive anthropology as one form of such fieldwork. As its name suggests, cognitive anthropology seeks to understand how people perceive the world by examining how they communicate. This leads to the production of *ethnographies*, or conceptually derived descriptions, of whole cultures, focussed on how people communicate. For instance, Basso (1972) discusses the situations in which native American Apache people prefer to remain silent and Frake (1972) shows how the Subanun, a people living in the Philippines, assign social status when talking together during drinking ceremonies.

Sociological work based on observational methods is usually assumed to originate in the 1920s, although many of the theoretical issues about group interaction raised in the nineteenth century by the German sociologist Georg Simmel (1950) offer an interesting basis for observational research.

The 'Chicago School', as it became known in the 1930s, had two strands. One was concerned with the sociology of urban life, represented by the work of Park and Burgess on the social organisation of the city into different 'zones' and the movement of population between zones over time. The second strand, associated with Everett Hughes, provided a series of vivid accounts of urban settings, particularly focussed on 'underdog' occupations and 'deviant' roles.

The Chicago School tradition continued for two decades after the Second World War. In the 1950s, Becker (1953) conducted a classic observational study of drug use. He was particularly concerned with the relationship between marihuana smokers' own understandings and the interactions in which they were involved. He discovered that people's participation in groups of users taught them how to respond to the drug. Without such learning, novices would not understand how to smoke marihuana nor how to respond to its effects. Consequently, they would not get 'high' and so would not continue to use it.

Becker outlines a number of stages through which novices pass on their path to become a regular smoker. These include:

1   Direct teaching – e.g. being taught the difference between how to smoke marihuana and how to smoke tobacco; learning how to interpret its effects and their significance.
2   Learning how to enjoy the effects – through interaction with experienced users, the novice learns to find pleasure in sensations which, at first, may be quite frightening.
3   Resocialisation after difficulties – even experienced users can have an unpleasant or frightening experience either through using a larger quantity or a different quality of marihuana. Fellow users can 'cool them out', explaining the reasons for this experience and reassuring them that they may safely continue to use the drug.
4   Learning connoisseurship – through developing a greater appreciation of the drug's effects, becoming able to distinguish between different kinds and qualities of the drug.

Becker stresses that it is only in the context of a social network, which provides a means of interpreting the effects of the drug, that people become stable marihuana users. It is unlikely, however, that such a network could have been identified by, say, survey research methods concerned with the attitudes of marihuana users.

A second example will show how the Chicago School encouraged research on 'underdog' occupations. Whyte (1949) carried out over a year's participant observation in a number of Chicago restaurants. He points out how, in a service trade like a restaurant, the organisation of work differs from other settings. Instead of the industrial pattern, whereby a supervisor gives orders to a worker, in a restaurant work originates from a customer's order.

Whyte shows shows this difference generates a number of problems for restaurant workers: Who originates action? For whom? How often? With what consequences? The social structure of the restaurant functions as an organised response to these problems.

This can be seen in the following three patterns:

1 Many of us will have had the experience of a member of staff snatching away a menu which we have innocently picked up on sitting down at a restaurant table. Whyte argues that this occurs because the skilful waitress/waiter attempts to fit customers into *her* pattern of work (e.g. her need to ensure that the table has been cleared before she takes an order). By not passively responding to the initiatives of customers, serving staff preserve their own work routines.

2 Back in the 1940s, widespread gender inequalities caused a particular problem for waitresses because they were expected to transmit orders to mainly male cooks. A structure emerged which concealed this initiation of work by waitresses: rather than shout out orders to the cooks, the women wrote out slips which they laid on the counter to be attended to in the cooks' own time.

3 Barmen also engaged in informal behaviour to distance themselves from the initiation of orders by waitresses. When they had lots of orders, they would not speed up. Moreover, at busy times, they would not mix one cocktail until they had several orders for it which could be mixed together.

Half a century later, Whyte's work remains impressive. Following Bryman's list, the restaurant study shows the importance of *context* and *process* in understanding behaviour. Thus Whyte cleverly focusses on how occupational and gender hierarchies are used to influence the flow of work and redefine apparently simple acts. Moreover, he does not let a preference for an unstructured research design lead to a study which merely tells anecdotes on a few choice examples. For instance, the restaurant study uses powerful *quantitative* measures of the number of times different types of people initiate actions.

However, although Whyte treats gender as a topic, it was not until twenty years later that social scientists began to think systematically about the impact of gender on the fieldwork process as a whole. In part, this reflected an interest in the interplay between gender and power. For instance, almost all the 'classics' of the Chicago School were written by men; and those researchers who rose up the academic hierarchy to become full professors were also almost all men (see Warren: 1988, 11).

Increasingly, the gender of fieldworkers themselves was seen to play a crucial factor in observational research. Informants were shown to say different things to male and female researchers. For instance, in a study of a nude beach, when approached by someone of a different gender, people emphasised their interest in 'freedom and naturalism'. Conversely, where the researcher was the same gender as the informant, people were far more likely to discuss their sexual interests (Warren and Rasmussen: 1977, reported by Warren: 1988).

In studies which involved extended stays 'in the field', people have also been shown to make assumptions based upon the gender of the researcher. For instance, particularly in rural communities, young, single women may be precluded from participating in many activities or asking many questions. Conversely, female gender may sometimes accord privileged access. For instance, Oboler (1986) reports that her pregnancy increased her rapport with her Kenyan informants, while Warren (1988, 18) suggests that women fieldworkers can make use of the sexist assumption that only men engage in 'important business' by treating their 'invisibility' as a resource. Equally, male fieldworkers may be excluded or exclude them-selves from contact with female respondents in certain kinds of situations (see McKeganey and Bloor: 1991).

One danger in all this, particularly in the past, was that fieldworkers failed to report or reflect upon the influence of gender in their fieldwork. For instance, in a study of a large local government organisation, referred to in Chapter 4, we reported but did not discuss the different kinds of situations to which the male and female researchers gained easy access (Silverman and Jones: 1976). Moreover, even as the role of doing fieldwork as a woman has become more addressed, hardly any attention has been paid by researchers to questions of male gender (McKeganey and Bloor: 1991, 198).

Nonetheless, as fashions change, it is possible to swing too far and accord gender issues too much importance. As McKeganey and Bloor (1991, 195–196) argue, there are two important issues relevant to the significance of gender in fieldwork. First, the influence of gender may be negotiable with respondents and not simply ascribed. Second, we should resist 'the tendency to employ gender as an explanatory catch-all' (196). For instance, McKeganey and Bloor suggest that other variables than gender, like age and social class, may also be important in fieldwork. Equally, I would argue, following Schegloff (1991), that we need to demonstrate that participants are actually attending to gender in what they are doing, rather than just work with our intuitions or even with statistical correlations.

None of this should imply that it would be correct to swing full circle and, like an earlier generation, ignore gender issues in research. It is incumbent upon fieldworkers to reflect upon the basis and status of their observations. Clearly, how the researcher and the community studied respond to their gender can provide crucial insights into field realities.

Indeed, we would do well to become conscious that even taken-for-granted assumptions may be culturally and historically specific. For instance, Carol Warren (1988) suggests that: 'The focal gender *myth* of field research is the greater communicative skills and less threatening nature of the female fieldworker' (64, my emphasis). As Warren notes, the important thing is to resist treating such assumptions as 'revealed truths' but to treat them as 'accounts' which are historically situated.

Organising Observational Research

Bearing in mind both Warren's and Whyte's work, it is now appropriate to think a little more systematically about how to organise an observational study. Simplifying, I will suggest five stages:

- beginning research
- writing fieldnotes
- looking as well as listening
- testing hypotheses
- making broader links

These steps are not arranged in any particular order. For instance, one should be making broader links at quite an early stage. Of course, making such links implies the relevance of theoretical perspectives on observational research – to be discussed in the subsequent section.

Beginning Research

In Chapter 1, I argued that premature definition of 'variables' was dangerous in field research. Early 'operational' definitions offer precision at the cost of deflecting attention away from the social processes through which the participants themselves assemble stable features of their social world. So, for instance, the qualitative social scientist may be reluctant to begin by defining, say, 'depression' or 'efficiency'. Instead, it may be preferable to examine how, in different contexts, 'depression' and 'efficiency' come to be defined.

The assumption that one should avoid the early specification of definitions and hypotheses has been common to field researchers since the 1930s. As Becker and Geer argued many years ago, for the field researcher:

> a major part of . . . research must consist of finding out what problems he [sic] can best study in this organisation, what hypotheses will be fruitful and worth pursuing, what observations will best serve him as an indicator of the presence of such phenomena as, for example, cohesiveness or deviance. (Becker and Geer: 1960, 267)

However, this does not mean that the early stages of field research are totally unguided. The attempt to describe things 'as they are' is doomed to failure. Without *some* perspective or, at the very least, a set of animating questions, there is nothing to report. Contrary to crude empiricists, the facts *never* speak for themselves.

One way to assemble data is to begin with a set of very general questions. A good example of such questions is provided by Wolcott:

What is going on here? What do people in this setting have to know (individually and collectively) in order to do what they are doing? How are skills and attitudes transmitted and acquired, particularly in the absence of intentional efforts at instruction? (Wolcott: 1990, 32)

Already here, we can see that Wolcott's questions are guided by a particular theoretical focus on people's knowledge and skills. This emerges out of a set of assumptions common to many field researchers. These assumptions may be crudely set out as follows:

1 *Common sense* is held to be complex and sophisticated rather than naive and misguided.
2 *Social practices* rather than perceptions are the site where common sense operates: the focus is on what people are doing rather than upon what they are thinking, e.g. talking to one another, having meetings, writing documents, etc.
3 *'Phenomena'* are viewed within such inverted commas. This means that we seek to understand how any 'phenomenon' is locally produced through the activities of particular people in particular settings.

Of course, any such list glosses over the range of theoretical directions to be found in field research. Later we will look at two key theories deriving from the work of Erving Goffman and Harvey Sacks. For the moment, however, let us assume that we have established a particular focus. How then do we proceed?

Writing Fieldnotes

Let us assume that you are not using electronic recordings (audio- or video-tapes) or that you wish to supplement such recordings with observational data. How should you write fieldnotes? (Working with transcripts deriving from recordings is discussed in Chapter 6.)

The greatest danger is that you will seek to report 'everything' in your notes. Not only does this overlook the theory-driven nature of field research, it gives you an impossible burden when you try to develop a more systematic analysis at a later stage: 'The critical task in qualitative research is not to accumulate all the data you can, but to "can" (get rid of) most of the data you accumulate. This requires constant winnowing' (Wolcott: 1990, 35).

At the outset, however, it is likely that you will use broad descriptive categories 'relating to particular people or types of people, places, activities and topics of concern' (Hammersley and Atkinson: 1983, 167). Moreover, items may be usefully assigned to more than one category in order to maximise the range of hypotheses that can be generated. To do this, it may help to make multiple copies of each segment of data, filed under several categories (*ibid*, 170).

One useful aid in filing and indexing is provided by computer software programs. ETHNOGRAPH allows you to code a text into as many as seven different categories. QUALPRO allows text to be broken into still more flexible units and codes. NUDIST will store information in tree-structured index systems with an unlimited number of categories and highly complex index structures. You can then search your data by these indexes or look for overlap between data indexed under different categories. The NUDIST program thus helps in the generation of new categories and the identification of relationships between existing categories (see Richards and Richards: 1987, Tesch: 1991).

In order to make this discussion of note-taking more concrete, I want to give an example from a piece of research I carried out in the early 1980s (see Silverman: 1987, Chs. 1–6). The study was of a paediatric cardiology unit. Much of my data derived from tape-recordings of an outpatient clinic that lasted between two and four hours every Wednesday.

Secure in the knowledge that the basic data were being recorded, I was free to use my eyes as well as my ears to record more data to help in the analysis of the audio-tapes. Gradually, with the help of my co-worker Robert Hilliard, I developed a coding sheet to record my observations.

As an illustration of how I coded the data, I append in Table 3.1 below the full coding sheet used in this study. In order to show how we derived the categories, I have included explanations of some of the categories in square brackets.

I ought to stress that this coding form was only developed after observation of more than ten outpatient clinics and after extensive discussions between the research team. During this time, we narrowed down what we were looking for. Increasingly, we became interested in how decisions (or 'disposals') were organised and announced. It seemed likely that the doctor's way of announcing decisions was systematically related not only to clinical factors (like the child's heart condition) but to social factors (such as what parents would be told at various stages of treatment). For instance, at a first outpatients' consultation, doctors would not normally announce to parents the discovery of a major heart abnormality and the necessity for life-threatening surgery. Instead, they would suggest the need for more tests and only hint that major surgery might be needed. They would also collaborate with parents who produced examples of their child's apparent 'wellness'.

This step-by-step method of information-giving was avoided in only two cases. If a child was diagnosed as 'healthy' by the cardiologist, the doctor would give all the information in one go and would engage in what we called a 'search and destroy' operation, based on eliciting any remaining worries of the parent(s) and proving that they were mistaken. In the case of a group of children with the additional handicap of Down's Syndrome, as well as suspected cardiac disease, the doctor would present all the clinical information at one sitting, avoiding a step-by-step method. Moreover, atypically, the doctor would allow parents to make the choice about further treatment, while encouraging parents to focus on non-clinical matters like their child's 'enjoyment of life' or friendly personality (see Chapter 8, pp. 186–188 for more details of this study).

The coding form in Table 3.1 allowed us to identify these patterns. For instance, by relating item 14 on the scope of the consultation to the decision-format (item 20), we were able to see differences between consultations involving Down's children and others. Moreover, it also turned out that there were significant differences between these two groups in both the form of the elicitation question (item 16) and the diagnosis statement (item 19).

The coding form in Table 3.1 followed a practice described elsewhere which derives from:

> that well-established style of work whereby the data are inspected for categories and instances. It is an approach that disaggregates the text (notes or transcripts) into a series of fragments, which are then regrouped under a series of thematic headings. (Atkinson: 1992, 455)

As Atkinson points out, one of the disadvantages of coding schemes is that, because they are based upon a given set of categories, they furnish 'a powerful conceptual grid' (459) from which it is difficult to escape. While this 'grid' is very helpful in organising the data analysis, it also deflects attention away from uncategorised activities.

In these circumstances, it is helpful to return occasionally to the original data. In our research, we had our tapes and transcripts which offered endless opportunities to redefine our categories. Lacking tapes of his data on medical education, Atkinson returned to his original fieldnotes. He shows how the same, original data can be reread in a quite different way.

Atkinson's earlier method had been to fragment his fieldnotes into relatively small segments, each with its own category. For instance, a surgeon's description of post-operative complications to a surgical team was originally categorised under such headings as 'unpredictability', 'uncertainty', 'patient career' and 'trajectory'. When Atkinson returns to it, it becomes an overall narrative which sets up an enigma ('unexpected complications') which is resolved in the form of a 'moral tale' ('beware, unexpected things can always happen'). Viewed in this way, the surgeon's story becomes a text with many resemblances to a fairytale, as we shall see in Chapter 4, pp. 73–75.

There is a further 'moral tale' implicit in using Atkinson's story. The field researcher is always torn between the need to narrow down analysis through category construction and to allow some possibility of reinterpretation of the same data. So, while the rush to categorise is laudable, it should always occur in the context of a solid body of original data. The ideal form for this is a tape-recording or original document. Where these cannot be used, the field researcher must attempt to transcribe as much as possible of what is said and done – and the settings in which it is said and done.

In such transcription, Dingwall (personal correspondence) notes how important it is to record *descriptions* rather than mere impressions. In practice, this means that we should always try to note concrete instances of

Table 3.1: *Outpatient Analysis*

1 Name of patient

2 Age

3 Clinic and date

4 Doctor

5 Family present

6 Non-family present

7 Length of co-presence of doctor and family [we wanted to record the time of the encounter not including periods when the doctor was out of the room]

8 Diagnosis

9 Stage of treatment:
   1st consultation
   Pre-inpatient
   Post-catheter [test requiring inpatient stay]
   Post-operation

10 Outcome of consultation:
    Discharge or referral elsewhere
    Non-inpatient follow-up
    Possible eventual catheter or surgery
    Catheter
    Surgery
    No decision

11 Consultation stages [this derived from Robert Hilliard's attempt to identify a series of stages from a greeting exchange to elicitation of symptoms, through to examination and diagnosis statement (see Silverman: 1985, especially pp. 265–269)]:
    Stage
    Questions asked
    Topics covered
    Notes/Markers

12 Does doctor invite questions?
    No
    Yes (When:)

13 Use of medical terminology:
    Stage
    Doctor/Family

14 Scope of consultation:

	Family	Doctor
Prior treatment history		
Extra-cardiac physical states		
Child development		
Child behaviour		
Family's practicalities of treatment or attendance		

Table 3.1: *Continued*

	Family	Doctor
Doctor's practicalities of treatment or attendance		
Anxieties and emotional problems of family		
Social situation of family		
External treatment agencies		

15   Family's presentation of a referral history

16   Format of doctor's initial elicitation question [e.g. how is she? is she well?]

17   Patency [this referred to whether symptoms or diseases were visible or 'patent' to the family]:
Family's presentation of problems/symptoms
Dr's mention of patent symptoms
Family's assent to problems/symptoms
'Not patent'?

18   Location of examination:
desk
couch
side-room

19   Diagnosis statement:
(a)   Use of 'well' (Dr/Family/Both)
(b)   Use of 'normal' (Dr/Family/Both)
(c)   Possible diagnoses mentioned (0/1/ > 1)

20   Decisions:
(a)   Possible disposals mentioned (0/1/> 1)
(b)   Medical preference stated (Yes/No)
(c)   Medical intention stated (Yes/No)
(d)   Family assent requested (Yes/No)
(e)   Family allowed to make decision (Yes/No)
(f)   Family wishes volunteered (Yes/No)
(g)   Family dissent from doctor's proposed disposal (Yes/No)

21   Uncertainty expressed by Dr:
(a)   over diagnosis
(b)   over treatment

what people have said or done, using verbatim quotations and 'flat' (or unadorned) descriptions.

Looking as Well as Listening

The attentive reader will have recognised that the coding frame used in Table 3.1 depended, in part, upon what we could *see* as well as hear (for instance, items 5 and 6 on the people present and item 18 on the location of the examination). As we have seen, W.F. Whyte (1949) also reaped rich rewards by paying attention to the spatial organisation of activities.

Using his observation of hospital wards, Anssi Peräkylä (personal correspondence) notes how spatial arrangements differentiate groups of people. There are the wards and patient rooms, which staff may enter anytime they need to. Then there are patient lounges and the like, which are a kind of public space. Both areas are quite different from areas like the nurses' room and doctors' offices where patients enter only by invitation. Finally, if there is a staff coffee room, you never see a patient there.

As Peräkylä points out, one way to produce different categories of human beings in a hospital is the allocation of space according to categories. At the same time, this allocation is reproduced in the activities of the participants. For instance, the perceptive observer might note the demeanour of patients as they approach the nurses' room. Even if the door is open, they may stand outside and just put their heads round the door. In doing so, they mark out that they are encroaching on foreign territory.

Unfortunately, we have all become a little reluctant to use our eyes as well as our ears when doing observational work (possible reasons for this are discussed in Chapter 4, p. 70). Notable exceptions are Humphrey's (1970) *Tea Room Trade* (a study of the spatial organisation of gay pick-up sites) and Lindsay Prior's (1988) work on hospital architecture. Michel Foucault's (1977) *Discipline and Punish* offers a famous example of the analysis of prison architecture, while Edward Hall's (1969) *The Hidden Dimension* coined the term 'proxemics' to refer to people's use of space – for instance, how we organise an appropriate distance between each other.

However, these are exceptions. Stimson (1986) has noted how 'photographs and diagrams are virtually absent from sociological journals, and rare in sociological books' (641). He then discusses a room set out for hearings of a disciplinary organisation responsible for British doctors. The Professional Conduct Committee of the General Medical Council sits in a high-ceilinged, oak-panelled room reached by an imposing staircase. There are stained-glass windows, picturing sixteen crests and a woman in a classical Greek pose. As Stimson comments:

> This is a room in which serious matters are discussed: the room has a presence that is forced on our consciousness . . . speech is formal, carefully spoken and a matter for the public record. Visitors in the gallery speak only, if at all, in hushed whispers, for their speech is not part of the proceedings. (Stimson: 1986, 643–644)

In such a room, as Stimson suggests, even without anything needed to be said, we know that what goes on must be taken seriously. Stimson aptly contrasts this room with a McDonald's hamburger restaurant:

> Consider the decorations and materials – plastic, paper, vinyl and polystyrene, and the bright primary colours. (Everything) signifies transience. This temporary character is further articulated in the casual dress of customers, the

institutionally casualised dress of staff and the seating that is constructed to make lengthy stays uncomfortable. (*ibid*, 649–650)

Exercise 3.2

This is a research exercise to improve your observational skills. These are your instructions:

1 Select a setting in which you regularly participate – good examples would be a student restaurant, a bus or train or a supermarket check-out queue.
2 Make a sketch map of the site. What sort of activities does the physical lay-out encourage, does it discourage or is it neutral towards? (Think of Stimson's comparison of the room for medical hearings and MacDonald's.)
3 How do people use the space you are studying? What do they show they are attending to? How do they communicate with one another or avoid communication? Do they look at one another or avoid it? What distance do they keep between one another?
4 In what ways are people using the space to co-operate with one another to *define* themselves (e.g. as a restaurant crowd but not bus passengers)?
5 Is there any difference between how people organise their activities when they are on their own, in pairs or in a crowd?
6 How do people use the setting as a resource for engaging in activities not specifically intended (but not necessarily inappropriate) in that setting (e.g. displaying particular personal characteristics such as wanting to communicate or not wanting to communicate)?

In a setting like McDonald's, we know that casual enjoyment and informality are appropriate. In addition to all its other differences from the oak-panelled room, this restaurant is not an area for confidences, cut off from the public gaze, but offers an open vista from street to kitchen. Imagine attempting to conduct a disciplinary hearing in such a setting!

Testing Hypotheses

One of the strengths of observational research is its ability to shift focus as interesting new data become available. For instance, during a study of two cancer clinics at a British National Health Service hospital, I unexpectedly gained access to a 'private' (fee-paying) clinic run by one of the doctors in his spare time. I was thus able to change my research focus towards a comparison of the 'ceremonial orders' of public and private medicine (Silverman: 1984).

However, a strength can also be a weakness. Some qualitative research can resemble a disorganised stumble through a mass of data, full of 'insightful' observations of a mainly 'anecdotal' nature. For instance, in a survey of qualitative papers in two journals in the area of health and social science, I was struck by the number of articles based on one or two 'convincing' examples (Silverman: 1989a).

There is absolutely no reason why observational research cannot combine insight with rigour. In other words, it is right to expect that such research should be *both* original *and* valid. This will involve testing hypotheses that we have generated in the field. Increasingly, however, as our knowledge of micro-social processes expands, it will mean that we can enter the field with a hypothesis we already want to test. So, in my comparative study of medical practice, Strong's (1979a) work on the 'ceremonial orders' of doctor–patient interaction gave me a clear hypothesis which became testable when I gained access to a private clinic.

But how then do we test hypotheses using qualitative data? Many years ago, Becker and Geer (1960) gave us some useful guidelines. In a study of the changing perspectives of medical students during their training, they found three ways of testing their emerging hypotheses:

1 Comparison of different groups at one time and of one cohort of students with another over the course of training. For instance, it could only be claimed with confidence that beginning medical students tended to be idealists if several cohorts of first year students all shared this perspective.

2 Ensuring that the responses given in interviews were also replicated by what students said and did in more 'naturally–occurring' situations (e.g. speaking to one another in classrooms and over lunch).

3 A careful inspection of negative or deviant cases leading to the abandonment, revision or even reinforcement of the hypothesis. For instance:

> if it can be shown that the person who acts on a different perspective is socially isolated from the group or that his deviant activities are regarded by others as improper, unnecessary, or foolish, then one can argue that these facts indicate use of the perspective by all but deviants, hence, its collective character. (Becker and Geer: 1960, 289)

4 The use of simple tabulations where appropriate. For instance, counting statements and activities by whether they were generated by the observer or were more naturally occurring.

More than thirty years later, Dingwall (1992) underlines this search for validity via the comparative method and the use of deviant cases. He adds two further ways of establishing validity:

5 The provision of sufficient 'raw' data (e.g. in long transcripts) to allow the reader to separate data and analysis. As Dingwall comments:

> Clearly, it is no more possible to reproduce all the data than it is for a film-maker to show every inch of film . . . What I am taking exception to, though, is the kind of report that is purely a redescription of the researcher's impressions or sensations. Empathy has its place in ethnography but it

should enter after recording rather than being confused with it. (Dingwall: 1992, 169)

6 Avoiding the temptation, at its height in the 1960s, to favour the 'underdog' at the expense of everybody else. One should have doubts about a study which fails to deal even-handedly with the people it describes or to recognise the interactive character of social life. Dingwall's ethic of 'fair dealing' implies that we should ask of any study: 'Does it convey as much understanding of its villains as its heroes? Are the privileged treated as having something serious to say or simply dismissed as evil, corrupt or greedy without further enquiry?' (*ibid*, 172). Clearly, this is as much a scientific as an ethical issue.

Provided it attends to these sorts of issues, observational research can produce findings every bit as 'hard' as those derived from other methods. Indeed, sometimes it can deliver valid information on topics which are intractable when we are limited by purely quantitative methods. For instance, Bloor *et al* (1991) show that it is possible to establish a reliable estimate of the proportion of drug-injecting female street prostitutes using observationals methods on a cohort of women and identifying new fieldwork contacts.

How we test hypotheses in qualitative research is a crucial matter which I have only touched upon here. It is treated in much greater depth in Chapter 7.

Exercise 3.3

This exercise is meant to encourage you to think about how you would test hypotheses derived from observational research. You need to go through the following steps:

1 Review your answers to Exercise 3.2 and consider how you might go about testing each of your conclusions, e.g.

  – comparison of different settings or of different groups or activities within the same setting
  – the use of simple tabulations
  – the use of negative or deviant cases.

2 Turn your answers to 3.2 into hypotheses (i.e. give them the form: if A then B). Return to the field and try to gather the kind of data which might test your hypotheses.

3 Distinguish those hypotheses which have been confirmed from those which have been disconfirmed and those which you remain unsure about.

4 What kind of further data (from this setting or other settings) would allow you (a) to test your initial hypotheses more thoroughly and (b) to generate other testable hypotheses?

Making Broader Links

No hypotheses are ever 'theory-free'. We only come to look at things in certain ways because we have adopted, either tacitly or explicitly, certain ways of seeing. This means that, in observational research, data collection, hypothesis-construction and theory-building are not three separate things but are interwoven with one another.

This process is well described by using an analogy with a funnel:

> Ethnographic research has a characteristic 'funnel' structure, being progress-ively focused over its course. Progressive focusing has two analytically distinct components. First, over time the research problem is developed or transformed, and eventually its scope is clarified and delimited and its internal structure explored. In this sense, it is frequently only over the course of the research that one discovers what the research is really 'about', and it is not uncommon for it to turn out to be about something quite remote from the initially foreshadowed problems. (Hammersley and Atkinson: 1983, 175)

For instance, my research on the two cancer clinics unexpectedly led into a comparison of fee-for-service and state-provided medicine. Similarly, my observation of a paediatric cardiology unit moved unpredictably in the direction of an analysis of disposal decisions with a small group of Down's Syndrome children.

We may note three features which these two cases had in common:

1 The switch of focus – through the 'funnel' – as a more defined topic arose.
2 The use of the comparative method as an invaluable tool of theory-building and testing.
3 The generation of topics with a scope outside the substantive area of the research. Thus the 'ceremonial orders' found in the cancer clinics are not confined to medicine, while the 'democratic' decision-making found with the Down's children had unexpected effects of power with a significance far beyond medical encounters.

Working this way parallels Glaser and Strauss' (1967) famous account of grounded theory. A simplified model of this involves these stages:

– an initial attempt to develop categories which illuminate the data
– an attempt to 'saturate' these categories with many appropriate cases in order to demonstrate their relevance
– developing these categories into more general analytic frameworks with relevance outside the setting.

Glaser and Strauss use their research on death and dying as an example. They show how they developed the category of 'awareness contexts' to refer to the kinds of situations in which people were informed of their likely fate. The category was then saturated and finally related to non-medical settings where people learn about how others define them (e.g. schools).

'Grounded theory' has been criticised for its failure to acknowledge implicit theories which guide work at an early stage. It also is clearer about the generation of theories than about their test. Used unintelligently, it can also degenerate into a fairly empty building of categories (aided by the computer software programs already discussed) or into a mere smoke-screen used to legitimise purely empiricist research (see Bryman: 1988, 83–87). At best, 'grounded theory' offers an approximation of the creative activity of theory-building found in good observational work, compared to the dire abstracted empiricism present in the most wooden statistical studies.

Styles of Theorising in Observational Work

Throughout this chapter, I have used relevant examples to give concrete illustrations of the methodological issues I have been covering. Now it is time to examine the competing claims of two different theories underlying observational research: interactionism and ethnomethodological ethnography.

However, I do not want to provide a purely theoretical discussion of rival 'schools' of sociology. My solution is to offer some illustrations of how different sociological traditions have provided different but fruitful ways of thinking about observational data.

Interactionism

Interactionist principles: Interactionism is concerned with the creation and change of symbolic orders via social interaction. For instance, Goffman (1964) has shown how social stigma is recognised by the rest of us and how stigmatised people manage their status. In another famous study, Goffman (1961a) outlines what he calls a 'mortifying process' whereby 'total institutions' (like armies, boarding schools and monasteries) strip away previous identities in order to create an identity that is consistent with the institution.

This concern with identity and the symbolic order has an important implication for how interactionists view methodology. While positivists can view methods as mere techniques of more or less efficient data-gathering, the interactionist is bound to view research itself as a symbolic order based on interactions. Consequently, Denzin properly points out that for him, as an interactionist, 'Methodology . . . represents the particular ways the sociologist acts on his environment' (1970, 5).

For Denzin, methods cannot be neutral instruments because they define how the topic will be symbolically constituted and how the researcher will adopt a particular definition of self vis-à-vis the data. For instance, interactionists are likely to define themselves in a subject-to-subject relation to their data, while positivists pursue an object-to-object model.

Denzin presents seven methodological principles which stem from this perspective. I have amalgamated some of his points in Table 3.2, while citing some examples for each principle taken from an early study by Becker (1953) 'Becoming a Marihuana User' (see p. 33, above).

Table 3.2: *Interactionism's Methodological Principles*

Principle	Implication	Example
1 Relating symbols and interaction	Showing how meanings arise in the context of behaviour	Behaviour of marihuana users in the presence of non-users (Becker 1953)
2 Taking the actors' points of view	Learning everyday conceptions of reality; interpreting them through sociological perspective	Becker's observations of a drug culture
3 Studying the 'situated' character of interaction	Gathering data in naturally-occurring situations	Observing people in their own environments
4 Studying process as well as stability	Examining how symbols and behaviour vary over time and setting	Studies of 'moral careers' (Becker 1953, Goffman 1961a)
5 Generalising from descriptions to theories	Attempting to establish universal interactive propositions	Goffman (1981) on 'forms' of interaction

Source: adapted from Denzin: 1970, 7–19

Following a practice common to interactionists, Denzin uses the term 'participant observation' rather than 'ethnography' to index the research methodology most appropriate to his perspective. Such a method involves sharing in people's lives while attempting to learn their symbolic world. The way it is used will depend on the precise role carved out by the researcher, varying from a 'complete participant' to the 'complete observer'.

Denzin rightly suggests that participant observation embodies the principles as set out in Table 3.2. It involves taking the viewpoint of those studied, understanding the situated character of interaction and viewing social processes over time, and can encourage attempts to develop formal theories grounded in first-hand data. Unlike survey research, Denzin points out, 'the participant observer is not bound in his field work by pre-judgements about the nature of his problem, by rigid data-gathering devices, or by hypotheses' (*ibid*, 216).

Unlike some interactionist work which may fail to improve upon good descriptive journalism, Denzin's principle 5 proposes that a description of content serves only as a prelude to analytic work. Basing himself on Glaser and Strauss' (1967) distinction between 'substantive' and 'formal' theory, he reminds us that the intrinsic fascination of much ethnographic data should be a stepping stone towards the attempt to establish 'universal interactive propositions' (Denzin: 1970, 19).

In this respect, Denzin's approach shares the analytic breadth that we found in cognitive anthropology. It underlines the point that good ethnography should not limit itself to a set of descriptions about how people behave in different settings. On the contrary, ethnography shares the social science programme of producing general, possibly even law-like, statements about human social organisation.

Denzin also notes that participant observation is not without its own difficulties. First, its focus on the present may blind the observer to important events that occurred before his entry on the scene. Second, as Dalton (1959) points out, confidants or informants in a social setting may be entirely unrepresentative of the less open participants. Third, observers may change the situation just by their presence and so the decision about what role to adopt will be fateful. Finally, the observer may 'go native', identifying so much with the participants that, like a child learning to talk, he cannot remember how he found out or how to articulate the principles underlying what he is doing.

It is now time to turn from principles and consider some exemplary interactionist studies.

Interactionist studies: When you observe face-to-face behaviour within a part of your culture with which you are familiar, it may all strike you as terribly 'obvious' and unremarkable. Perhaps that was your experience when you attempted some of the early exercises in this chapter.

If so, you would have been helped by reading the early work of Erving Goffman. Goffman shows us two recurrent kinds of rules used to organise social interaction:

1 Rules of courtesy, manners and etiquette (who is able to do and say what to whom and in what way?).
2 Depending upon the definition of the situation, rules of what is relevant or irrelevant within any setting.

As Goffman points out, these rules give us a clue to understanding what is going on in definitions of situations in face-to-face encounters. For: 'instead of beginning by asking what happens when this definition of the situation breaks down, we can begin by asking what perspectives this definition of the situation *excludes* when it is being satisfactorily sustained' (Goffman: 1961b, 19, my emphasis). In Goffman's later terminology, rules of relevance and irrelevance constitute the *frames* through which a setting is defined.

Viewing 1000 doctor–parent consultations in Scottish clinics in the 1970s, Strong at first struggled to see anything remarkable about what was going on. Only when he gathered some comparative data on private and 'charity' clinics in the United States did the relevance of 'frame' become so apparent. Now he saw cases where medicine was individualised and parents identified their child's medical history in terms of named specialists. He also saw cases (in the 'charity' clinic) where mothers' 'good intentions' were openly challenged by doctors.

Strong (1988) reports that interaction in the Scottish clinics could now be seen to be framed in the following ways:

1 Parents were portrayed as passive and technically ignorant.
2 Nonetheless parents' behaviour towards their children was never publicly challenged: 'every Scottish mother was nominally treated as loving, honest, reliable and intelligent' (*ibid*, 240).
3 Mothers were portrayed as more knowledgable than fathers and mothers of many children or foster-mothers were held to be more reliable witnesses than other mothers.
4 Doctors were anonymous and interchangeable – enjoying 'collegial' authority.

Strong's study shows how Goffman's concept of frame allows the observer to generate important questions. Following Sherlock Holmes, what may be most significant is 'the dog that did not bark at night', i.e. what does *not* happen or seems irrelevant.

In a more recent study of a ward for terminally ill patients, Anssi Peräkylä (1989) has shown how staff can use four different frames to define themselves and their patients:

1 *The practical frame* defines staff in terms of the practical tasks they need to carry out in the ward; patients become the mere objects of such tasks.
2 *The medical frame* defines staff in terms of the activities of diagnosis and therapeutic intervention; once again patients become objects.
3 *The lay frame* makes staff into ordinary people, able to feel anguish and grief; it redefines the patient as a feeling and experiencing subject.
4 *The psychological frame* defines staff as objective surveyors of the emotional reactions of patients; patients are both subjects (who feel and experience) and objects (of the knowing psychological gaze).

However, Peräkylä's study, which is very rich, goes beyond a mere attempt to catalogue different frames. First, he shows the contingencies associated with a move between different frames. It turns out, for instance, that the psychological frame is a powerful means of resolving the identity-disturbances found in other frames – where a patient is resisting practical or medical framing, for instance, this can be explained in terms of his psychological state. Second, the psychological frame also seemed to be a convenient means for the staff to talk about their activities to Peräkylä himself and to define his presence to each other and to patients.

As used by Strong and Peräkylä, within a broadly interactionist perspective, Goffman's concept of 'frame' offers a powerful way to ask questions about observational data. Moreover, in related studies like Dingwall and Murray (1983) and Silverman (1984), an ever-growing, *cumulative* body of knowledge is emerging about how framing works in professional–client settings.

Exercise 3.4

This is an exercise to give you some experience of using the concept of 'frame' which is concerned with what people treat as 'relevant' or 'irrelevant' in any social activity.

Choose any setting with which you are familiar (e.g. a meeting with friends in a restaurant or bar, a family gathering, a college class, a religious ceremony, a television soap-opera). When you next participate in (or watch) this setting, consider the following questions:

1   Which frames are people using to organise their activities?
2   What functions are served by each frame?
3   How and why do people move between frames?
4   Do any 'out-of-frame' activities occur? If so, how are these handled? If not, what would they look like?

As Peräkylä (1989) shows, such studies open up a series of questions with a strongly practical relevance. Following my work on the hidden 'power-plays' of apparently 'democratic' consultations, Peräkylä reveals that the 'psychological' frame serves a multiplicity of purposes which is not coterminous with 'greater understanding'. As he argues:

> Instead of arguing for or against the use of social-psychological models in medicine, sociology should explicate the way these models are used, the circumstances that they are applied in, and the intended and unintended consequences of their use. These are social issues, permeated by power relations. (Peräkylä: 1989, 131)

It is now time to turn to an alternative way of exploring these questions.

Ethnomethodological Ethnography

Ethnomethodological principles: Several decades ago, the links between good interactionist ethnography and ethnomethodology were noted by Harvey Sacks:

> Instead of pushing aside the older ethnographic work in sociology, I would treat it as the only work worth criticising . . . where criticising is giving some dignity to something . . . the relevance of the works of the Chicago sociologists is that they contain a lot of information about this and that. And this-and-that is what the world is made up of. (Sacks: 1989, 254)

In this transcript of a lecture given in the 1960s, Harvey Sacks suggests that there is a continuity between the older Chicago School work and the then newly emerging ethnomethodological studies. The basis for this continuity, Sacks suggests, is not theoretical but methodological.

Sacks admires the painstaking attention to detail ('this-and-that') of the Chicago School which we glimpsed in Whyte's account of restaurant work.

He implies that, in this respect, it surpasses that kind of sociology which deals merely in huge generalisations.

Like the older ethnographers, Sacks also rejected the crass empiricism of certain kinds of quantitative sociology. In particular, its assumptions that research is based on finding some indices and explaining why they rise and fall by *ex post facto* interpretations of significant correlations.

Sacks was convinced that serious work paid attention to detail and that, if something mattered, it should be observable. For instance, in a fascinating passage, Sacks noted the baleful influence on sociology of Mead's proposal that we need to study things which are not available to observation, e.g. 'society', 'attitudes'. He comments:

> But social activities are observable, you can see them all around you, and you can write them down. The tape recorder is important, but a lot of this can be done without a tape recorder. If you think you can see it, that means we can build an observational study. (1992a, 28)

If Chicago School ethnography ultimately fails, its failure lies in not going far enough in its pursuit of detail. The proper model of scientific enquiry, Sacks assumes, derives from the natural sciences in the sense that such sciences provide precise information about their data and research instruments. The aim is to give the reader as much information as the author and the ability to reproduce the analysis. This leads Sacks to identify two methodological limitations of Chicago School ethnography:

1 It fails to reproduce its data in a form which allows the reader to reproduce the analysis.
2 It often depends on using native informants. This reveals the categories that people use but 'they're not investigating the categories by attempting to find them in the activities in which they're employed' (*ibid*, 254).

Sacks' problem is that most ethnography depends upon generalisations made on the basis of truncated data extracts and/or responses elicited from informants. There are, he implies, five simple solutions:

1 Provide the reader with transcripts based on tape-recordings of naturally occurring activities.
2 Always focus on what is *observable*, like behaviour, and avoid that which is not observable, like motivations or attitudes (although we may study how people talk about one another's 'motivations' and 'attitudes').
3 Avoid abstractions and early generalisations, while carefully sorting through your material:

> the more material you have at your command, the more you ought to be able to pick up items and see their recurrence and get some idea of what they might be doing. But the way to proceed is item by item. (*ibid*)

4 Reject the anti-scientific position of some interactionists (e.g. Blumer). Sacks wanted to do a *better* science. For instance, he criticised

laboratory studies only for their lack of success, not for their aim of producing a 'science of society'. So laboratory studies of, say, 'short-term memory' fail because they ask the wrong question, namely 'do people understand what somebody else says?'. Instead, researchers should be asking: 'is there some *procedure* people use which has, as its product, a showing that they heard and understood?' (Sacks: 1992b, 30, my emphasis).

5 Make common sense, as Garfinkel (1967) put it, a 'topic' not just a tacit 'resource'. Thus the problem with *both* survey research and much ethnography is that they fail to topicalise their understandings. As Sacks says:

> Now (w)hat I want to do is turn that around: to use what 'we' know, what any Member [i.e. member of society] knows, to pose us some problems. What activity is being done, for example. And then we can see whether we can build an apparatus which will give us those results. (1992a, 487)

Ethnomethodological studies: I have only space for two examples of the kind of work that follows from Sacks' recommendations. One example is sociological (Maynard: 1989) and one is anthropological (Moerman: 1974).

Writing twenty years after Sacks, Maynard notes how ethnographers are still trying to picture how people see things rather than focussing on what is observable. As he puts it:

> In doing ethnography, researchers attempt to draw a picture of what some phenomenon 'looks like' from an insider's account of the phenomenon and for some audience who wants to know about it. The ethnographer, in general, is in the business of describing culture from the members' point of view. (Maynard: 1989, 130)

Maynard notes how such concerns have shaped research in one part of the sociology of law. 'Plea bargaining' has been identified as a process by which defendants plead guilty to a 'lesser' offence, thereby minimising their punishment and speeding up the work of the courts (evidence does not need to be heard if the defendant pleads guilty). Ethnographers have assumed that this process works on the basis of shared perceptions held by prosecution and defence lawyers.

However, Maynard suggests that such ethnographic work, based on the identification of people's perceptions, has at least three deficiencies:

1 It depends upon common-sense knowledge: 'ethnographers rely on unnoticed abilities to record and recognise such features, just as participants rely on basically uninvestigated abilities in producing them' (*ibid*).

2 It glosses over what 'plea bargaining' actually is – the diversity of discourse that gets called 'plea bargaining'.

3 It fails to treat the common orientation of the parties concerned as an outcome of their interaction, preferring to make such 'mutuality appear to be a matter of cognitive consensus' (*ibid*, 134).

Instead, following Sacks' emphasis on what is observable, Maynard studies 'how a sense of mutuality is accomplished' (*ibid*). This involves examining how plea bargaining sequences are introduced into the talk. For instance, a bargaining proposal can be solicited or it can be announced, as shown in Table 3.3.

Table 3.3: *Two Forms of Plea Bargaining*

SOLICITATION		
(solicit)	PD[1]:	Is there an offer in this case?
(proposal)	DA[2]:	I would say in this case a fine, seventy five
ANNOUNCEMENT		
(announcement)	PD:	I'll propose a deal to you
('go-ahead' signal)	DA:	Tell me what ya got
(proposal)	PD:	If ya dismiss the 242, I might be able to arrange a plea to 460 for a fine

[1] PD = Public Defender.
[2] DA = District Attorney.
Source: Maynard 1989, 134

Maynard's study draws attention to how the phenomenon of 'plea bargaining' is itself locally constituted in the activities of the participants. As I argued earlier, in Chapter 2, there is a danger that, if ethnography reduces social life to the definitions of the participants, it becomes a purely 'subjectivist' sociology which loses sight of *social* phenomena.

Instead, the point is to narrow the focus to what people are *doing*. As Maynard puts it:

> The question that ethnographers have traditionally asked – 'How do participants see things?' – has meant in practice the presumption that reality lies outside the words spoken in a particular time and place. The . . . [alternative] question – 'How do participants do things?' – suggests that the microsocial order can be appreciated more fully by studying how speech and other face-to-face behaviours constitute reality within actual mundane situations. (Maynard: 1989, 144)

Maynard underlines Sacks' position on the need to provide transcripts, to focus on what is observable and to proceed in a cautious, step-by-step manner. We can see the full force of Sacks' arguments in the experiences of one ethnographer who attempted a study of a tribe living in Thailand. As a cognitive anthropologist, Michael Moerman was interested in learning the categorisation systems employed by this native people.

Like most anthropologists and Chicago School ethnographers, he used native informants. His aim was to elicit from them what 'being a Lue' (the name of the tribe) meant to them. However, he was troubled about what sense to read in their accounts.

First, his questions often related to issues which were either obvious or irrelevant to the respondents. As he puts it: 'To the extent that answering an ethnographer's question is an unusual situation for natives, one cannot reason from a native's answer to his *normal* categories or ascriptions' (Moerman: 1974, 66, my emphasis).

Second, it was not so straightforward to switch to observational methods while pursuing the tribe's 'identity'. Even when the ethnographer is silent and merely observes, his presence indicates to people that matters relevant to 'identity' should be highlighted. Consequently, people may pay particular attention to what both he and they take to be relevant categorisation schemes – like ethnic or kinship labels. In this way, the ethnographer may have 'altered the local priorities among the native category sets which it is his task to describe' (*ibid*, 67).

What, then, is to be done? A clue is given by the initially opaque sub-headings of his article: 'Who are the Lue?' 'Why are the Lue?' 'When are the Lue?'

Moerman argues that there are three reasons why we should *not* ask: 'Who are the Lue?' First, it would generate an inventory of traits. Like all such inventories it could be endless because we could always be accused of having left something out. Second, lists are retrospective. Once we have decided that the Lue *are* a tribe, then we have no difficulty in 'discovering' a list of traits to support our case. Third, the identification of the Lue as a tribe depends, in part, on their successful presentation of themselves as a tribe. As Moerman puts it: 'The question is not "Who are the Lue?" but rather when how and why the identification "Lue" is preferred' (62).

Moerman adds that this does *not* mean that the Lue are not really a tribe or that they fooled him into thinking they were one. Rather their ethnic identity arises in the fact that people in the area use ethnic identification labels some of the time that they are talking about each other.

Of course, some of the time is not all the time. Hence the task of the ethnographer should be to observe when and *if* ethnic identification labels are used by the participants being studied.

Moerman neatly summarises ethnomethodology's alternative to other forms of ethnography:

> Anthropology [has an] apparent inability to distinguish between warm . . . human bodies and one kind of identification device which some of those bodies sometimes use. Ethnic identification devices – with their important potential of making each ethnic set of living persons a joint enterprise with countless generations of unexamined history – seem to be universal. Social scientists should therefore describe and analyse the ways in which they are used, and not merely – as natives do – use them as explanations. (Moerman: 1974, 67–68)

Conclusion: The Unity of the Ethnographic Project

I want to conclude this chapter by trying to locate points of contact between the two forms of ethnography that I have been considering. Consonant with the argument deployed throughout this book, researchers have more to learn by exploring the interstices between analytic positions than by dwelling on one side of fine-sounding polarities. Moreover, it

would be entirely mistaken to believe that all the certainties in observational work derive from ethnomethodological insights.

In fact, as I have argued already, a number of ethnographers have either
taken on board many of these insights or reached them independently. For
instance, a recognition that social phenomena are locally constituted
(through the activities of participants) is not confined to Moerman and
Maynard. Using the example of studies of the 'family', I want to show
another direction from which one can draw the same conclusion.

Exercise 3.5

This exercise is meant to test how well you have acquired the skills
outlined in the work of Sacks, Maynard and Moerman.

Your task is to describe the outline of a small-scale observational study
of a group of people near at hand to you (e.g. students, family, workers).

1   What is your topic (i.e. which group are you going to study and what
    are you interested in about them?)?
2   What methods can you use to gather data (e.g. observation, tape-
    recording, interview, etc.)? What will each method tell you?
3   How can you study 'when', 'how' and 'why' this is a group rather
    than 'who' or 'what' is the group?
4   What will you learn in this way that you would not learn by asking
    'who' or 'what' is the group?
5   Imagine that you later discover that the members of the group do not
    agree with your conclusions. Should you modify them?

In a paper on methodological issues in family studies, Gubrium and
Holstein (1987) show how much sociological work assumes that 'family life'
is properly depicted in its 'natural' habitat – the home. Conversely, they
argue that 'the family' is not a uniform phenomenon, to be found in one
setting, but is 'occasioned' and 'contexted'.

We can see more clearly what they are saying in Table 3.4, which
contrasts the 'conventional understanding' with Gubrium and Holstein's
alternative.

Gubrium and Holstein's alternative direction for family studies closely
fits Sacks' approach, while opening up a number of fascinating areas for
family studies, as set out below:

1   Once we conceive of 'the family' in terms of a researchable set of
    descriptive practices, we are freed from the methodological and ethical
    nightmare of obtaining access to study families 'as they really are', i.e.
    in their own households.
2   We can now study how the structures of family organisation are
    depicted in different milieux (e.g. employment agencies, schools,
    clinics, etc.).

Table 3.4: *Two Ways of Describing 'Family Life'*

THE CONVENTIONAL UNDERSTANDING

1 Families have 'inner' and 'outer' sides

2 The 'inner' side is located in the household

3 Outside households we obtain only a 'version' of this 'prime reality'

4 Members of the household have a privileged access to family order

5 Participant observation is required to obtain 'authentic understanding' of family life

AN ALTERNATIVE

1 'Family' is a way of interpreting, representing and ordering social relations

2 The family is not private but inextricably linked with public life

3 The household does not locate family life

4 The household is not 'trivial' because it is often appealed to by laypeople and professionals alike as the determinant of family life

Source: adapted from Gubrium & Holstein: 1987

3 This links to studies of the social distribution of 'knowledge' about the family (e.g. when, where and by whom theories of the nature and consequences of 'broken homes' are employed).

4 It also ties in with the study of how different organisational routines constrain particular depictions of family order.

As already noted, issues of household location and privileged access now become redefined as topics rather than troubles – for example, we might study the claims that professionals make for such access. This underlines Gubrium and Holstein's point that family knowledge is never purely private. Family members themselves appeal to collective representations (like maxims and the depictions of families in soap-operas) to explain their own behaviour. Family members also present the 'reality' of family life in different ways to different audiences and in different ways to the same audience (see Gubrium and Holstein: 1987 for a fuller elaboration of this argument).

Gubrium and Holstein offer an exciting prospectus for family studies and an appropriate way to conclude this chapter on observation. For this kind of work (elsewhere termed 'articulative ethnography' by Gubrium: 1988), together with ethnomethodology, offers three crucial insights for observational studies, as follows:

1 It switches attention away from a more psychological orientation around what people are thinking towards what they are doing.

2 It shows the analytic issues that lie behind methodological puzzles.

3 It firmly distinguishes social science observational work from journalism and common sense, thus, in a certain sense, fulfilling Durkheim's project.

As Michael Moerman once commented: 'Folk beliefs have honourable status but they are not the same intellectual object as a scientific analysis' (Moerman: 1974, 55).

Exercise 3.6

This exercise encourages you to use the 'alternative' version of describing family life.

Imagine that you wish to do an observational study of the family. Now consider the following questions:

1   What are the advantages and disadvantages of obtaining access to the family household?
2   In what ways may families be studied outside the household setting? What methodology might you use and what questions could you ask?
3   What might observation tell you about 'the family' in each of the following settings:

    – law courts
    – doctor–patient consultations
    – television soap-operas?

    (EITHER do a study of ONE of these settings OR write hypothetically about all THREE.)
4   What does it mean to say you are studying 'the family' (i.e. within inverted commas)?

4
Texts

British and American social scientists have never been entirely confident about analysing texts. Perhaps, in (what the French call) the Anglo-Saxon cultures, words seem too ephemeral and insubstantial to be the subject of scientific analysis. It might seem better, then, to leave textual analysis to literary critics and to concentrate on definite social phenomena, like actions and the structures in which they are implicated.

This uncertain, occasionally cavalier, attitude to language is reflected in the way in which so many sociological texts begin with fairly arbitrary definitions of their 'variables'. The classic model is Durkheim's *Suicide* which offers a 'conclusive' definition of the phenomenon in its first few pages and then rushes off to investigate it in these terms. As Atkinson (1978) has pointed out, this method rules out entirely any analysis of the very social processes through which suicide is socially defined – particularly in the context of coroners' own definitional practices.

In most sociology, then, words are important simply as a jumping-off point for the real analysis. Where texts are analysed, they are usually presented as 'official' or 'common-sense' versions of social phenomena, to be undercut by the underlying social phenomena displayed in the sociologist's analysis of social structures. The model is: people *say* X, but we can *show* that Y is the case.

There are four exceptions to this general rule:

Content Analysis

Content analysis is an accepted method of textual investigation, particularly in the field of mass communications. It involves establishing categories and then counting the number of instances when those categories are used in a particular item of text, for instance a newspaper report.

Content analysis pays particular attention to the issue of the *reliability* of its measures – ensuring that different researchers use them in the same way – and to the *validity* of its findings – through precise counts of word use (see Selltiz *et al*: 1964, 335–342). However, its theoretical basis is unclear and its conclusions can often be trite. Because it is a quantitative method, it will not be discussed in detail in this text. However, I will later present a study of political articles (Silverman: 1982) which combines qualitative textual analysis with some simple word-counts.

Ethnography

As we saw in Chapter 3, ethnographers seek to understand the organis-ation of social action in particular settings. Most ethnographic data are based on observation of what people are saying and doing (and of the territories in which this talk and action takes place). However, in literate societies, written accounts are an important feature of many settings, as Hammersley and Atkinson (1983, 128) point out. Therefore, ethnogra-phers must not neglect the way in which documents, tables and even advertisements and cartoons exemplify certain features of those settings. More recently, as we shall see, what Dingwall (1981) calls ethnomethod-ological ethnography has provided an analytic framework for the analysis of texts. In the work of Garfinkel (1967) and Zimmerman (1974), for instance, attention has been paid to the common-sense practices involved in assembling and interpreting written records. This work has refused to reduce texts to a secondary status and has made an important contribution to our understanding of everyday bureaucratic practices.

Semiotics

Anglo-Saxon culture, in which these first two approaches have arisen, makes clear-cut disciplinary boundaries. Perhaps this is why, generally speaking, 'words' are allocated to the humanities and 'structures' to the sciences. French culture, on the contrary, creates unities around 'methods' rather than disciplines. We shall shortly see how concepts deriving from the Swiss linguist Ferdinand de Saussure provided a vital apparatus for the analysis of texts. The signal contribution of Saussure was to generate a method which showed that 'structures' and 'words' are inseparable.

Ethnomethodology

Following Garfinkel (1967), ethnomethodology attempts to understand 'folk' (*ethno*) methods (*methodology*) for organising the world. It locates these methods in the skills ('artful practices') through which people come to develop an understanding of each other and of social situations. Following an important paper by Sacks (1974), a major focus of ethno-methodology has been on the skills we all use in producing and understand-ing descriptions – from a remark in a conversation to a newspaper headline. I will, therefore, conclude this chapter by an account of Sacks' concept of 'membership categorisation'.

Ethnographic Analysis

The presence and significance of documentary products provides the ethnogra-pher with a rich vein of analytic topics, as well as a valuable source of information. Such topics include: How are documents written? How are they read? Who writes them? Who reads them? For what purposes? On what occasions? With what outcomes? What is recorded? What is omitted? What is taken for granted? What does the writer seem to take for granted about the reader(s)? What do readers need to know in order to make sense of them? (Hammersley and Atkinson: 1983, 142–143)

Hammersley and Atkinson show the many interesting questions that can be asked about documents. In this section, I will examine some of the answers that ethnographers have given to these questions. This will involve a consideration of different kinds of documents, taken in the following order:

– files
– statistical records
– records of official proceedings
– images.

It should be stressed that this is not a hard-and-fast or an all-embracing list of every kind of document. It is organised in this way purely for ease of presentation. Nonetheless, the discussion that follows tries consistently to pursue the analytic issues involved in dealing with data. Although there are always practical problems which arise in data-analysis and techniques that can offer assistance, methodological problems should never be reduced to merely practical issues and 'recipe' solutions.

For instance, people who generate and use such documents are concerned with how accurately they *represent* reality. Conversely, ethnographers are concerned with the *social organisation* of documents, irrespective of whether they are accurate or inaccurate, true or biased.

Files

Like all documents, files are produced in particular circumstances for particular audiences. Files never speak for themselves. The ethnographer seeks to understand both the format of the file (for instance, the categories used on blank printed sheets) and the processes associated with its completion.

Selection interviews provide a good example of a setting where an interaction is organised, at least in part, by reference to the categories to be found on some document that will later constitute a 'file'. For instance, a large British local government organisation used the following record of job-selection interviews with candidates in their final year at university:

Name
Appearance
Acceptability
Confidence
Effort
Organisation
Motivation

Any other comments
(Silverman and Jones: 1976)

Following Hammersley and Atkinson's set of questions (above), the ethnographer can immediately ask about which items are represented on this list and which are omitted. For instance, the fact that 'appearance' and 'acceptability' are cited and located at the top of the list, while 'ability' is omitted, gives us clues about the culture of the organisation. So: 'successful candidates will be recognised in their preparedness to defer to "common sense" and to the accumulated wisdom of their seniors; to "sell themselves" without implying that a university degree provides any more than a basis for further training' (Silverman and Jones: 1976, 31).

Some of this is seen in the completed file of one (unsuccessful) applicant to whom we gave a fictitious name – see Table 4.1.

Table 4.1: *A Completed Selection Form*

Name: Chadwick
Appearance: Tall, slim, spotty-faced, black hair, dirty grey suit
Acceptability: Non-existent. Rather uncouth
Confidence: Awful. Not at all sure of himself
Effort: High
Organisation: Poor
Motivation: None really that counts
Any other comments: Reject

Source: Silverman and Jones: 1976, 31–32

It is tempting to treat such completed forms as providing the *causes* of selection decisions. However, two important points must be borne in mind before we rush to such a conclusion. First, such forms provide 'good reasons' for any selection decision. This means that we expect the elements of the form to 'fit' the decision recorded. For instance, we would be surprised if the 'reject' decision had been preceded by highly favourable comments about the candidate.

Thus the language of 'acceptability' provides a rhetoric through which selectors define the 'good sense' of their decision-making. It does not *determine* the outcome of the decision. A telling example of this was provided when we played back tapes of selection interviews to selectors several months later without meeting the selectors' request to remind them of their decision. Predictably, on hearing the tapes, selectors often made a different decision than they had made at the time. Nevertheless, when told of their earlier decision, they were able to adjust their comments to take account of it. The 'acceptability' criterion (and its converse 'abrasiveness') thus served more as a means to 'rewrite history' (Garfinkel:1967) than as a determinant of a particular selection decision.

The second point is that the files themselves are not simple 'records' of events but are artfully constructed with a view to how they may be read. For instance, in a study of a promotion panel at the same organisation, I showed how the committee organised their discussion in a way which made their eventual decision appear to be sound. In particular, I identified a three-stage process:

1 Beginning with premises all can accept (e.g. 'facts' everyone can agree upon).
2 Appealing to rules in ways which make sense in the present context.
3 Reaching conclusions demonstrably grounded in the rules as applied to the facts (Silverman: 1975b).

In order to produce 'sound' decisions, committees attend to relevant background circumstances which shape how 'facts' are to be seen. For instance, in the case of one candidate who had not made much progress, the following was said:

> Chair: and, um, is no doubt handicapped in, you know, his career development
> by the fact that that Department suddenly ha, ha
> ?: yes, yes
> Chair: came to an end and he was, had to be pitched forth somewhere

Even when the facts are assembled, they ask themselves further questions about what the facts 'really mean'. For instance:

> May: He's been there a long while in this job has he not? Does he do it in
> exactly the same way as when he started?

Or again:

> May: supposing he had people under his control who needed the softer form of
> encouragement (. . .) assistance rather than pushing and driving; could
> he handle that sort of situation?
> ?: Yes, and not only could he, but he has done
> May: He has, ah good (adapted from Silverman and Jones: 1976, 157–158)

Gubrium and Buckholdt's (1982) study of a U.S. rehabilitation hospital shows that a concern to assemble credible files may be a common feature of organisational activities. The authors show how hospital staff select, exchange and present information about the degree of physical disability and rehabilitation of patients and potential patients. Like reports of selection interviews, such descriptions are never context-free but are assembled or 'worked up' with reference to some audience: 'staff members work up descriptions of activities . . . using their knowledge of audience relevance in organising what they say and write' (Gubrium and Buckholdt: 1982, ix).

I will briefly illustrate such 'work up' in the context of what the authors call 'third-party description'. This refers to descriptions assembled for insurers and U.S. government agencies rather than for patients or their families.

Exercise 4.1

The following is a completed selector's report using the same form as found in Table 4.1:

Name: Fortescue

Appearance: Tall, thin, straw-coloured hair. Neat and tidy

Acceptability: High. Pleasant, quite mature sensible man

Confidence: Very good. Not conceited but firm, put himself across very well

Effort: Excellent academic record

Organisation: Excellent, both at school and university

Motivation: Keen on administration and very well informed on it. Has had considerable experience. Quite well informed about both Organisation and its functions generally.

Any other comments: Call for interview. First-rate.

1 What conclusions may be drawn from how the selector has completed this form (e.g. what sort of features does he find praiseworthy or not needing comment?)?
2 Does the completed form help us in understanding why certain candidates are selected at this organisation? If so, how? If not, why not?
3 If you were told that this selector came to a different decision when played a tape-recording of the same interview some months later, what would you make of this fact? What sociological questions could be asked now?

Rehabilitation at the hospital was paid for through government funds (via Medicare and Medicaid programmes) and insurance companies. An essential constraint, established by the U.S. Congress in 1972 was a review agency called the Professional Standards Review Organization (PSRO). The PSRO looks at decision-making over patient intake and discharge with a view to limiting costs. For instance, the acceptable average stay for a rehabilitation patient had been calculated at thirty-eight days.

A further constraint on the organisation of patient care was two rules of insurance companies. First, the hospital's charges would not be paid if a patient could not have rehabilitation because of additional medical problems (e.g. pneumonia). Second, if a patient's stay is very short, the insurance company may decide, retrospectively, that the patient should not have been admitted in the first place. These constraints shape how admissions are organised and how patient 'progress' is described.

Admissions staff have to make an initial decision about whether or not a potential patient is suitable for rehabilitation or needs other services involving chronic or acute care. A rule of thumb when considering whether a patient should be admitted is that the patient should be able to benefit from at least three hours of therapy per day. However, staff recognise that the files they are sent are not conclusive and may 'shade the truth'. For instance, another institution may wish to discharge the patient or the family may have exerted pressure for a transfer to the rehabilitation hospital. Consequently, admissions staff appeal to 'experience' and 'professional discretion' in working out what a potential patient's notes 'really mean'.

Appealing to these kinds of grounds, staff establish a basis for deciding what is 'really' meant by any file. Thus, in sorting out 'facts' from 'fancy', participants use a body of interpretive and rhetorical resources to define what will constitute 'reality' or 'the bottom line'.

Once a patient is admitted, the 'work-up' of descriptions continues. 'Progress notes' are prepared at regular intervals and staff work at making them internally consistent and appropriate to the recommendation (just like selectors). For instance, staff talk about 'the need to make sure that the figures tell the right story' and regularly try out their accounts on colleagues by asking 'how does that sound?'. The institutional interest is to show some sort of progress which will be sufficient to satisfy the funding agencies. Consequently, there is a pressure to identify simple problems where progress can readily be made and to seek patient statements which accord with the therapist's version of progress.

Gubrium and Buckholdt's work shows that hospital files can be treated as the outcome of a series of staff decisions grounded in the contingencies of their work. Similarly, Silverman and Jones reveal how records of selection interviews satisfy organisational conceptions of what is appropriate.

Both studies confirm that qualitative researchers are not primarily concerned with whether files are factually 'true' or 'false'. Instead, they focus on how such files reveal the practical decision-making of employees in the context of the constraints and contingencies of their work.

Statistical Records

Until the 1960s, official statistics, like files, were treated as a more or less accurate *representation* of a stable reality. Of course, this did not mean that their reliability or validity was taken for granted. Particular statistics or measures were often found to be of dubious scientific status. However, it tended to be assumed, in these cases, that such data or measures could always be improved.

The 1960s saw a massive shift of focus among sociologists as documented below:

- Cicourel and Kitsuse (1963) showed how school statistics on educational performance depended upon the organised, practical judgments of school staff.
- Garfinkel (1967) revealed how coroners writing death certificates formulated accounts 'of how death *really*-for-all-practical-purposes happened' (12). As Garfinkel noted, 'really' in these cases, referred, unavoidably, to common-sense understandings in the context of organisational contingencies.
- Sudnow (1968a) showed how hospital 'death' was recognised, attended to and disattended to by hospital staff.
- Sudnow (1968b) revealed that U.S. criminal statistics depended, in part, on a socially organised process of 'plea bargaining' through which defendants were encouraged to plead guilty.

Now, of course, many of these processes had already been recognised by sociologists and demographers. The difference was that such processes were no longer viewed as 'problems' which distorted the validity or reliability of official statistics. Instead, they were now treated in their own right, not as distortions of the phenomena they ostensibly measured but as *constitutive* of those phenomena. In other words, inspired by these studies, many sociologists now treated such phenomena ('death', 'guilt', 'ability') as *arising* within the very record-keeping activity which was supposed passively to record them.

This shift of focus did not mean that demography, based on official statistics, suddenly became worthless. As Hindess (1973) showed, one can pay attention to the social context of statistical production and still make use of statistics for both practical and analytical purposes. So the work that developed out of the insights of the 1960s is properly seen as having taken a divergent but non-competitive path to the continuing studies based on the use of official statistics.

For instance, Prior (1987) follows Garfinkel by looking at how 'deaths' are investigated by coroners. Prior puts it this way:

> men are more likely to have their deaths investigated, and to have their deaths regarded as 'unnatural', than are women. The same is true of the middle class as against the working class, the married as against the unmarried, widowed or single, and the economically active as against the inactive. (368)

However, in the case of decisions to do a post-mortem (autopsy) after 'violent' deaths, Prior finds that the figures go in the other direction: manual workers and the single, widowed or divorced are more likely to have an autopsy than the middle class or married.

Prior suggests that coroners use their 'common-sense knowledge' to treat sudden and violent death as more suspicious among the former groups. Although autopsy is generally more common after a death defined as 'violent', Prior notes that: 'in its search for the origins of death, forensic pathology tends to reserve the scalpel as an investigatory instrument for distinct and specific segments of the population' (371).

The implication is that statistical tables about causes of death are themselves the outcome of a decision-making process which needs to be described. Consequently, for the qualitative researcher, statistics, like files, raise fundamental questions about the processes through which they are produced.

Exercise 4.2

In a discussion of how records are assembled on 'juvenile delinquents' in the U.S. justice system, Cicourel (1968) considers the case of Linda, aged 13. Linda first came to the attention of the police when she reported that she had been kidnapped by four boys. She said that she had been coaxed away from a party by them and admitted that she had told them that she would get drunk and then have sexual intercourse with one of them. After stealing some alcohol, the boys took her to a club where they all got drunk and she had sex with the youngest boy. Although the boys sought to depict Linda as a 'slut', the police viewed Linda as an 'attractive' victim with no prior record. However, some weeks later, acting on information from Linda's parents, the police saw Linda in a drunken state and obtained an admission that she had had sex with ten boys. She was now charged as in danger of leading a 'lewd and immoral life'.

Here are extracts from an interview between Linda (L) and a female Probation Officer (PO) after Linda's arrest:

```
 1 PO: You're not pregnant?
 2 L:  No
 3 PO: Have you used anything to prevent a pregnancy?
 4 L:  Once X (one of her boyfriends) used one of those things
 5 PO: Did you ever feel scared about getting pregnant?
 6 L:  No, I was always trying to get even with my parents
 7 PO: You sort of wanted to get even with them?
 8 L:  Yes. I always wanted to get even with other people. My
 9      mother gets mad at me. I love my father. I know that's
10      what's wrong with me. I talk about this with my parents.
11      I don't know why.
```

The Probation Officer's report suggests that Linda needs psychotherapy and suggests that she be institutionalised for three to six months' treatment.

1 How does the PO organise her questioning to support her eventual recommendation?
2 Is there any evidence that Linda is colluding with the PO in a particular interpretation of her past behaviour?

Public Records

Public or official records are not limited to statistical tables. A common feature of democracies is a massive documentation of official business covering legal proceedings, certain business meetings and the work of parliaments and parliamentary committees.

Such public records constitute a potential goldmine for sociological investigation. First, they are relevant to important issues – revealing how public and private agencies account for, and legitimate, their activities. Second, they are accessible; the field researcher does not have the problem, so common in observational work, of negotiating access.

Despite the potential of such work, it has been sadly neglected by field researchers. However, an important, relatively new source of studies in this area has been provided by the journal *Discourse and Society*.

I will take just one example: a study of the 1973 Watergate Hearings in the U.S. Congress. Molotch and Boden (1985) show how their work on the text of these hearings arises in the context of a debate about the nature of power. They are not concerned with explicit power battles or with the ability to set agendas. Instead, they are concerned with a 'third face of power': 'the ability to determine the very grounds of the interactions through which agendas are set and outcomes determined . . . the struggle over the linguistic premises upon which the legitimacy of accounts will be judged' (273).

As they show, a problem resolved in all talk is that, while accounts are context-bound, a determinate account has 'somehow' to be achieved (see Garfinkel: 1967). Molotch and Boden apply this insight to the interrogation of President Nixon's counsel (John Dean) by a pro-Nixon Senator (Sen. Gurney). Dean had made public charges about the involvement of the White House in the Watergate 'cover-up'. Gurney's strategy is to define Dean as someone who avoids 'facts' and just relies upon 'impressions'. This is seen in the following extract:

(G = Sen. Gurney; D = John Dean) (Transcription conventions are given in Chapter 6, p. 118)

G: Did you dis*cuss* any aspects of the *Water*gate at that meeting with the President? For example, did you *tell* him anything about (1.4) what *Halde*man *knew* of or what Ehrlichman knew?

D: Well, given the– given the fact that he *told* me I've done a good job I assumed he had been very pleased with what ha– what had been going on
    . . .

G: Did you discuss what Magruder knew about Watergate and what involvement *he* had?

D: No, I didn't. I didn't get into any – I did not give him a report at that point in time

G: Did you discuss *cover*-up money *money* that was being raised and paid?

D: No, sir
    . . .

G: Well now how can you say that the President knew all about these *things* from a *simple* observation by him that 'Bob tells me you are doing a good job'?

(Molotch and Boden: 1985, 280, adapted)

As Molotch and Boden show, Gurney's strategy is to insist on literal accounts of 'facts' not 'impressionistic' ones. Throughout this extract, for instance, Gurney demands that Dean state that he actually discussed the cover-up with Nixon. When Dean is unable to do this, Gurney imposes limits on Dean's ability to appeal to a context (Dean's 'assumptions') which might show that Dean's inferences were correct.

However, as Gurney knows, all accounts can be defeated by demonstrating that *at some point*, since they depend upon knowing the context, they are not 'really objective'. Hence: 'Demands for "just the facts", the simple answers, the forced-choice response, preclude the "whole story" that contains another's truth . . . [consequently] Individuals can participate in their own demise through the interactional work they do' (*ibid*, 285).

Exercise 4.3

Here is a further extract from the Watergate Hearings. At this point, Dean is trying to implicate Nixon in the 'cover-up' operation:

```
 1 D: When I discussed with him (Nixon) the fact that I thought
 2     he ought to be aware of the fact I thought I had been
 3     involved in the obstruction of justice . . . He told me,
 4     John, you don't have any legal problems to worry about
 5     . . .
 6 G: Did you discuss any specific ob– instances of obstruction
 7     of justice?
 8 (1.3)
 9 D: Well, I'd– Senator, from– based on conversations I'd had
10     with him– I had worked from–
11 G: I am talking about this meeting.
12 D: Yes, I understand. I'm answering your question. Uh– the–
13     eh–you c– y– I can tell when– when uh I am talking with
14     somebody if they have some conception of what I am
15     talking about– I had the impression that the President
16     had some conception of what I was talking ab[out
17 G:                                              [But I am not
18     talking about impressions. That is what I am trying to
19     get away from. (0.8) I am talking about specific
20     instances
```

1 Using this material, show what strategies Sen. Gurney is using to discredit John Dean's evidence

2 Show how Dean tries to sustain the credibility of what he is saying

3 Why might Dean's appeal to what 'I can tell when I am talking with somebody' be seen as 'a risky strategy' by Molotch and Boden?

Visual Images

Images are another neglected source of data for field research. There are both good and bad reasons for this neglect:

1 In societies where television is central to leisure, there are grounds to believe that, somewhat ironically, we have become lazy with our eyes. Thus what we see is taken for granted and our first thought tends to associate social research with what we can read (texts, statistics) or hear (interviews, conversations).

2 The analysis of images raises complex methodological and theoretical issues. Thus it is difficult, but not impossible, to transcribe images as well as words (see Peräkylä and Silverman: 1991b). Moreover, the theoretical basis for the analysis of images is complex. The two very different traditions of semiotics (see Barthes: 1967) and conversation analysis (see Chapter 6) offer competing ways into such work.

3 It is sometimes argued that attention to the image alone can detract attention from the social processes involved in image-production and image-reception. For instance, Slater (1989) argues that semiotic analysis of advertisements has neglected the way in which such images are shaped by the economic logic and social organisation of the relationship between advertising agencies and their clients. A similar argument lies behind the switch of film analysis in the 1980s away from the semiotics of film and towards understanding the logic of movie-production in terms of such structures as the studio system.

Nonetheless, despite these problems, the analysis of images has provoked much interesting work. This ranges from advertisements (e.g. Barthes, 1972 analysis of a pasta ad), to films (e.g. Silverman's: 1993 analysis of the film *Bad Timing*), to parenting manuals (e.g. Dingwall *et al*: 1991).

Once again, I have space for only one example. This is Emmison's (1983) fine analysis of cartoons about the economy. According to his analysis, it turns out that there are at least three phases in how 'the economy' is represented:

1 Before the 1930s, 'economy' refers only to the classical notion of 'economising' through cutting back unnecessary expenditure.

2 In the 1930s, Keynesian ideas about a national economic structure, able to be modified by government intervention, start to be represented. Thus a contemporary cartoon shows 'Slump' as a half-ghost, half-scarecrow figure, while a jaunty Father Christmas dismisses the slump with a wave of his hand. For the first time, then, 'the economy' becomes embodied (as a sick person) and collective solutions to economic problems are implied (Father Christmas dispensing gifts via government spending).

3 By the 1940s, the economy is understood as a fully collective, embodied being. Often cartoons of that period use animals to represent both the

economy and economic policy. One cartoon depicts the economy as a sea-monster. Another shows the Budget as a box of snakes charmed by a finance minister.

As already noted, however, one of the difficulties in working with images is the range of complex theoretical traditions available. One tradition that has been used to considerable effect in this area is concerned with the analysis of sign systems. Following Saussure, it has now been called semiotics.

Semiotics

Stubbs (1981) has criticised the *ad hoc* selection of linguistic units for study. Before this century, however, such an approach was the accepted form of analysis. Linguistics viewed language as an aggregate of units (words), each of which had a separate meaning attached to it. Linguistic research concentrated on historical changes in the meanings of words.

In the early years of this century, Saussure revolutionised this approach. Hawkes (1977) has identified the two crucial aspects of Saussure's reform of linguistic research:

1 His rejection of a substantantive view of language – concerned with the correspondence between individual words and their meanings – in favour of a relational view, stressing the system of relations between words as the source of meaning.
2 His shift away from historical or 'diachronic' analysis towards an analysis of language's present functioning (a 'synchronic' analysis). No matter what recent change a language has undergone, it remains, at any given point in time, a complete system. As Hawkes puts it: 'Each language has a wholly valid existence apart from its history as a system of sounds issuing from the lips of those who speak it now' (1977, 20).

Saussure now makes a distinction between language (*langue*) and speech (*parole*). We need to distinguish the system of language (*langue*) from the actual speech acts (*parole*) that any speaker actually utters. The latter are not determined by language, which solely provides the system of elements in terms of which speech occurs. Saussure uses the analogy of a chess game to explain this. The rules and conventions of chess constitute a language (*langue*) within which actual moves (*parole*) take place. For Saussure, the linguist's primary concern is not to describe *parole* but to establish the elements and their rules of combination which together constitute the linguistic system (*langue*).

Having identified *langue* as the concern of linguistics, Saussure now notes that language is comparable to other social institutions like systems of writing, symbolic rites and deaf-sign systems. All these institutions are systems of signs and can be studied systematically. Saussure calls such a science of signs semiology (from the Greek *semeion* = 'sign'). Signs have four characteristics:

1 They bring together a concept and an image (e.g. 'horse' and a pictorial image – as in a road sign – or a written English word or a spoken English 'sound-image').

2 Signs are not autonomous entities – they derive their meaning only from the place within an articulated system. What constitutes a linguistic sign is nothing but its difference from other signs (so the colour red is only something which is not green, blue, orange, etc.).

3 The linguistic sign is arbitrary or unmotivated. This, Saussure says, means that the sign 'has no natural connection with the signified' (Saussure: 1974, 69). Different languages simply use different terms for concepts. Indeed they can generate their own concepts – think, for instance, how difficult it is to translate a game into another culture where, because the game is not played there, they lack the relevant terms.

4 Signs can be put together through two main paths. First, there are combinational possibilities (e.g. the order of a religious service or the prefixes and suffixes that can be attached to a noun – for example, 'friend' can become 'boyfriend', 'friendship', 'friendly', etc.). Saussure calls these patterns of combinations *syntagmatic relations*. Second, there are contrastive properties (e.g. choosing one hymn rather than another in a church service; saying 'yes' or 'no'). Here the choice of one term necessarily excludes the other. Saussure calls these mutually exclusive relations *paradigmatic oppositions*.

An example may help to pull these various features of signs together. Think of traffic lights: (1) they bring together concepts ('stop', 'start') with images ('red', 'green'); (2) these images are not autonomous: red is identifiable by the fact that it is not green, and vice versa; (3) they have no natural connection with what they signify: red has simply come to mean 'stop' and green to mean 'start'; finally (4) they express syntagmatic relations (the order in which the traffic lights can change: from red to green and back again but much more complicated in countries where there is also an amber light). They also express paradigmatic oppositions: imagine the chaos created if red and green light up simultaneously!

This, then, is a simplified version of the apparatus provided by Saussure. In order to show how it can be used in the analysis of texts, I will briefly examine Propp's work on narratives and Laclau's analysis of the articulation of political discourses.

Narrative Structures

The organisation of systems of narration, within literature and elsewhere, has been of constant interest to writers influenced by Saussure. I shall briefly discuss V.I. Propp's study *The Morphology of the Folktale*, written in Russia in 1928 (Propp 1968) and its subsequent development by the French sociologist A.J. Greimas (1966).

Exercise 4.4

This is an exercise to help you to use Saussure's abstract concepts. Imagine you are given a menu at a restaurant. The menu reads as follows (for convenience we will leave out the prices):

Tomato soup
Mixed salad

Roast beef
Fried chicken
Grilled plaice

Ice cream (several flavours)
Apple pie

Your task is to work out how you can treat the words on the menu as a set of related signs. Try to use all the concepts above: i.e. *langue*, *parole*, syntagmatic relations and paradigmatic oppositions.
Here are some clues:

1 What can you learn from the *order* in which the courses are set out?
2 What can you learn from the *choices* which are offered for each course?

Propp argues that the fairytale establishes a narrative form which is central to all story-telling. The fairytale is structured not by the nature of the characters that appear in it, but by the function they play in the plot. Despite its great detail and many characters, Propp suggests that 'the number of functions is extremely small' (1968, 20). This allows him to attend to a favourite distinction of structuralists between appearances (massive detail and complexity) and reality (a simple underlying structure repeated in different ways).

Propp suggests that fairytales in many cultures share similar themes, e.g. 'A dragon kidnaps the king's daughter.' These themes can be broken into four elements, each of which can be replaced without altering the basic structure of the story. This is because each element has a certain *function*. This is shown in Table 4.2.

Following this example, we could rewrite 'A dragon kidnaps the king's daughter' as 'A witch makes the chief's wife vanish', while retaining the same function of each element. Thus a function can be filled by many different role-players. This is because the function of a role arises in its significance for the structure of the tale as a whole.

Using a group of 100 tales, Propp isolates thirty-one 'functions' (actions like 'prohibition', 'violation' or, as we have seen above, 'disappearance'). These functions are played out in seven 'spheres of action': the villain, the provider, the helper, the princess and her father, the dispatcher, the hero and the false hero.

Table 4.2: '*A Dragon Kidnaps the King's Daughter*'

Element	Function	Replacement
Dragon	Evil force	Witch
King	Ruler	Chief
Daughter	Loved one	Wife
Kidnap	Disappearance	Vanish

Source: adapted from Culler: 1976, 207–208

These functions and 'spheres of action' constitute an ordered set. Their presence or absence in any particular tale allows their plots to be classified. Thus plots take four forms:

1 Development through struggle and victory.
2 Development through the accomplishment of a difficult task.
3 Development through both 1 and 2.
4 Development through neither.

Although any one character may be involved in any sphere of action, and several characters may be involved in the same sphere, we are dealing with a finite sequence: 'the important thing is to notice the number of spheres of action occurring in the fairytale is infinite: we are dealing with discernible and repeated structures' (Hawkes: 1977, 69).

Writing in 1960, Greimas agrees with Propp about the need to locate narrative form in a finite number of elements disposed in a finite number of ways. However, he modifies Propp's list of each element. This is set out below.

1 Propp's list of seven spheres of action can be reduced into three sets of structural relations: subject versus object (this subsumes 'hero' and 'princess' or 'sought-for person'); sender versus receiver (includes 'father' and 'dispatcher'); and helper versus opponent (includes 'donor', 'helper' and 'villain'). As Hawkes shows, this reveals the simple structure of many love stories, i.e. involving relations between both subjects and objects and receivers and senders.
2 Propp's thirty-one functions may be considerably reduced if one examines how they combine together. For instance, although Propp separates 'prohibition' and 'violation', Greimas shows that a 'violation' presumes a 'prohibition'. Hence they may be combined in one function: 'prohibition versus violation'. Hawkes points out that this allows Greimas to isolate several distinctive structures of the folk narrative. These include: contractual structures (relating to establishing and breaking contracts); performative structures (involving trials and struggles); and disjunctive structures (involving movement, leaving, arriving, etc.).

This summarised presentation of the work of Propp and Greimas has underlined two useful arguments. First, the structuralist method can be an important aid to what C. Wright Mills called 'the sociological imagination'. It reminds us that meaning never resides in a single term (Culler: 1976) and consequently that understanding the articulation of elements is our primary task. Second, more specifically, it shows some aspects of how narrative structure works. When one reflects how much of sociological data (interviews, documents, conversations) takes a narrative form, as indeed do sociological reports themselves, then the analysis of the fairytale stops looking like an odd literary pursuit.

Exercise 4.5

This is part of the life story of a Finnish man attending an alcohol clinic:

> When I was a child, the discipline was very strict. I still remember when my younger brother broke a sugar cup and I was spanked. When my father died, my mother remarried. The new husband did not accept my youngest brother. When I was in the army, my wife was unfaithful to me. After leaving the army, I didn't come home for two days. I started to drink. And I began to use other women sexually. I drank and I brawled, because I was pissed off and because her treacherousness was in my mind.
>
> When I came to the alcohol clinic, it made me think. I abstained for a year. There was some progress but also bad times. I grew up somewhat. When the therapist changed, I was pissed off and gave it all up. (adapted from Perti Alasuutari, *Desire and Craving: Studies in a Cultural Theory of Alcoholism*, University of Tampere, Finland, 1990)

1 Using what you have read about Propp and Greimas, identify the following elements in this story:
   (a) functions (e.g. 'prohibition' or 'violation')
   (b) spheres of action (e.g. the villain, the provider, the helper, the princess and her father, the dispatcher, the hero and the false hero)
   (c) structures (e.g. subject versus object (this includes 'hero' and 'princess' or 'sought-for person'); sender versus receiver (includes 'father' and 'dispatcher'); and helper versus opponent (includes 'donor', 'helper' and 'villain')).
2 What can be said about the *sequence* of actions reported?
3 Having done this analysis, what features would you look for in other life stories?

However, although textual analysis, following Propp and Greimas, seems very attractive, we need to proceed carefully. If we are analysing how a text works, we should not forget how our own text has its own narrative structure, designed to persuade the reader that, confronted with any given textual fragment, 'we can see that' a favoured reading applies.

This question arose when I examined (Silverman:1982) a collection of papers discussing the future of the British Labour Party (Jacques and Mulhern:1981). Although written before Labour's 1983 election defeat, many of the contributions provided a good instrument for predicting the election outcome in relation to Labour's shrinking social base.

I selected two short papers by little-known trade union leaders which seemed to propose alternative versions of Labour's political past and future. In this discussion, I shall only consider the four-page text by Ken Gill. Gill argues that the post-1950 period has seen a 'picture of advance' for the Labour Party. This advance is indexed by a move towards left-wing policies and left-wing leaders in both unions and the Labour Party.

One immediate critical rejoinder to this argument is that organisational and ideological advances have to be judged in relation to popular support – which, with one or two exceptions, dropped continuously at general elections after 1950. However, this is to remain in a sense *outside* of Gill's text. Such arguments tend to use isolated extracts and summaries as a means of deploying critiques or deconstructions. Outside structuralism, contrasts between texts and 'theory', or texts and 'reality', are the very stuff of academic and practical debates. Inevitably, however, they can result in empty victories in mock battles.

Following a structuralist method, my aim was to avoid interpreting Gill's text in terms of alternative versions of reality but, instead, to enter within it. Such *internal* analysis must seek to establish the realities the text itself sets into play. There was no difficulty in the programme. The problem was to find a method which would allow these realities to be described without appealing to the 'we see that . . . ' strategy.

In order to get a sense of Gill's paper as a whole, I went through the text listing the subjects or agents mentioned. The agents named fell into four broad categories. References to trade unions and to groups defined by class were counted as instances of economic agents. These were distinguished from references to theorists, to political parties or tendencies. This produced Table 4.3.

Table 4.3 was used to support the suggestion that Gill's analysis concentrates on economically defined subjects or subjects defined with reference to other formal institutions. This apparent preference for formal structures was underlined when I counted the 'level' of agent to which Gill refers. Although not all the agents were classifiable in these terms, I discovered a clear preference for agents with an official or high-level position, as shown in Table 4.4.

Tables 4.3 and 4.4 substantiated the impression that Gill has constructed a narrative which tells its tale from the top down. It is largely a tale of economic subjects, organised by existing institutions and their leaders. Moreover, further analysis revealed that Gill's text concentrates on

Table 4.3: *Gill's Agents*

Agent	Number
Economic	16
Theoretical	5
Political	9
None of the above	1
Total	31

Table 4.4: *Agents' Level*

Level of agent	Number
Leader or theorist	14
No rank or lower rank	3
Unclear	14
Total	31

activities relating to policy-making, or occupying particular political positions, like passing resolutions opposing the government. In only five cases did he refer to an agent's action; all these cases related to economic struggles.

These simple tabulations supported my argument that Gill's practice contradicted his theory. While Gill theorises about movements towards socialism and democracy, the structure of his text is consistently élitist. Put another way, the élitist form of his tale runs directly contrary to its democratic message.

Some of this could, of course, be demonstrated by the use of brief extracts from Gill's piece followed by critical exegesis. However, this standard procedure of traditional (political, literary) criticism cannot generate such an analysis so forcefully or economically. Critical exegesis is prone to two damaging limitations: it may appeal to extra-textual realities, while de-emphasising the realities constructed in the text under consideration and/or, it may base its case on isolated fragments of a text supported by a 'persuasive' argument.

At this point, the reader may ask: doesn't your own method bear a striking resemblance to content analysis? If so, doesn't it risk the charges of triviality and of imposing (extra-textual) realities on the data through its methods of classification? In which case, can't your argument against traditional criticism be turned against yourself?

Now, of course, the tabulations I have just presented do share with content analysis one characteristic: both involve counting instances of terms used in a text. However, unlike naive forms of content analysis, the terms counted are *not* determined by an arbitrary or common-sense version of what may be interesting to count in a text. It is not coincidental that I have counted Gill's agents or 'subjects'. In Western cultures, at least, subjects are intrinsic to narratives: by analysing the construction of subjects, we get to the heart of the work of the text.

Moreover, I have sought to show how Gill's subjects are positioned in relation to particular activities and 'spheres of action'. This follows Propp's analysis of fairytales and Saussure's crucial argument that signs are not autonomous.

This means that signs derive their meaning only from their relations with and differences from other signs. This further implies that the meaning of signs cannot be finally fixed. It is always possible to extend the signifying chain.

Two examples may help to explain this. Colours, as already noted, are constituted by their differences. Hence red is not orange (or any other colour). Now think of the way in which some great artists use palettes which make us rethink the way particular colours stand in relation to others. Although the spectrum of colours is fixed, the *relation* between particular colours can be endlessly rearticulated.

This process is, however, not limited to aesthetics. Think of the symbolic potential of two examples from the 1980s: 'People's Airline' (flying = everybody's right) and, from an attempt by the Greater London Council to gain support for its cheap fares policy, 'Fares Fair' (payment equality). These examples reflect only some of the myriad connections that have been made between these elements: compare 'People's Airline' with 'People's Republic'. The connotations of such articulations and their popular success are entirely dependent on the particular historical and cultural context in which they are deployed. However, they emphasise that Saussure's concept of the sign does allow an understanding of (political, aesthetic) practice consisting of a struggle over the articulation of the relations between elements.

So the only arbitrary aspect of the sign is the relation of signifier to signified. Without some fixing, the sign would not exist. But no sign is totally fixed. Politics is not an expression of the 'hidden' movement of history (or of anything else). It is concerned with the articulation and disarticulation of the ensemble of signs and sign-systems (or discourse).

Let us now follow this up with the example of nationalism. A relational view of language shows how nationalism only gets a meaning in relation to other terms – hence the Nazi success in identifying a relation between nationalism or patriotism and Fascism (e.g. National Socialism). Conversely, as Laclau (1981) has shown, left-wing politicians can make appeals to the apparently indissoluble links between being a patriotic Italian, German, etc. and supporting a party of the Left. Since terms have no fixed meaning derived from their past use, populist politicians will try to incorporate popular signs (such as 'patriotism') into their vocabulary. Think, for instance, of the power of the name of Senator McCarthy's

Exercise 4.6

The following is an extract from a speech made by an English Member of Parliament in the late 1960s. The topic was a Race Relations Bill then going through the British Parliament. The M.P. was Enoch Powell and the speech became (in)famous as the 'Rivers of Blood' speech because Powell concludes his argument against laws on racial discrimination by saying: 'Like the Roman, I see the River Tiber foaming with much blood.' The extract below occurs earlier in the speech:

1 Nothing is more misleading than comparison between the
2 Commonwealth immigrant in Britain and the American Negro.
3 The Negro population of the United States, which was
4 already in existence before the United States became a
5 nation, started literally as slaves and were later given
6 the franchise and other rights of citizenship ( ).
7 The Commonwealth immigrant came to Britain as a full
8 citizen, to a country which knew no discrimination between
9 one citizen and another, and he entered instantly into the
10 possession of the rights of every citizen, from the vote
11 to free treatment under the National Health Service ( ).
12 But while to the immigrant entry to this country was
13 admission to privileges and opportunities eagerly sought,
14 the impact upon the existing population was very
15 different. For reasons which they could not comprehend,
16 and in pursuit of a decision by default, on which they
17 were never consulted, they found themselves made strangers
18 in their own country.
19   They found their wives unable to obtain hospital beds in
20 childbirth, their children unable to obtain school places,
21 their homes and neighbourhoods changed beyond recognition
22 ( ). At work they found that employers hesitated to apply
23 to the immigrant worker the standards of discipline and
24 competence required of the native-born worker; they began
25 to hear, as time went by, more and more voices which told
26 them that they were now the unwanted.
27   On top of this, they now learn that a one-way privilege is
28 to be establish by Act of Parliament: a law, which cannot,
29 and is not intended, to operate to protect them or to
30 redress their grievances, is to be enacted to give the
31 stranger, the disgruntled and the agent-provocateur the
32 power to pillory them for their private actions. (extracted from Kobena
     Mercer, 'Powellism as a Political Discourse', unpublished Ph.D., Gold-
     smiths' College, London University, 1990)

1 Identify the subjects that the text constructs (e.g. 'immigrants', 'native-born') and show the relations that are established between them, looking for how Powell uses a version of national identity.
2 On this basis, why was Powell's speech so powerful? (Here is a clue: look at how the term 'stranger', first used in line 17, takes on a different meaning in line 31.)
3 How could the same textual strategies be used to *oppose* his arguments?

red-baiting hearings in the early 1950s: the Un-American Activities Committee.

Membership Categorisation: Description as a Socially Organised Activity

As we saw in Chapter 3, Sacks' work has raised some vital methodological questions for ethnographers and anyone else attempting to construct sociology as an 'observational' discipline. Sacks puts the issue succinctly:

> Suppose you're an anthropologist or sociologist standing somewhere. You see somebody do some action, and you see it to be some activity. How can you go about formulating who is it that did it, for the purposes of your report? Can you use at least what you might take to be the most conservative formulation – his name? Knowing, of course, that any category you choose would have the[se] kinds of systematic problems: how would you go about selecting a given category from the set that would equally well characterise or identify that person at hand? (1992a, 467–468)

The classic statement of this problem is found in Moerman's (1974) self-critical treatment of his attempt to do a standard ethnography upon a Thai tribe. But the message has also been taken by intelligent ethnographers who, like Gubrium (1988), are centrally concerned with the descriptive process.

Sacks shows how you cannot resolve such problems simply 'by taking the best possible notes at the time and making your decisions afterwards' (468). Instead, our aim should be to try to understand when and how members do descriptions, seeking thereby to describe the apparatus through which members' descriptions are properly produced.

Consider this description in which the identities of the parties are concealed:

> The X cried. The Y picked it up.

Why is it that we are likely to hear the X as, say, a baby but not a teacher? Furthermore, given that we hear X as a baby, why are we tempted to hear Y as an adult (possibly as the baby's mother)?

In fact, Sacks looks at the first two sentences of a children's story: 'The baby cried. The mommy picked it up.' Why do we hear the 'mommy' as the mother of this 'baby'? Why do we hear the baby's cries as the 'reason' why the mommy picks him up?

Not only are we likely to hear the story this way, but we hear it as 'a possible description' without having observed the circumstances which it characterises. Sacks asks: 'Is it some kind of magic? One of my tasks is going to be to construct an apparatus for that fact to occur. That is, how we come to hear it in that fashion' (1992b, 236).

No magic lies behind such observations. Instead:

> What one ought to seek is to build an apparatus which will provide for how it is

that any activities, which members do in such a way as to be recognisable as such to members, are done, and done recognisably. (*ibid*)

The issue is 'how a human gets built who will produce his activities such' that they're graspable in this way' (1992a, 119). On this basis, 'culture' is approached as an 'inference-making machine': a descriptive apparatus, administered and used in specific contexts.

In this concluding section, I shall briefly outline Sacks' attempt to build such an apparatus for 'description'. The aim will be to emphasise the broad sweep of his concerns. This links up this chapter with themes in both Chapters 5 and 6.

For reasons of space, I shall telescope Sacks' account into four related points:

Categories

One only has to read accounts of the 'same' event in two different newspapers to realise the large number of categories that can be used to describe it. For instance, as feminists have pointed out, women, but not men, tend to be identified by their marital status, number of children, hair colour and even chest measurement. Such identifications, while intelligible, carry massive implications for the sense we attach to people and their behaviour. Compare, for example:

    A. 'Shapely, blonde, mother of 5'

with:

    B. '32-year old teacher'.

Both descriptions may 'accurately' describe different aspects of the same person. But each constitutes very definitely how we are to view that person (for instance, in A, purely in terms of certain physical characteristics).

Collections

Each identity is heard as a category from some collection of categories (what Sacks calls a membership categorisation device – MCD). For instance, in A and B above, we hear 'mother' as a category from the collection 'family', and 'teacher' as located in a collection of 'occupation'. The implication is that to choose one category from an MCD excludes someone being identified with some other category from the same device. So MCDs are organised around what Saussure calls 'paradigmatic oppositions' (see p. 72 above). They generally involve polar oppositions so that to call someone a 'mother' excludes her being seen as a 'father'.

Consistency

Sacks suggests a 'hearing rule' which structures how we hear descriptions. When a speaker uses two or more categories to describe at least two members of a population and it is possible to hear the categories as belonging to the same collection, we hear them that way. That is why, in the story with which Sacks begins, we hear 'baby' and 'mommy' in relation to the collection 'family'. Furthermore, a related 'consistency rule' (Sacks: 1974, 333) suggests that once one category from a given collection has been used to categorise one population member, then other categories from the same collection may be used on other members of the population.

The import of the consistency rule may be seen in a simple example. If we use an abusive term about someone else, we know that a term from the same collection can be used on us. Hence one of the reasons we may avoid name-calling is to avoid the development of this kind of slanging-match.

Category-Bound Activities

Many kinds of activities are commonsensically associated with certain membership categories. So, by identifying a person's activity (say, 'crying'), we provide for what their social identity is likely to be (in this case, a 'baby'). Moreover, we can establish negative moral assessments of people by describing their behaviour in terms of performing or avoiding activities inappropriate to their social identity. For instance, it may be acceptable for a parent to 'punish' a child, but it will be unacceptable for a child to 'punish' a parent. Notice that, in both cases, 'punish' serves as a powerful picture of an activity which could be described in innumerable ways. Social life, unlike foreign films, does not come with subtitles attached. Consequently, how we define an activity is morally constitutive of it. So if, like other sociologists, Sacks is talking here about norms, unlike them (and members) he is not treating norms as descriptions of the causes of action. Instead, he is concerned with how 'viewers use norms to provide some of the orderliness, and proper orderliness, of the activities they observe' (*ibid*, 39).

In order to put some flesh on these conceptual bones, I will give some examples that Sacks himself uses. Later, I will show how we can use his concepts on a range of textual materials.

Sacks shows the importance of categorisation by using data from his Ph.D. dissertation on calls to a suicide prevention centre. He points out that people may only become suicidal *after* they have reviewed various categories of people and found 'no one to turn to'. For instance, a caller's statement 'I'm nothing' is not to be heard as having a purely psychological reference or as indicating some mental disturbance, but, as Schegloff points out in his 'Editor's Introduction':

> the outcome of a procedure, as announcing 'a finding' by its speaker. [Sacks] asked what that procedure was and how it could arrive at such a finding, in such a fashion that other participants would find understandable and even 'correct'. He took seriously the particular form in which conduct appeared – the participants had said this thing, in this way, and not in some other way. (Sacks: 1992a, xxx)

However, we see our use of a descriptive apparatus in much more mundane situations. For instance, certain things are known about any category, e.g. people of a certain age or gender. If you want to escape such category-bound implications, you can counter by accounting for why the category should not be read in this way here (e.g. 'I'm 48 but . . .'). However, people use sayings like 'boys will be boys' which serve as 'anti-modifier modifiers', asserting that, in the last instance, the category is omni-relevant (45). The precise relevance of a category is also established by categorising the categoriser, e.g. if B categorises C as 'old', you might categorise B in order to decide how *you* would categorise C (*ibid*).

Similarly, categories can usually be read off the activities in which people engage. Thus, as we have seen, to hear a report of someone crying *may* be heard as the activity of a baby. Similarly, a person who properly picks a baby up *may* be hearable as a 'mother'. Moreover, if both baby and mother are mentioned, we will try to hear them as a 'team' – so that, if the mother picks up the baby, we will hear the mother as not any mother but the mother of this baby.

However, people may try to avoid the normally category-bound implications of certain activity-descriptions. For instance, Sacks discusses the American South where, according to some whites, even when blacks engage in activities appropriate to anybody, they are not to be seen as 'anybody', but as 'blacks-*imitating*-whites'.

Sacks also notes the commonplace assumption that members of sub-cultures resist being categorised by other groups. For instance, he shows how 'hotrodder' may be preferred to 'teenager' by a young person. The logic of this is fully understood by reference to Sacks' account of the apparatus of descriptive categories (membership categorisation devices) and activities (category-bound activities). For, when adults refer to 'teenagers', they give themselves access to the known category-bound activities in which teenagers may engage. By preferring an alternative term ('hotrodders') with category-bound activities known only to the 'in-group', young people assert ownership of the descriptive apparatus (1992a, Fall 1965, Lecture 7).

Moreover, Sacks notes, this attention to descriptive categories occurs even in those many situations where we are talking to strangers and there is no apparent battle over which category to use. He mentions the case of people telling interviewers doing surveys that they watch less television than they actually do. Sacks comments: 'It's interesting in that they're controlling an impression of themselves for somebody who couldn't matter less' (1992a, 580). Sacks argues that this happens because we can be held responsible not only for our descriptions but for the *inferences* that can be drawn from them, i.e. the sort of person who would say such a thing about themselves or others.

However, descriptions are not just assembled for ourselves but are recipient-designed for others. We help others infer certain things from our descriptions by indicating if the hearer should seek to use them to find

some person already known to them. So using descriptions like 'Joe',
'Tom' or 'Harry' allows hearers to search for someone already known.

These Type 1 descriptions are different from Type 2 descriptions (like 'a
guy' or 'someone') where we signal that the description should *not* be used
by the recipient to find out who is being referred to. Moreover, Sacks
argues that the usual rule is: use Type 1 if you can, but correct or repair
into Type 2 if Type 1 is inappropriate (1992a, 445).

Using MCD Analysis

I now want to show you how analysis of descriptions, using Sacks'
concepts, can be a relatively simple and illuminating activity. To do so, I
will use examples from a newspaper headline, a lonely hearts advertisement and two conversations.

The Headline

FATHER AND DAUGHTER IN SNOW ORDEAL

This headline appeared in the inside pages of a recent copy of the London
Times. I want to examine how we can understand the sense it makes using
MCD analysis. In doing so, we will see the skill involved in constructing
headlines which encourage us to read the story beneath. The analysis of the
headline is set out in schematic form in Table 4.5.

The Lonely Hearts Advertisement

> Active attractive cheerful blonde widow graduate no ties many interests. Seeks
> mutually fulfilling life with fit considerate educated 60 year old. Details please to
> Box 123. (*The Times*, 30.1.93)

Like the headline, this advertisement was chosen at random in order to
show how MCD analysis can fruitfully analyse *any* material of this kind.
Let us begin by focussing upon the category 'widow'. Now I take it that,
while successful newspaper headlines make you want to read the story, the
success of a lonely hearts advertisement is judged by the number of
appropriate responses that it elicits. If we look at 'widow' in this light, it
may evoke a series of contrasting category-bound activities as follows:

Type 1: miserable (dressed in black); given up on life
Type 2: freed from monogamy, light-hearted and ready for multiple
relationships ('the merry widow').

Note how this advertisement attends to both these types of category-
bound activities. Type 1 is rejected primarily by the use of the adjective
'cheerful', although 'blonde' also neatly contrasts with the black of
mourning. Moreover, this is not a description of someone who has given up
on life. This widow is 'active' and has 'many interests'. On the other hand,

Table 4.5: *'Father and Daughter in Snow Ordeal'*

Concept	Explanation	Headline
Category	Any person can be labelled in many 'correct' ways	Persons later described as 'supermarket manager' and 'student'
Membership categorization device (MCD)	Categories are seen as grouped together in collections	MCD = 'Family'
Economy rule	A single category *may* be sufficient to describe a person	Single categories are used here
Consistency rule	If one person is identified from a collection, then a next person *may* be identified from the same collection	'Daughter' is from same MCD as 'father'
Duplicative organisation	When categories can be heard as a 'team' hear them that way	'Daughter' is the daughter of *this* 'father'
Category-bound activities	Activities may be heard as 'tied' to certain categories	'Snow ordeal' is *not* heard as tied to 'father–daughter' categories; this is why the story is newsworthy
Standardised relational pairs (SRPs)	Pairs of categories are linked together in standardised routine ways	'Father' and 'daughter' assumed to be linked together through 'caring' and 'support'; how could 'snow ordeal' have happened?

we are specifically not encouraged to assume that this is a 'merry widow'. She is, after all, an intelligent person ('graduate') who seeks one person for a 'mutually fulfilling life'.

Note throughout how the consistency rule applies. She is 'active' and seeks someone who is 'fit'. She is a graduate and seeks someone who is educated. However, the subtleties of the descriptive apparatus particularly stand out in what the advertisement does *not* say as follows:

- we are not told the age of the 'widow' (although the consistency rule might imply that she is close to 60 like the man she seeks, this is not necessarily so)
- we are not told the gender of the person she is seeking.

How can the reader resolve these puzzles? First, the advertiser uses the term 'active' to describe herself. Now we may assume that someone, say, in their twenties is 'active'. To state that you are active is thus hearable as what we have seen Sacks calls a category-modifier. Consequently, we can assume that this is at least a middle-aged person. Second, since the advertiser describes herself in the context of a previous heterosexual

---

Exercise 4.7

This exercise allows you to use MCD analysis on a newspaper headline:

Engagement was broken – Temperamental young man gassed himself

Using what you have learned from MCD analysis, why might we assume:

1 that the engagement was for marriage (not dinner)
2 that the young man was engaged (not someone else)
3 that the engaged parties were engaged to each other (and not to others)
4 that the broken engagement was the young man's (not another's)
5 that the gassing was a suicide (not an accident, and not less than terminal)
6 that first the engagement was broken and then the young man gassed himself (not the reverse)
7 that the second happened *because* of the first (not independently of it)
8 that it happened because of desperation arising from the 'loss' assisted by the 'temperamental' aspect of the young man's behaviour (rather than from, say, religious ecstasy or moral outrage)?

Now consider the following:

1 Why might the headline make us want to read the story?
2 Invent *two* equally 'accurate' headlines of the 'same' events which make the story less newsworthy.

(The headline and the questions about it are taken from Eglin and Hester: 1992.)

---

relationship ('widow'), we may assume that, without contrary evidence and following the consistency rule, she is seeking a man here.

Two Conversations

Sacks provides us with a method for analysing texts that fully attends to how all of us are concerned with fine-tuning our descriptions. So, as social scientists, we cannot describe and classify without attending to how members describe and classify. As Sacks puts it:

> All the sociology we read is unanalytic, in the sense that they simply put some category in. They make sense to us in doing that, but they're doing that simply as another Member. They haven't described the phenomena they're seeking to describe – or that they ought to be seeking to describe. What they need to do is to give us some procedure for choosing that category which is used to present some piece of information. And that brings us back to the question, are there

---

Exercise 4.8

Here is another lonely hearts advertisement, chosen from the same newspaper:

> Good looking (so I am told!) Englishman, 35, tall, professional, seeks very attractive lady, preferably nonsmoker, to wine, dine and make her smile. Age unimportant. Photo appreciated. Please reply to Box 789.

1   Analyse this advertisement using the following concepts:

   Categories
   MCDs
   The economy rule
   The consistency rule
   Category-bound activities
   Standardised relational pairs

2   What does this advertisement *imply* about the advertiser or the 'lady' sought even though it does not tell us these things directly?

---

procedures that Members have for selecting categories? One of my aims is to show that there are. (1992a, 41–42)

As we have seen, Sacks argues that any number of descriptive labels may adequately describe a person or an activity. Choosing any particular label (or 'membership categorisation device') carries with it many implications. For instance, it implies:

- the sort of activities in which a person so described may engage (e.g. friendship is associated with the activity of 'giving support'; thus 'giving support' may be heard as a 'category-bound activity' linked to such persons as 'friends')
- the kind of role-partners associated with the description (e.g. 'friend/ friend' or 'child/parent' both of which constitute 'standardised relational pairs')
- the collection of categories from which other persons may appropriately be named (e.g. 'friendship' or 'family').

Below you will find two brief examples of talk. These show how we can make further use of these concepts. The first example is a question asked by a counsellor (C) during an HIV-test interview in a U.S. gay men's clinic. Numbers in brackets indicate pauses in seconds and underlined words are emphasised:

> C: when was the last time that you had what you may consider er (1.0) er being (1.0) not *too safe* er encounter (0.7) with another er (1.8) person?

Presumably, this question might have been conveyed as follows:

> *C: when did you last have unsafe sex with a man?

What does the counsellor gain by her 'expressive caution'? We can seek an answer by noting three features of her descriptions:

1   They may be heard as 'non-judgmental': she says 'what you may consider', thus abstaining from her own judgments and implying that her client does indeed consider such matters.
2   They avoid making a charge against her client: she says 'not too safe' rather than 'unsafe' which might imply that she thought her client was the sort of person who *might* engage in clearly 'unsafe' activities.
3   They avoid specifying the precise nature of the activity described: by saying 'encounter', the counsellor leaves it to her client to define the nature of the act.
4   They avoid the counsellor defining what type or gender of people with whom the client has 'encounters'. By using the term 'person', no category-bound activities are implied (other than, perhaps, that her client does not have 'encounters' with animals!).

We can also observe multiple hesitations before the counsellor produces her descriptions. One such hesitation is also found in the final extract below, which is drawn from the film *Bad Timing*. Further discussion of both the text and the images in this film can be found in Silverman (1993), while McHoul (1987) offers a discussion of how we can use Sacks' methods on fictional texts like novels and films.

(1, 2 and 3 list the speakers)

1: Husband?
2: no
1: relation?
2: no
1: er boyfriend?
3: (   )
1: look what connection do you have with her?
2: you could say I'm a friend

The first speaker (1) is seeking to elicit 2's description of his relationship with a woman. Each description that he offers implies a particular set of role-partners associated with certain obligations and activities, appropriate to standardised relational pairs (SRPs). For instance, husbands can be expected to have greater obligations than relations. In addition, certain SRPs, like husband–wife or relation–relation, can be heard as engaged in stable, routinised activities based on fairly clear-cut obligations. This is less true of other SRPs, such as boyfriend–girlfriend, where the expected obligations are less stable and associated with more 'delicate' activities such as 'wooing:being wooed' which, in a potentially unstable way, constitute the material and sexual status of the relationship.

Now note two features of this conversation:

–   1 hesitates ('er') before producing the MCD which can be heard as the most delicate description of 2's relationship

– 2 chooses an MCD ('friendship') which avoids the delicate implications of 'boyfriend' by bracketing any issues of sexual involvement i.e. one can have 'friends' of either sex. Unlike any of the three MCDs offered by 1, all of which imply specific obligations and activities, 'friendship' is much vaguer and ill-defined.

Conclusion

I hope that, by the end of this chapter, the reader is not feeling punch-drunk! We have indeed covered an enormous amount of ground.

The wide scope of the chapter arose for two reasons. First, I am convinced that qualitative sociologists make too little of the potentialities of texts as rich data. Second, I am also convinced that there are several powerful ways of analysing such data.

In examining ways, we have rapidly moved between several complex and apparently different theories – all the way from semiotics to ethnomethodology. However, if the reader has grasped at least one useful way of thinking about textual analysis, then I will have achieved my purpose.

Let me also add that I will return to some of these concepts in the next two chapters. In Chapter 6, we will see the other side of Sacks' work – on the sequential organisation of conversation. Moreover, immediately, in Chapter 5, I will show how his analysis of description can be applied to understanding interview data.

5

Interview Data

As we saw in Chapter 4, Sacks (1974) examines the way descriptions are applied and invoked in constructing intelligible narratives. It is worth pointing out that the apparatus that he develops directs attention to quite traditional sociological concepts like norms and roles. Although his concern is naturally with the formal procedures through which hearers and viewers may use norms to generate descriptions, he does not question that members' accounts are replete with descriptions based on appeals to norms and roles.

Carolyn Baker puts it this way:

> When we talk about the world we live in, we engage in the activity of giving it a particular character. Inevitably, we assign features and phenomena to it and make it out to work in a particular way.
>
> When we talk with someone else about the world, we take into account who the other is, what that other person could be presumed to know, 'where' that other is in relation to ourself in the world we talk about. (Baker: 1982, 109)

Here Baker is questioning the attempt to treat interview questions and answers as passive filters towards some truths about people. Instead, she is telling us, interviewer and interviewee actively *construct* some version of the world appropriate to what we take to be self-evident about the person to whom we are speaking and the context of the question.

Baker is raising a number of issues about the status of interview data, including:

1 What is the relation between interviewees' accounts and the world they describe? Are such accounts potentially 'true' or 'false' or is neither concept always appropriate to them?
2 How is the relation between interviewer and interviewee to be understood? Is it governed by standardised techniques of 'good interviewing practice'? Or is it, inevitably, based on taken-for-granted knowledge of interpersonal relations?

These issues are central to this chapter. Shortly, I will return to how Baker addresses them in her own interview study of adolescents.

First, however, I want to set out *two* different ways in which most social scientists would answer Baker's questions:

– According to *positivism*, interview data give us access to 'facts' about the world; the primary issue is to generate data which are valid and reliable, independently of the research setting; the main ways to achieve this are the random selection of the interview sample and the administration of standardised questions with multiple-choice answers which can be readily tabulated.

- According to *interactionism*, interviewees are viewed as experiencing subjects who actively construct their social worlds; the primary issue is to generate data which give an authentic insight into people's experiences; the main ways to achieve this are unstructured, open-ended interviews usually based upon prior, in-depth participant observation (for an example of a feminist argument along these lines, see Oakley: 1981).

These two positions are set out in Table 5.1.

Table 5.1: *Two Versions of Interview Data*

	Status of data	Methodology
Positivism	Facts about behaviour and attitudes	Random samples, standard questions, tabulations
Interactionism	Authentic experiences	Unstructured open-ended interviews

Let me now describe these two different approaches in greater detail.

Positivism

Type of Knowledge

In standard methodology texts, geared to a statistical logic based principally on survey research, interview data give access to 'facts' about the world. Although these facts include both biographical information and statements about beliefs, all are to be treated as accounts whose sense derives from their correspondence to a factual reality. Where that reality is imperfectly represented by an account, checks and remedies are to be encouraged in order to get a truer or more complete picture of how things stand.

Here are the six kinds of topics to which, according to a standard text, interview questions are addressed. Notice how these writers envisage problems and remedies in relation to each topic:

Facts: These relate primarily to biographical information about the respondent, to statements from informed sources about the structures, policies and actions of organisations, and to descriptions of an event or a community. In this last case, it is possible to weed out 'inaccurate' descriptions by comparing different people's statements:

> If respondents occupying widely different positions in the community agree on a statement, there is much better ground for accepting it as true than if only one of

these respondents makes the statement. On the other hand, contradictions between the reports of apparently reliable informants provide important leads for further investigation. (Selltiz *et al*: 1964, 245)

Beliefs about facts: In questions about beliefs or attitudes, no inter-personal cross-checking of statements is appropriate. However, Selltiz *et al* point out that it is always important to check first whether the respondent has any beliefs about the topic in question, otherwise, the researcher may put words into his mouth (*ibid*, 246).

Feelings and motives: Here, 'because emotional responses are frequently too complex to report in a single phrase' (*ibid*, 248), Selltiz *et al* recommend the use of open-ended questions, allowing the respondents to choose their own terms.

Standards of action: These relate to what people think should or could be done about certain stated situations. Here it helps to link such standards to people's experiences. Where someone has actually faced a situation of the type described, his/her response is likely to be more reliable.

Present or past behaviour: Again, specific questions related to actual rather than hypothetical situations are recommended.

Conscious reasons: (for the preceding five topics): Rather than simply ask 'Why?', Selltiz *et al* recommend that the researcher should examine broad classes of considerations that may have determined this outcome (e.g. 'the history of the actor's feeling', or 'the characteristics in a given entity that provoke a given reaction') (*ibid*, 253).

In each of these six topics, the task of the interview is to elicit a body of facts 'out there' in the world. For positivists, an observation that interview responses might be an outcome of the interview setting would be heard as a charge against the reliability of the technique. To the extent that this possibility arises, checks and remedies are built into the research design. Similarly, for positivists, the language of the interviewee serves primarily as an instrument for the communication of social or psychological facts.

Reliability and Validity

The aim of interviews for positivists is to generate data which hold independently of both the research setting and the researcher or inter-viewer. One way of achieving this is by attempting standardised interviews. Consequently, Selltiz *et al* are rather suspicious of unstructured interviews. Although they concede that they are more flexible than pre-scheduled interviews and can allow more intensive study of perceptions and feelings, they have inherent problems for positivists: 'The flexibility frequently results in a lack of comparability of one interview with another.

Moreover, their analysis is more difficult and time-consuming than that of standardised interviews' (*ibid*, 264).

Even more important for reliability than the type of interview selected is the need to follow a standardised protocol. So Selltiz *et al* offer an Appendix entitled 'The Art of Interviewing' which provides a set of rules and taboos. Interviewers should ask each question precisely as it is worded and in the same order that it appears on the schedule. They should not show surprise or disapproval of an answer, offer impromptu explanations of questions, suggest possible replies or skip certain questions. Similarly, Brenner offers a list of 'do's' and 'don'ts' ('basic rules of research interviewing' — Brenner: 1981, 129–130), which are defended in terms of the necessity of standardisation:

> In order to ensure adequacy of measurement in a data collection programme it is of primary importance to secure, as much as is possible, the equivalence of the stimulus conditions in the interviews. If these are not equivalent, measurement may be biased, and it may be unwarranted to group responses together for the purposes of statistical analyses. (*ibid*, 115)

Although Brenner is more sceptical than Selltiz *et al* about the prospects of obtaining 'literal measurement' in the interview situation (*ibid*, 156), the statement quoted indicates that he shares with them the same statistical and behaviourist (or stimulus–response) logic. Following that logic, he calls for more research on social interaction in interviews as a means of: 'improving the quality of research interviews . . . and increasing the degree of social control over the measurement process' (*ibid*, 156).

From a critical position, Mäseide (1990) summarises the most significant premises of the positivist approach to interview data. According to positivists:

1 The aim of social science is to discover unknown but actual social facts or essentials.
2 Reality is supposed to be 'out there'. Thus it is a matter of finding the most effective and unbiased methods that, as precisely and objectively as possible, could bring out information about this reality.
3 The existence of typical respondents is explicitly presupposed. These respondents are implicitly supplied with standardised mental structures that match the analyst's reasoning and use of language.
4 Methodological problems are more technical than theoretical or interpretive (adapted from Mäseide: 1990, 4).

As Mäseide points out, positivists' 'belief in standardised forms of interviewing relies on an exclusive emphasis on the referential functions of language' (1990, 9). However, interview responses 'are delivered at different descriptive levels. The informant does different things with words and stories' (*ibid*, 11).

We will later see that we can extend Mäseide's critique of positivism. As Carolyn Baker's research shows, *both* informant *and* interviewer do many 'different things with words and stories'.

To what extent can we understand these 'things' if we switch away from the standardised interview forms of positivism towards more open-ended interviews or even conversations? To answer this question, we must review the arguments of interactionist sociologists.

Interactionism

Type of Knowledge

For positivists, interviews are essentially about ascertaining facts or beliefs out there in the world. While it is acknowledged that interviewers interact with their subjects, such interaction is strictly defined by the research protocol. Consequently, positivists only become seriously interested in interviewer–interviewee interaction when it can be shown that interviewers have departed from the protocol (Brenner: 1981). Conversely, for interactionists, interviews are essentially about symbolic interaction: 'I wish to treat the interview as an observational encounter. An encounter . . . represents the coming together of two or more persons for the purpose of focused interaction' (Denzin: 1970, 133).

Whatever the topic addressed by the questions, interviews are social events based on mutual participant observation:

> Interviews must be viewed, then, as social events in which the interviewer (and for that matter the interviewee) is a participant observer . . . Interview data, like any other, must be interpreted against the background of the context in which they were produced. (Hammersley and Atkinson: 1983, 126)

Consequently, for interactionists, the social context of the interview is intrinsic to understanding any data that are obtained. While positivists aim for a clear-cut distinction between research interviews and other forms of social interaction, interactionists argue that that aim is unobtainable. The distinction between these two positions is summarised in Table 5.2.

Table 5.2:   *Two Versions of the Interview Relationship*

	Positivism	Interactionism
Interviewer	Object – following research protocol	Subject – creating interview context
Interviewee	Object – revealing items relevant to the research protocol	Subject – complying with or resisting definition of the situation

Reliability and Validity

When interactionists assess what makes interview responses valid, they continue to depart from the positivist position. If interviewees are to be viewed as subjects who actively construct the features of their cognitive world, then one should try to obtain intersubjective depth between both sides so that a deep mutual understanding can be achieved. As Reason and Rowan argue: 'Humanistic approaches favour "depth interviews" in which interviewee and interviewer become "peers" or even "companions"' (Reason and Rowan: 1981, 205). In this 'humanistic' version of the interview, *both* the type of knowledge gained *and* the validity of the analysis are based on 'deep' understanding. This is because 'the humanistic framework' supports 'meaningful understanding of the person . . . and wholeness in human inquiry' (206).

Similarly, in Burgess' (1980) paper, significantly entitled 'The Unstructured Interview as a Conversation', the interview is seen to give greater depth than other research techniques. This is because, Burgess claims, it is based on 'a sustained relationship between the informant and the researcher' (Burgess: 1980, 109).

For this reason, most interactionists tend to reject pre-scheduled standardised interviews and to prefer open-ended interviews. Denzin offers three reasons for this preference:

1 It allows respondents to use their 'unique ways of defining the world' (Denzin: 1970, 125).
2 It assumes that no fixed sequence of questions is suitable to all respondents.
3 It allows respondents to 'raise important issues not contained in the schedule' (*ibid*).

The Limits of Interactionism

These positions might seem to be a welcome alternative to the purely technical version of interviews espoused by positivists. After all, isn't it both more valid and more ethical to recognise that interviews are encounters between human beings trying to understand one another?

This 'humanistic' position is seductive. It seems to blend a self-evident truth about humanity with political correctness about the need for mutual understanding and dialogue. However, it *neglects* three issues which I want briefly to explore:

– the assumptions made in preferring open-ended interviews
– the difference between a 'humanistic' and a 'sociological' position
– the role of common-sense knowledge, rather than 'empathy', in allowing us to conduct and analyse interviews.

I will consider each issue in turn.

Open-endedness: As Hammersley and Atkinson (1983: 110–111) point out, it is somewhat naive to assume that open-ended or non-directive interviewing is not in itself a form of social control which shapes what people say. For instance, where the researcher maintains a minimal presence, asking few questions, this can create an interpretive problem for the interviewee about what is relevant. Moreover, the passivity of the interviewer can create an extremely powerful constraint on the interviewee to talk (as seen in 'non-directive' styles of psychotherapy and counselling).

I would also add that this preference for a particular form of interview can be defined in terms of avoiding bias which is entirely appropriate to a positivist approach. Conversely, in certain feminist writings, where value-freedom is rejected, structured interviews are criticised on political grounds as maintaining a hierarchical relationship in research (see Stanley and Wise: 1983).

Humanism:　Why are interviews so self-evidently based on an exchange of unique human experiences? Indeed, may not this self-evident 'truth' derive not from a sociological insight but from a widespread cultural assumption?

Think of our fascination with interviews with celebrities on television news or 'chat-shows'. Or consider the way in which sporting events or even Nobel Prize ceremonies are now incomplete without 'pre-match' and 'post-match' interviews. Do the latter give us insights into 'unique' experiences or do they simply reproduce predictable forms of how it is appropriate to account for sporting or academic success or failure (see Emmison: 1988, Mulkay: 1984)?

Only occasionally do sportsmen and women resist their depiction as heroes or villains. For instance, the British decathlete Daley Thompson was well known for nonplussing the media by producing the 'wrong' account – claiming he was 'over the moon' when he had failed and 'sick as a parrot' when he had won. Again, in this vein, a British boxer was recently termed 'arrogant' by a reporter because he had refused to engage in the usual pre-fight slanging-match with his next opponent.

This, of course, is the irony. The media aim to deliver us immediate 'personal' experience. Yet what they (we) want is simple repetition of familiar tales. Perhaps this is part of the post-modern condition. Maybe we feel people are at their most authentic when they are, in effect, reproducing a cultural script.

Those approaches in sociology which, to some extent, take on board the media's approach and imply that people's experiences are individually meaningful and authentic raise many questions. For instance, from what do these experiences derive? If you can see uniformity in even the most intimate kinds of accounts, I think there we would see a job for the sociologist or the anthropologist.

The well-meaning 'humanistic' social scientist may thus have uncritically taken on board a common-sense assumption about the immediacy and validity of accounts of human experience. This leads to analytic laziness in considering the status of interview data.

Common sense:　As already noted, interactionists are inclined to follow Hammersley and Atkinson's (1983) suggestion that: 'accounts are not simply representations of the world; they are part of the world they describe' (107). Often, however, this insight merely leads into a concern with 'misunderstandings' between interviewer and interviewee (or respondent). Thus, in an early text, Denzin lists a number of 'problems' which can 'distort' interviewees' responses (Denzin: 1970, 133–138):

(a) Respondents possessing different interactional roles from the interviewer.
(b) The problem of 'self-presentation' especially in the early stages of the interview.
(c) The problems of 'volatile', 'fleeting' relationships to which respondents have little commitment and so 'can fabricate tales of self that belie the actual facts' (*ibid*, 135).
(d) The difficulty of penetrating private worlds of experience.
(e) The relative status of interviewer and interviewee.
(f) The 'context' of the interview (e.g. home, work, hospital).

However, interviews can also be seen to possess basic properties of all social interaction deriving from both parties' employment of their everyday, common-sense knowledge of social structures. It follows that such properties should be *investigated* rather than treated as a 'problem'.

The earliest attempt to set out this version of interview data was made by Cicourel (1964). For Cicourel, previous advice about good interview technique offers a revealing insight into our dependence on everyday knowledge of social structures. As he writes:

> The subtleties which methodologists introduce to the novice interviewer can be read as properties to be found in the everyday interaction between members of a society. Thus the principles of 'good and bad interviewing' can be read as basic features of social interaction which the social scientist presumably is seeking to study. (Cicourel: 1964, 68)

For Cicourel, the remedies recommended by methodologists derive from the very knowledge of the social world which should be made problematic. Moreover, the 'errors' they detect are not really obstacles to social research but rather exhibit basic properties of social interaction. We must learn, he suggests, to 'conceive of the error as evidence not only of poor reliability but also of "normal" interpersonal relations' (*ibid*, 74).

Cicourel parallels Garfinkel's (1967) awe at the 'amazing, practical accomplishment' of research findings which, inevitably, are reflexively linked to everyday procedures for 'looking' and 'finding'. Ironically, he is full of praise for methodology texts like Hyman (1954), which is dubbed 'excellent' on two occasions (Cicourel: 1964, 85 and 93). The irony arises because he wants to utilise their desired success in achieving a degree of invariance not as a resource but as a topic:

> In spite of the problem of interviewer error, 'somehow' different interviewers with different approaches produce(d) similar responses from different subjects. The question then becomes one of determining what was invariant or, more precisely, how were invariant meanings communicated despite such variations. (*ibid*, 75).

For Cicourel, there is no distinction between the practical skills of methodologists, researchers and interviewers. All are uniformly concerned with what he calls 'the synchronisation of meaning'. All use 'rules of evidence' deriving from a single conceptual scheme based on assumed common relevances, stocks of knowledge, typifications, recipes, rules for managing one's presence before others, and so on. These shared 'common sense devices for making sense of the environment' (*ibid*, 100) are presupposed in conducting or analysing interviews. We must, therefore, learn to 'conceive of the error as evidence not only of poor reliability but also of "normal" interpersonal relations' (*ibid*, 74).

Cicourel's position derives from ethnomethodology, an approach we have already encountered in earlier chapters of this book (most notably in Chapters 3 and 4). His work allows us to develop a three-part table of approaches to interview data. This is set out in Table 5.3, which extends Table 5.1.

Table 5.3: *Three Approaches to Interview Data*

Approach	Type of knowledge	Claim to reliability
Positivism	Facts, beliefs	Standardised protocol to ensure unbiased measurement
Interactionism	Orientations of people involved in symbolic orders	Intersubjective depth (the open-ended or humanistic interview)
Ethnomethodology	Versions of persons and activities as sequentially constructed	Elucidating the basic properties of social interaction

For many years, positivist survey research provided the main source of data for sociology. For instance, Brenner (1981) reports studies which indicate that, during the 1960s, around 90 per cent of all the papers in the two leading American sociology journals were based on data derived from interviews and questionnaires.

Although the interactionists' critique of the positivist approach appears to be convincing, the interactionists' own position seems to have problems and inconsistencies. Moreover, Cicourel's ethnomethodological concern with the basic properties of social interaction would seem to deny the value of treating interview data as saying anything about any other reality than the interview itself. Put simply, according to one reading of Cicourel, we would focus on the conversational skills of the participants rather than on the content of what they are saying and its relation to the world outside the interview.

However, contemporary interactionist sociologists are familiar with these critiques and sometimes offer practical solutions to the problems suggested. Let us look at a relevant example based on a study of adolescents. I will then compare this study to other research on adolescents which uses interview data for different purposes.

Glassner and Loughlin: Drugs in Adolescent Worlds

Barry Glassner and Julia Loughlin (1987) conducted a major interview study of American adolescents' perceptions and uses of drugs. At first glance, their approach is highly positivist. For instance, they used structured interviews with pre-tested, scheduled questions and computer-assisted data analysis. They were also concerned about the representativeness of their sample. Although their sample was small (100 adolescents aged from 12 to 20) it was randomly selected.

However, Glassner and Loughlin's methodology exemplified many standard interactionist strategies. No multiple-choice answers were offered to respondents and the interviews were in-depth, each lasting between four and twelve hours. Moreover, the questions asked were based on a one-year participant observation study. The two fieldworkers each spent approximately twenty hours per week for more than a year with adolescents in the neighbourhoods studied (1987, 18). This meant that: 'The interviewers had spent a great deal of time with . . . the subjects during the fieldwork phase of the study, so that rapport and depth of probing were enhanced in interviews' (24).

The fieldwork allowed interview questions to be based upon the subjects' vocabulary learned from the period of observation. Unlike most survey research, the data-analysis was largely qualitative. Although some data are quantified (e.g. how people perceived drugs in relation to their drug use and gender), Glassner and Loughlin recognise that such counting may be misleading (e.g. subjects change their responses to seemingly factual questions as a result of probes by the interviewer) (*ibid*, 28–29).

Instead, tapes were transcribed and coded by: 'identifying topics, ways of talking, themes, events, actors and so forth . . . Those lists became a catalogue of codes, consisting of 45 topics, each with up to 99 descriptors' (25).

This approach to data analysis is different from positivistic, survey research studies:

> In more positivistic research designs, coder reliability is assessed in terms of agreement among coders. In qualitative research one is unconcerned with standardising interpretation of data. Rather, our goal in developing this complex cataloguing and retrieval system has been *to retain good access to the words of the subjects*, without relying upon the memory of interviewers or data analysts. (27, my emphasis)

However, Glassner and Loughlin do suggest that their analysis fits conventional criteria of reliability (e.g. every finding was discovered independently by at least two analysts). Moreover, the authors make strong claims about the validity of their analysis, because:

1 The coding and data-analysis were done 'blind' – both the coding staff and the analysts of the data 'conducted their research without know-ledge of [the] expectations or hypotheses of the project directors' (30).
2 The computer-assisted recording and analysis of the data meant that one could be more confident that the patterns reported actually existed throughout the data rather than in favourable examples.

However, in the light of critiques of interactionism how do the authors address the status of their data? Following Cicourel, Glassner and Loughlin acknowledge that their interview tapes could be treated as displays of purely conversational activities, but they argue that their transcripts are not sufficiently precise to allow such an analysis.

They respond more directly to the alternative argument about the problematic status of 'experience' in a section of their methodology chapter entitled 'Can we believe the kids?' (1987, 32–38).

The authors treat interview responses *both* as culturally defined narra-tives and as possibly factually correct statements. So, for instance, when someone says she uses marihuana because her friends do, Glassner and Loughlin take this to suggest *two* findings:

1 'She has made use of a culturally prevalent way of understanding and talking about these topics' (NARRATIVE).
2 'We now have evidence that marijuana smoking is part of peer gatherings' (FACTUAL STATEMENT) (35).

Glassner and Loughlin argue that narrative analysis works through examining the nature and sources of the 'frame of explanation' used by the interviewee. However, the character of what the interviewee is saying can also be treated as a factual statement and validated by observation (e.g. of the series of interactions through which her friends' use comes to affect her own).

If we treat interviewees' responses as factual statements, then it becomes crucial to ask: 'Can we believe the kids?' Clearly, the authors take this to be a serious question, arguing that, indeed, we should trust (their report of) what the kids are saying. They base this assertion on a set of claims about how '*rapport*' was established with subjects: interviewers were accepted as peer-group members, showed 'genuine interest' in understand-ing the interviewee's experiences and guaranteed confidentiality (35).

Calling their approach, a 'methodology for listening', Glassner and Loughlin are thus centrally concerned with 'seeing the world from the perspective of our subjects' (37). In this respect, they share the same assumptions about the 'authenticity' of 'experience' as do other inter-actionists (and many feminists). However, their sensitive address of the narrative forms from which perspectives arise suggests an alternative path for interview analysis to which I shall return (see Baruch: 1982, discussed below).

Exercise 5.1

This exercise gives you an opportunity to think through the debate about whether it is appropriate to assess whether interview accounts are true or false. The following extract is taken from a study in which scientists were interviewed about the factors that influence changes in scientific theories:

(S = Scientist)

1 S: To make changes you have to be highly articulate,
2   persuasive, and devastating. You have to go to the heart
3   of the matter. But in doing this you lay yourself open to
4   attack. I've been called fanatical, paranoid, obsessed
5   ... but I'm going to win. Time is on my side. (quoted by Gilbert and
     Mulkay: 1983, 10)

1 How might this extract be used to support the view that scientific research is largely influenced by scientific politics?
2 Why might you *not* be convinced by this view on the basis of this extract?
3 Why might it be important to understand the different *social contexts* in which scientists give an account of their work?
4 Can it be said *definitively* whether or not science is *essentially* a political process? If not, why not?

For the moment, I will use Carolyn Baker's (1982) work to show another way of analysing interviews with adolescents.

Baker: Membership Work in Adolescent–Adult Talk

Baker's research is based on her comparative studies of interviews with teenagers in Canada and Australia. Her initial concern was to use the interviews to learn about how adolescents see themselves relative to children and adults.

However, she soon saw that the participants themselves were constructing a version of adolescent–adult relations for each other. As she puts it:

> at the same time as these passages contain comment about adolescent–adult talk, they are instances *themselves* of adolescent–adult talk. They are conversations between a researcher who could commonsensically be understood to be an adult, and persons who could similarly be describable as adolescents, given their age. (Baker: 1982, 111)

To show how Baker proceeds, let us take just one extract from one of her interviews. The respondent is Pam, aged 14:

(P = Pam; I = Interviewer)

1 I: Are there any ways in which you consider yourself to

2   still be partly a child?
3 P: Well, I like to watch TV and, uh,
4 I: Well, adults do that
5 P: Yeah, I still read the comics ((laugh))
6 I: Adults do that
7 P: That's about, only thing I can think of
(Baker: 1984, 316)

Note how I assigns P to a place between childhood and adulthood (1–2) and how P enters into the discussion in these terms. Moreover, as Baker (1984, 317) notes, in lines 4 and 6, I treats as invalid P's nominated instances of 'childish' behaviour. By showing that a valid response would involve depicting something exclusive to children, I proceeds on the basis that, although child–adolescent overlap can properly arise (being 'partly a child'), child–adult overlap constitutes an unacceptable answer. The interview continues as follows (Baker: 1984, 317):

(// = overlap)
 8 I: Do you notice any leftovers of childhood in your
 9   personality?
10 P: Well, my food tastes have all changed differently, like I
11   used to hate lots of things, now I like most, almost
12   everything. I used to really hate vegetables, and now I'd
13   rather have vegetables than anything else! And um, when I
14   was a child, I used to really be worried about what I
15   looked like and that an now I don't, I don't really care.
16   If peop//
17 I: // You really don't care?
18 P: Pe, I don't care what people think, I just, think well I
19   like this, and if no one else does, that's too bad
20 I: At what point were you, so terribly self conscious about
21   your appearance?

Baker draws our attention to the way in which I picks up and pursues the topic of P's feelings about her appearance, while paying no attention to what P says about vegetables. In this way, she shows Pam that her tastes in food are not entirely compatible with I's attempt to depict overlaps between childhood and adolescence. As Baker suggests:

> by doing this, [I] shows Pam how adolescence should be done in the interview. While Pam's 'vegetable eating' is passed by, her 'not caring' about her appearance becomes the basis for an identity rich puzzle and solution whose pursuit by the interviewer binds this activity to her category 'adolescence'. (Baker: 1984, 317–318)

Anssi Peräkylä (personal correspondence) has also pointed out that I's first questions, in both extracts, treat P as a subject who might be puzzled by her identity. This can amount to treating P as a *non-child* (because children are not supposed to have that kind of self-consciousness about their identity) and simultaneously as a *non-adult* (because adults are not supposed to be puzzled about who they are). So, straight off, I constitutes P as neither child nor adult (i.e. as an 'adolescent').

Baker's analysis draws upon Sacks' MCD apparatus, already discussed in Chapter 4. It will be recalled that membership categorisation devices are used by members to group together collections of 'similar' identities or categories. Any category is a potential member of more than one MCD. One MCD that can be heard in these attempts to position people as 'children', 'adolescents' or 'adults' is 'stage of life'.

Now MCDs like 'stage of life' have three features noted by Sacks:

1 Like all MCDs, they are associated with category-bound activities (CBAs). So, in categorising someone as a child, within a stage of life MCD, certain activities are predictable (e.g. being irresponsible, having 'fads', etc.). Similarly, in defining an activity (irresponsibility, faddishness) one also implies the kinds of categories of people who might engage in it (e.g. children).

2 In a stage-of-life MCD, unlike some other MCDs, the members of the collection are differentially positioned so that, in this case, adult is higher than adolescent, adolescent is higher than child and thus adult is higher than child.

3 It follows that if an adult (A) or an adolescent (B) engages in a CBA appropriate to a child (C) then:

> a member of either A or B who does that activity may be seen to be degrading himself, and may be said to be 'acting like a child'. Alternatively, if some candidate activity is proposedly bound to A, a member of C who does it is subject to be said to be acting like an A, where that assertion constitutes 'praising'. (Sacks: 1974, 222, quoted by Baker: 1984, 302)

All of these features are present in the brief interview extracts above. First, in the exchanges between lines 1 and 7, I requests, and P attempts to provide, a set of activities hearable as bound to the category 'still partly a child'. I's comments at lines 4 and 6 now may be heard as attending to the unclear category-bounding of activities such as 'watching TV' or 'reading comics'. Similarly, I's pursuit of P's comment about her looks makes sense in terms of the association between the way in which the activity 'being concerned about one's appearance' is category-bound to the category 'adolescent'.

Second, the hierarchical relationship between each of these stage of life categories is attended to by both speakers. I uses the term 'leftovers' to describe elements left behind from childhood, while P describes her 'non-childlike' self in terms of greater independence and maturity. By reporting her activities in this way, P can be heard to be acting more like an adult than a child.

Most stage-of-life categories are mutually exclusive, i.e. you are either an 'adult' or a 'child' but, usually, cannot be both at the same time. Hence to refer to an 'adult's' behaviour as 'childish' is hearable as quite a powerful charge.

People recognisable as 'adolescents' may, therefore, want to set up a mutually exclusive framework between such categories. In the extract above, notice how Pam makes a sharp distinction between the past ('when I was a child') and the present (when she has more 'adult' qualities).

At the same time, as Baker notes: '"adolescence" can be made to overlap with "childhood" or "adulthood" by discovering "childness" or "adultness" in the "adolescent"' (1984, 303).

The interviewer's question about 'leftovers' (at line 1) depends precisely on the availability of this sense of overlap. Indeed, people can use both 'childness' and 'adultness' as simultaneous descriptions of the 'adolescent'. Indeed, as Baker notes, 'this is a classic "problem of adolescence"' (1984, 304) to be found in everyday life just as much as in this interview.

It is worth noting how Baker's analysis departs from more conventional approaches to interview data. According to these approaches:

1 Standardised sets of questions are part of 'good interview practice', designed to ensure that the interview is a reliable research instrument, free from interviewer-error.
2 Any similarities in interviewees' answers are to be explained in terms of 'fact-sheet variables' (e.g. social class, gender, ethnicity) external to the interview context.

Conversely, Baker shows that:

1 Standardised questions (and follow-up questions) derive their sense from commonly available conceptions about people's behaviour. Hence, whatever 'scientific' character they have builds upon common-sense knowledge about how the everyday social world operates.
2 Similar answers relate to the interviewees' skills in deploying shared knowledge about this shared social world.

The contrast is very clear. While many interview studies define their approach by technical criteria and treat 'society' simply as an external social fact, Baker shows how *both* interviewer and interviewee rely upon their common sense knowledge of social structures in order to produce locally 'adequate' utterances. The former approach can be characterised as *interview-as-technique*; the latter can be called the *interview-as-local-accomplishment*. This is shown in Table 5.4.

Table 5.4: *Two Versions of Interview Data*

	Questions	Answers
Interview-as-technique	Technical criteria (e.g. pre-testing of questions)	Reflect respondents' place in the social structure
Interview-as-local-accomplishment	Common-sense knowledge of social structures used to produce 'adequate' utterances	
	(e.g. to bring science into line with common sense)	(e.g. to trade off what everyone knows about categories)

From the point of view of interview-as-local-accomplishment, interview data are not 'one side of the picture' to be balanced by observation of what respondents actually do, or to be compared with what their role partners say. Instead, such data reproduce and rearticulate cultural particulars grounded in given patterns of social organisation.

Exercise 5.2

The extract below is taken from Carolyn Baker's study of 'adolescents':

(I = Interviewer; V = Victor, age 12)

```
 1 I: Are there any ways in which you consider yourself still
 2    to be a child, or to have child-like interests or habits
 3    or attitudes?
 4 V: Yeah I still like doin' things that I did when I was a
 5    kid you know like, y'know, Lego 'n that just building
 6    stuff you know like when I, I was a kid you know.
 7 I: Yeah. You still take pleasure in that kind of thing.
 8 V: Yeah, I get a friend over and we just build a, great big
 9    house 'n that, it's still just like doing it.
10 I: Do you feel at the same time that you're too – really too
11    old for it or do you not feel it's too
12 V: Well when people say 'ah, he's still doin' that stuff' I
13    don't really care. I just do it in the living room 'n
14    that, 'n it's still fun. Pretty soon I'll, I'll stop
15    doin' it but, when I get too old for it.
16 I: Or when you no longer think it's fun.
17 V: Yeah.
18 I: Which one?
19 V: How do you mean?
20 I: What would make you stop, feeling you were too old for it
21    or
22 V: Yeah, like everyone buggin' me too much y'know 'n, it's
23    not really that bad just building a house or something
24    y'know like, just show my mom it'n everything just take
25    it apart y'know, sort of something to do on a rainy day
```
(Baker: 1984, 308–309)

1 In what sense does this interview give us reliable information about how Victor seems himself?
2 With close attention to the text, and identifying MCDs and CBAs show:

   – how Victor accounts for potentially child-like activities
   – how the interviewer identifies child-like activities
   – how both Victor and the interviewer attend to the implications of what the other is saying.

To take another concrete example, to be discussed shortly: when parents of handicapped children are first interviewed, they often offer 'atrocity' stories, usually about the late discovery or inadequate treatment of their child's condition. It is tempting to compare what they say with observations of what has happened and with medical workers' accounts. However, as Baruch (1982) notes, such a comparison is based on the assumption that interview responses are to be valued primarily because of their accuracy as objective statements of sets of events. Conversely, we might address the moral forms that give force to 'atrocity' stories, whatever their accuracy. Right or wrong, biased or unbiased, such accounts display vividly cultural particulars about the moral accountability of parenthood. Shortly, I will discuss Baruch's work. Before doing so, I want to try to pull together some of the threads of the argument so far and to fill in some gaps in what I have been saying.

Summary

The value of interview data: Positivists argue that interviews based upon pre-tested, standardised questions are a way of increasing the reliability of research. However, both interactionism and ethnomethodology bring into question the value of data derived from standardised, survey-research style interviews.

Interactionists, like Glassner and Loughlin, assume that people's cultural worlds are more complex than most positivists will allow. Consequently, it is insufficient simply to 'pre-test' an interview schedule by asking questions of a few respondents. Instead, for Glassner and Loughlin, it is more appropriate to engage in systematic observation *before* any interviewing takes place.

Ethnomethodologists take the argument far further, rarely using interview methods as a way of gathering data. Instead, ethnomethodologists tend to concentrate on purely 'naturally occurring' settings which are observed and/or recorded at first hand.

It should at once be noted that the critique of the value of interview data unknowingly shares an assumption with more traditional approaches. As Hammersley and Atkinson (1983) have pointed out, an attachment to 'naturally occurring data' is a kind of 'naturalism'. Naturalism, they argue, unwittingly agrees with positivism that the best kind of data are somehow 'untouched by human hands' – neutral, unbiased and representative. In some senses, then, naturalists are the inheritors of the positivist programme, using different means to achieve the same unquestioned ends.

In an earlier book (Silverman: 1985), I argued that the opposition between artificial and naturally occurring data is a methodological red herring. Neither kind of data is intrinsically better than the other; everything depends on the method of analysis.

Despite the power of naturally occurring data, it does not follow that it is illegitimate to carry out our own research interviews. Everything depends on the status which we accord to the data gathered in such interviews.

The 'truth' of interview data: One important dimension which distinguishes positivists from ethnomethodologists is whether interviews are treated as straightforward reports on another reality or whether they merely report upon, or express, their own structures.

According to the former ('externalist') position, interviews can, in principle, be treated as reports on external realities. The only condition is that strict protocols are observed. According to the latter ('internalist') position, interviews do present interesting data. But these data express interpretive procedures or conversational practices present in what both interviewer and interviewee are *doing* through their talk and non-verbal actions (see Baker: 1982, discussed above).

Interactionists probably are closer to the former position, while recognising that the complexity of the interview situation is not fully grasped by positivist notions of bias or error. However, as already noted, there is a tension in interactionism between internalist and externalist versions of interview data. Put in simpler terms, interactionists are not too sure whether interviews are purely 'symbolic interaction' or express underlying external realities. We have found this tension in the work of Glassner and Loughlin.

The debate is seen in its clearest form in discussions about whether interview data can be biased. Within positivist work, there is an assumption that bias is a problem because of both bad interviewers *and* bad interviewees. Thus we hear about the inability of 10 per cent of the adult population to fill out 'even simple questionnaires' (Selltiz *et al*: 1964, 241), and about the untrustworthiness of some respondents and their unfortunate lack of comprehension of social scientific language (Brenner: 1981, 116–117).

These fears of bias are reflected in interactionist concerns about how informants may distort social reality (Hammersley and Atkinson: 1983, 105–107) or conceal what the interviewer most wants to know (Denzin: 1970, 130). Both positivists and interactionists find a common concern, then, in the various ways in which interviewees are not fully moral or not intellectually up to scratch.

However, there are exceptions. For instance, in what is largely a positivist argument, Brown and Sime claim that: 'an account is neither naive nor an apology for behaviour, but must be taken as an informed statement by the person whose experiences are under investigation' (Brown and Sime: 1981, 160).

Equally, there is a more helpful tendency in interactionism. This suggests that we need not hear interview responses simply as true or false *reports* on reality. Instead, we can treat such responses as *displays* of perspectives and moral forms.

The need to preserve and understand the reality of the interview account is central to the argument of many interactionists. Indeed, the interactionist tradition contains a way of looking at respondents' accounts which goes beyond categorising them as 'true' or 'false'. William F. Whyte has observed:

> In dealing with subjective material, the interviewer is, of course, not trying to discover the *true attitude or sentiment* of the informant. He should recognise that ambivalence is a fairly common condition of man – that men can and do hold

conflicting sentiments at any given time. Furthermore, men hold varying sentiments according to the situations in which they find themselves. (Whyte: 1980, 117, original emphasis)

Unlike Burgess and Denzin, but like Glassner and Loughlin, Whyte shows us how it is not always necessary to treat respondents' accounts as if they were scientific statements and subject them to possible refutation. This leads Whyte to ask questions about the causes of respondents' accounts ('the events and interpersonal relations out of which [they] arise' (*ibid*)).

Of course, this pays scant attention to the form and structure of such accounts, as discussed by Baker. However, in a paper first published in 1960, we can forgive Whyte neglecting the study of the interview as a narrative. An alternative approach, following Gilbert and Mulkay (1983), would be to treat interviews as giving us access to the *repertoire* of narratives that we use in producing accounts (see Chapter 9).

The question remains whether any bridging position is possible between these two apparently incompatible perspectives. Must we choose between seeing interviews *either* as potentially 'true' reports or as situated narratives?

Let me make two observations which I hope are helpful. First, everything depends on our purposes at hand. Sometimes, as in Baker's work, it makes sense consistently to concentrate on the local or situational character of interview talk. At the other extreme, for instance in quantitative studies of voting intentions or patient satisfaction, it becomes appropriate to treat what interviewees say as potentially 'true' reports. And again, sometimes, not without some difficulty, one can try to follow up both issues, using Glassner and Loughlin's apparently 'twin-track' approach.

My second observation relates only to work like Baker's. It might seem that, if, as she does, we focus on the local character of interview talk, we have privileged form over content. However, this is yet another misleading polarity. By analysing how people talk to one another, one is directly gaining access to a cultural universe and its content of moral assumptions. Such a position is intrinsic to Garfinkel's (1967) argument that accounts are part of the world they describe.

Let me try to demonstrate this position by looking in detail at an interview study of 'parenthood' which adopts a similar approach to Baker's discussion of the 'adult–adolescent' relationship.

Baruch: Moral Tales of Parenthood

One of the striking aspects of Baker's data is the way in which her interviewees' accounts have recurrent features in common. This parallels Baruch's (1982) comments about studies of parents' responses to different congenital illnesses in their children.

As an example, Baruch compares data extracts from Burton's (1975) study of parents of children with cystic fibrosis to his own study of parents of children with congenital heart disease. Here is the extract from Burton's study:

> Parent: I went to the baby clinic every week. She would gain one pound one week and lose it the next. They said I was fussing unnecessarily. They said there were skinny and fat babies and I was fussing too much. I went to a doctor and he gave me some stuff and he said 'You're a young mother. Are you sure you won't put it in her ear instead of her mouth?' It made me feel a fool. (quoted by Baruch: 1982, Appendix 2, 1)

This is the extract that Baruch quotes from his own study:

> Parent: When she was born, they told me was perfectly all right. And I accepted it. I worried about her which most mothers do, you know. Worry about their first child.
> Int: Hm
> Parent: She wouldn't eat and different things. And so I kept taking her to the clinic. Nothing wrong with her my dear. You're just making yourself . . . worrying unnecessarily, you see. (*ibid*)

Despite the different illnesses, there are striking similarities in the content of what each mother is saying. Both mothers report their concern about the baby's eating habits. Both complain that the clinic doctor dismissed their worries as groundless.

Nonetheless, Baruch notes that each account is treated very differently by each researcher. More specifically:

> Burton treats her findings as an accurate report of an external event and argues that parents' early encounters with medical personnel can cause psychological damage to the parents as well as lasting damage to the relationship with doctors. On the other hand, I see parents' talk as a situated account aimed at displaying the status of morally adequate parenthood. In this instance, the display is produced by the telling of an atrocity story. (Baruch: 1982, Appendix 2, 2)

If we return to Table 5.4, we can find the basis for this difference of approach. Burton treats parents' answers as deriving from the social structure of mother–doctor interactions, coupled with a given psychological reality to do with parents' feelings of guilt and responsibility. For Burton, then, the interview is a technique used by social scientists to get closer to such 'facts'.

Conversely, Baruch is arguing that mothers are trading on common-sense knowledge of 'what everyone knows' about the concerns of young mothers. Treating the interview as a local accomplishment, he invites us to see how the construction of an 'atrocity story' is an effective way for mothers to display their moral responsibility.

It might appear that Burton and Baruch are offering *competing* versions of mothers' behaviour. Burton seems to be stressing the mothers' goodwill in difficult circumstances, while Baruch appears to be offering a more cynical account which seems to argue that mothers are mainly concerned with how they will look in the eyes of others. However, it must be stressed that, for Baruch at least, the two accounts are *not* competitive.

This is because Baruch is not treating what his mothers tell him as either true or false accounts of what actually happened to them when they took their babies to the clinics. Consonant with his view of these interviews as 'local accomplishments', he is instead focussing on how, in telling their story to a stranger, mothers skilfully produce demonstrably 'morally adequate' accounts.

Once more following Sacks, we can hear the category of 'mother-of-baby-with-newly-discovered-illness' as associated with a category-bound activity (CBA) of 'mother-who-did-not-monitor-her-baby-sufficiently'. Notice now how, in both extracts, the mothers' reports that they noticed that their babies had eating problems *prior to the disease diagnosis* specifically contradict this possible charge. Coupled with their reports that doctors had, at first, played down their fears, this effectively shifts the category of 'mother-of-baby-with-newly-discovered-illness' to a new CBA, namely 'mother-who-thoroughly-monitored-her-baby-but-was-spurned-by-the-doctor'.

So Baruch is asking about the *functions* of the mothers' accounts rather than casting doubt on their motives. He is not competing with what Burton says about the reality of what happens in mother–doctor encounters because he is refusing to treat interviewees' accounts as simple *reports* on such an external reality. If anything, however, Baruch's analysis offers a more human account of the capacities of his respondents. While Burton's mothers' responses seem determined by social and psychological structures, Baruch reveals that human subjects actively participate in the construction of social and psychological realities.

So far, however, we been depending on brief extracts to show how such an analysis works. As I shall argue in Chapter 7, a danger of depending on such extracts is that one can use them to support a preconceived argument rather than to test it. Baruch (1982) overcomes such dangers by two effective strategies:

- tabulating many cases
- investigating deviant cases.

Let me briefly review each strategy in turn.

Following Sacks, Baruch shows how interview accounts can be investigated in terms of the membership categorisation devices (MCDs) employed by respondents. The MCDs used by Baruch's parents were mainly 'parent', 'child' and 'medical professional'. In turn, these MCDs were grouped in various pairs at different parts of the account according to who had a duty towards the other (e.g. parent–child, professional–parent).

Baruch used only the parents' initial responses to the interviewer's opening question: 'So could you just tell me the story?' He then tabulated these responses in terms of pairs of MCDs. Table 5.5 indicates the pairs identified – in each case, the category mentioned first is described by the parent as having an implied duty towards the second category.

Baruch notes that earlier studies (e.g. Voysey: 1975) have stressed the

Table 5.5: *Membership Categories*

Categories	Number	%
Parent–child	160	51
Parent–professional	86	28
Professional–child	49	16
Professional–parent	16	5
Total	311	100

Source: Baruch 1982, Appendix 2, 17

perceived importance of parental responsibilities towards their children. Table 5.5 supports this finding, showing that:

> Parent–child norms are central to parents' accounts and, on their own, amount to all the other norms put together. Thus, when parents provide an account of their responses, they are heard to attend to their duties, rights and obligations towards their child, even though they might have been expected to emphasise the medical aspects of their child's career, e.g. professional–child relationships. (Baruch: 1982, Appendix 2, 18)

In Sacks' terms, each of these pairs of MCDs implies common expectations about what sorts of activities are appropriate. For instance, the parent–child pairing implies a standard obligation of parental responsibility such that we can describe the collection 'parent–child' as a standardised relational pair (SRP).

Looking just at the SRP 'parent–child', Baruch finds the kinds of activities described in the interviews that are listed in Table 5.6.

Table 5.6: *Parent–Child Activities*

Type of Activity	Number	%
Emotional responses to the child's illness and treatment	101	63
Action taken in relation to the child's illness	38	24
Taking responsibility for the child's illness	11	7
Showing knowledge about the child's development and illness	10	6
Total	160	100

Source: Baruch: 1982, Appendix 2, Table 3

We see from Table 5.6, as Baruch puts it, that: 'One of the central features of these stories is the way parents appeal to their emotionality as a normal, moral response of anyone who is in their situation' (*ibid*, 21).

This emotional response (described in 63 per cent of all such descriptions of parents and children) appears to set the backdrop for the other accounts of action taken (24 per cent) in the context of responsibility (7 per cent) and knowledge (6 per cent). Thus parents describe their relationship to their children as primarily grounded in emotion but leading to actions embodying the more cognitive dimensions of responsibility and knowledge.

Using such tabulations, Baruch demonstrates that the construction of what he calls 'moral tales' (see also Baruch: 1981) is not just an isolated feature of one or two extracts but runs throughout his corpus of data. When grounded on MCD analysis, Baruch's systematic 'content analysis' makes generalisation possible without violating the recognition of the interview as a situated encounter.

Nonetheless, as in all data-sets, there are always exceptions. As already mentioned, Baruch stringently seeks to identify such exceptions and, through the method of *deviant case analysis*, uses them to refine his analysis. The most important deviant case is discussed briefly below.

One set of parents, when asked to tell their story, responded entirely in terms of descriptions of what medical professionals had done for their child. They made no mention of their own emotional responses, nor of their own actions as parents. The following extract gives a brief taste of their response:

```
 1 Parent: Well the story really started with him going in for
 2          a minor op last year and the anaesthetist just er
 3          investigations discover a murmur which she wasn't
 4          very happy about and referred us to a paediatrician
 5          after the op who agreed that it was an unusual sight
 6          and um
 7          murmurs are commonplace really
 8 Int:    um
 9 Parent: But on the sight and nature of it, it sort of wanted
10          further investigation. (*ibid*, Appendix 2, 28)
```

While all Baruch's other interviews contained several descriptions of parent–child SRPs, they are totally absent here where the tale is told simply in terms of professional–child activities. If you compare this extract with the ones given earlier, the absence here of references to parents' worries is quite striking.

Baruch suggests that the key to understanding this deviant case lies in P's statement in line 7 that 'murmurs are commonplace really'. As he notes, this involves: 'the use of a technical language . . . which is never heard in other parents' accounts at this stage of the child's career' (*ibid*, 29).

It turns out that these parents are themselves medical professionals and are treating the interviewer's question as a request for a reasonably 'objective' account of events seen from a medical point of view. This 'deviant case' thus highlights the way in which, for parents without these medical resources, the request for a story is heard as an opportunity to display that one is still an adequate parent.

Two points of clarification perhaps need to be made. First, this extract is being viewed as deviant purely in a statistical sense. As Baruch argues:

> we are not viewing [P's] account as deviant in terms of preconceived assumptions about what constitutes adequate parenthood. Rather, the claims we are making about its status are based on a comparison of the considerable differences between its normative character and that of the rest of the sample.

> As Strong (1979) has argued, such limiting cases are extremely valuable in illuminating consistent features of social life. (*ibid*, 30)

The second point derives from this: it might be suggested that Baruch is arguing that the occupation of these parents is the *cause* of why they give their account in this way. If so, Baruch would be treating the interviewees' account as stemming from their place in the social structure and, thereby, be reverting to a version of the interview-as-technique (see Table 5.4 above).

However, although Baruch is not explicit on this matter, his method would suggest that this is *not* his argument at all. Following Sacks, we must recognise that any person can describe themselves (or be described) in a multiplicity of ways. These parents could have elected to have heard the interviewer's request for 'the story' to be addressed to them purely as 'parents' rather than as 'health-care-professionals-who-happen-to-be-parents'. By choosing the latter format, they display other, equally moral, qualities, e.g. as people who are, for the moment, able to put their feelings on one side and seek to offer an admirably 'objective' account.

Exercise 5.3

This exercise gives you an opportunity to work with some of Baruch's data and to compare his approach with others. Here are some extracts from interviews with mothers of children with congenital heart disease:

1
Well um ... the first thing the nurse who delivered him said was: 'Don't worry, it's alright. Everything's alright'. And I didn't even realise there was anything wrong with him to start with

2
When she was born they told me everything was perfectly alright. And I accepted it.

3
He was very breathless and I kept saying to midwives and doctors and various bods that came round, um I said the midwife look, I said, he's breathing so fast

4
He was sitting in his buggy just looking absolutely lifeless. So I thought right up to the doctor's and see what she says

Now answer the following questions:

1 Attempt a psychological interpretation of what these mothers are saying (refer to the discussion of Burton on pp. 108–109 above).
2 Attempt a sociological interpretation, using Baruch's concepts of 'moral adequacy' and 'atrocity stories'.
3 Is it helpful to check the accuracy of what these mothers are saying (e.g. by comparing them to case-notes, medical accounts, etc.)? Explain your answer.

In neither case do we have to see an external, pre-given social structure as the determinant of the account. Rather, all the interviewees invoke a sense of social structure in order to assemble recognisably 'sensible' accounts which are adequate for the practical purposes at hand.

The implications are clear-cut. First, in studying accounts, we are studying displays of cultural particulars as well as displays of members' artful practices in assembling these particulars. Second, there is no necessary contradiction in seeking to study *both* particulars and practices. Sacks himself, for instance, seeks to establish the norms at work in children's stories in order to give an account of the artful practices through which they are assembled. It is equally possible, as Baruch has shown, to study the cultural norms at work within a narrative and to understand how their power derives from *both* their cultural base and their use in relation to a set of formal rules with an apparently inexorable logic.

As Sacks acknowledges, the *content* of his formal membership categorisation devices is cultural through and through, arising, for instance, in how the collection 'family' is put together in a particular society. However, as he points out, once a category from one collection is used there are powerful pressures to draw on the same collection in subsequent descriptions. This can have unintended consequences – slanging-matches, for instance, can get locked into a pattern of mutual insult once the first insulting term is used.

Following Sacks, Baruch's research reveals that, for analytic purposes and in real life, form and content depend upon each other. It underlines my first argument: interviews (like other narratives) display cultural particulars – which are all the more powerful, given the connections which members make between them.

Conclusion

Interviews share with any account an involvement in moral realities. They offer a rich source of data which provide access to how people account for both their troubles and good fortune.

Such observations are hardly surprising since the evidence for them is immediately before our eyes in our everyday experience. Only by following misleading correspondence theories of truth could it have ever occurred to researchers to treat interview statements as *only* potentially accurate or distorted reports of reality.

Ironically, however, when such 'distortion' is diagnosed, it is often treated as an indication of a moral shortcoming on the part of the respondent (i.e. as 'concealment', 'lack of intelligence', etc.). We are led ineluctably to the Durkheimian conclusion that moral forms suffuse the social world. This further supports the emphasis in this chapter upon treating interview accounts as compelling narratives.

6

Transcripts

Language

In this part of the book, we have so far examined three sources of data in field research: observations, texts and interviews. Despite the different uses that can be made of each kind of data, all share a common feature – their focus on language.

The linguistic character of field data is most obvious in the case of texts and interviews. Even if our aim is to search for the supposedly non-linguistic, social 'realities' purportedly present in such data (e.g. social class, gender, power), our raw material is inevitably the words written in documents or spoken by interview respondents. Moreover, while observational data should properly include descriptions of non-verbal aspects of social interaction (what Stimson: 1986 calls 'the sociology of space and place'), much of what we observe in formal and informal settings will inevitably consist of conversations.

An analysis of why linguistic phenomena are so important lies beyond the scope of this book. However, we can make a few relevant observations:

1 Twentieth-century thought has resisted earlier assumptions that words are simply a transparent medium to 'reality'. From the linguist Saussure (1974), as we saw in Chapter 4, we learn that signs derive meaning from their relation to other signs. From the philosopher Wittgenstein, we understand that the meaning of a word largely derives from its *use*. Consequently, as Wittgenstein puts it:

> When philosophers use a word – 'knowledge', 'being', 'object' (etc.) . . . – and try to grasp the *essence* of the thing, one must first ask oneself: is the word ever actually used in this way in the language-game which is its original home? – What *we* do is to bring words back from their metaphysical to their everyday use. (Wittgenstein: 1968, para. 116)

Wittgenstein's critique of some philosophers can, of course, be turned upon social scientists who arbitrarily construct 'operational definitions' of phenomena without ever studying the 'language-game' in which the phenomenon has its everyday home. This explains, for instance, Atkinson's (1978) attempt to understand 'suicide' in terms of its everyday construction in the work of coroners' courts.

2 Although talk is sometimes seen as trivial ('merely' talk), it has increasingly become recognised as the primary medium through which social interaction takes place. In households and in more 'public' settings,

families and friends assemble their activities through talk. At work, we converse with one another and have our activities placed on dossiers and files. As Heritage argues: 'the social world is a pervasively conversational one in which an overwhelming proportion of the world's business is conducted through the medium of spoken interaction' (Heritage: 1984, 239). Indeed, as Heritage notes, 'the world's business' includes such basic features as the child's entry into the social world through learning how to converse with its mother.

3 If our concern is with more 'formal' or institutional settings, it may not seem immediately apparent why we need to know about how 'informal' or mundane conversation is organised. However, as we shall see, a strong case has been made out that 'institutional' talk operates through the modified use of patterns deriving from ordinary conversation (Heritage: 1984, 239–240). Moreover, attempts to analyse such talk which fail to problematise these patterns will inevitably be based on the analyst's own taken-for-granted knowledge about how to understand ordinary conversation.

Transcripts

Even if we concede the centrality of language (and, more specifically, conversation) to social life, why should we give priority to recording and transcribing talk? Given the usefulness of other kinds of data derived, say, from observations and interviews, what is the special value of transcripts of tape-recordings of conversation?

One way to start to answer this question is to develop the arguments for using 'naturally occurring' data, first discussed in Chapter 2. Conversely, in interviews, as Heritage puts it: 'the verbal formulations of subjects are treated as an appropriate substitute for the observation of actual behaviour' (Heritage: 1984, 236).

The temptation is then to treat respondents' formulations in terms of their one-to-one relationship with a pre-existing social world (i.e. as 'true' or 'false'). One way round this, as we have seen, is to treat interview accounts as 'narratives' and, like Baker and Baruch, to focus on their linguistic structure. An alternative is to concentrate on how 'interviews' depend upon the modified use of certain properties of everyday conversation.

A basic sequence of actions in a recognisable interview is a series of questions and answers (Silverman: 1973). After a question, as Sacks puts it, 'the other party properly speaks, and properly offers an answer to the question and says no more than that' (Sacks: 1972, 230). However, after the answer has been given, the questioner can speak again and *can* choose to ask a further question. This chaining rule can provide 'for the occurrence of an indefinitely long conversation of the form Q–A–Q–A–Q–A . . .' (*ibid*).

Although question–answer sequences do arise in mundane conve
they seem to provide a defining characteristic of interview ta
chaining rule gives a great deal of space to the interviewer to shape i
of topics, while interviewees depend upon being granted a right ιο ask
questions themselves (Silverman: 1973).

Hughes has noted this asymmetry of interactional rights, based on a
question–answer format. In medical consultations:

> The asking of a question in itself constrains the patient to give an answer on the
> same topic. Having heard the answer to the question as the end of the patient's
> utterance, the doctor is free to interrupt and the turn to initiate continually
> comes back to him. To introduce a new point he simply moves on to the next
> question without necessary recourse to certain practices common in everyday
> conversations. (Hughes: 1982, 369)

The reader will have noticed that such work involves a shift of interest
away from using the interview as a means of obtaining data about a pre-
existing social world and *towards* a focus on the organisation of 'interview-
talk' itself. Moreover, since interview-talk is only a sub-set of various kinds
of talk-in-interaction, it has no special status as a *tool* of social research.

However, can the same be said about observation? After all, unlike the
research interview, observational data are precisely of value because they
focus on naturally occurring activities. What do we lose if we base our
analysis purely on such data?

The first thing to bear in mind is that, to become data, observations have
to be recorded in some way, e.g. through fieldnotes or pre-coded
schedules. However sophisticated such recording devices may be, they
cannot offer the detail found in transcripts of recorded talk.

Detailed transcripts of conversation overcome the tendency of trans-
cribers to 'tidy up' the 'messy' features of natural conversation. Sacks *et al*
(1974) offer an Appendix which provides a detailed description of the
notation they use and the interested reader is recommended to study it. An
alternative source is Atkinson and Heritage (1984). In Table 6.1 I provide
a simplified set of transcription symbols.

However, it should not be assumed that the preparation of transcripts is
simply a technical detail prior to the main business of the analysis. As
Atkinson and Heritage (1984) point out, the production and use of
transcripts are essentially 'research activities'. They involve close, repeated
listenings to recordings which often reveal previously unnoted recurring
features of the organisation of talk. The convenience of transcripts for
presentational purposes is no more than an added bonus.

As an example, the reader might examine Extract 6.1 below, drawn
from Heritage (1984) and based on transcribing conventions, listed in
Table 6.1, which report such features as pauses (in parts of a second) and
overlapping talk:

Table 6.1:   *Simplified Transcription Symbols*

[	C2: quite a [while Mo: [yea	Left brackets indicate the point at which a current speaker's talk is overlapped by another's talk
=	W: that I'm aware of = C: = Yes. Would you confirm that?	Equal signs, one at the end of a line and one at the beginning, indicate no gap between the two lines
(.4)	Yes (.2) yeah	Numbers in parentheses indicate elapsed time in silence in tenths of a second
(.)	to get (.) treatment	A dot in parentheses indicates a tiny gap, probably no more than one-tenth of a second
————	What's *up*?	Underscoring indicates some form of stress, via pitch and/or amplitude
: :	O:*kay*?	Colons indicate prolongation of the immediately prior sound. The length of the row of colons indicates the length of the prolongation
WORD	I've got ENOUGH TO WORRY ABOUT	Capitals, except at the beginnings of lines, indicate especially loud sounds relative to the surrounding talk
.hhhh	I feel that (.2) .hh	A row of h's prefixed by a dot indicates an inbreath; without a dot, an outbreath. The length of the row of h's indicates the length of the in- or outbreath
( )	future risks and ( ) and life ( )	Empty parentheses indicate the transcriber's inability to hear what was said
(word)	Would you see (there) anything positive	Parenthesised words are possible hearings
(( ))	confirms that ((continues))	Double parentheses contain author's descriptions rather than transcriptions
. , ?	What do you think?	Indicate speaker's intonation

Extract 6.1
(S's wife has just slipped a disc)
1 H: And we were *w*ondering if there's *a*nything we can do to
2   help
3 S: [Well 'at's
4 H: [I mean   can we do any shopping for her or something
5   like tha:t?
6   (0.7)
7 S: Well that's *most* ki:nd Heather*ton* .hhh At the moment
8   no:. because we've still got two bo:ys at home

Heritage (1984, 237) has noted the gains of working with such transcripts. His observations can be summarised as follows:

1   It is very difficult for the ethnographer working with fieldnotes to record such detail.

2 The tape-recording and the transcript allow both analyst and reader to return to the extract either to develop the analysis or to check it out in detail.

3 What may appear, at first hearing, to be interactionally 'obvious' can subsequently (via a transcript) be seen to based on precise mechanisms skilfully used by the participants, for instance, how S delays his refusal of H's offer.

Exercise 6.1

This is a task designed to help you familiarise yourself with the transcription conventions used in conversation analysis. As a consequence, you should start to understand the logic of transcribing this way and be able to ask questions about how the speakers are organising their talk.

You are asked to tape-record no more than five minutes of talk in the public domain. One possibility is a radio call-in programme.

Avoid using scripted drama productions, as these may not contain recurrent features of natural interaction (such as overlap or repair). Do not try to record a television extract, as the visual material will complicate both transcription and analysis.

Now go through the following steps:

1 Attempt to transcribe your tape using the conventions in Table 6.1. Try to allocate turns to identified speakers where possible but don't worry if you can't identify a particular speaker (put ? at the start of a line in such cases).

2 Encourage a friend to attempt the same task independently of you. Now compare transcripts and re-listen to the tape-recording to improve your transcript.

3 Using this chapter as a guide, attempt to identify in your transcript any features in the organisation of the talk (e.g. adjacency pairs, chaining rule, preference organisation, interview format, etc.)

It is worth concluding here with Heritage's summary of the advantages of transcripts:

the use of recorded data is an essential corrective to the limitations of intuition and recollection. In enabling repeated and detailed examination of the events of interaction, the use of recordings extends the range and precision of the observations which can be made. It permits other researchers to have direct access to the data about which claims are being made, thus making analysis subject to detailed public scrutiny and helping to minimise the influence of personal preconceptions or analytical biases. Finally, it may be noted that because the data are available in 'raw' form, they can be re-used in a variety of investigations and can be re-examined in the context of new findings. (Heritage: 1984, 238)

The detailed transcription symbols in Extract 6.1 derive from the approach called *conversation analysis* (CA). CA is based on an attempt to describe people's methods for producing orderly social interaction. In turn, CA emerged out of Garfinkel's (1967) programme for *ethnomethodology* and its analysis of 'folk' ('ethno') methods. Sacks' MCD analysis, discussed in Chapter 5, derives from this programme.

As we shall see, CA's concern with the *sequential* organisation of talk means that it needs precise transcriptions of such (commonsensically) trivial matters as overlapping talk and length of pauses. As Sacks once put it:

> What we need to do . . . is to watch conversations . . . I don't say that we should rely on our recollection for conversation, because it's very bad . . . One can invent new sentences and feel comfortable with them (as happens in philosophy and linguistics). One cannot invent new sequences of conversation and feel happy with them. You may be able to take 'a question and answer', but if we have to extend it very far, then the issue of whether somebody would really say that, after, say, the fifth utterance, is one which we could not confidently argue. One doesn't have a strong intuition for sequencing in conversation. (1992b, 5)

CA has established itself as the leading approach in this area and most of this chapter will be devoted to it. However, CA is not the only way to work with transcripts.

Discourse Analysis

Discourse analysis (DA) describes a heterogeneous range of social science research based on the analysis of recorded talk. It shares with CA a common intellectual ancestor in the Oxford philosopher J.L. Austin.

In *How to Do Things with Words*, Austin (1962) showed that many utterances do not simply describe a state of affairs but perform an action. For instance:

Help
I thee wed

In both cases, the speakers are not heard to describe the state of their mind nor to picture reality but to perform some action ('asking for help', 'getting married'). Uttering such 'performatives', as Austin calls them, commits speakers to their consequences. For instance, when people come to give you help and find nothing amiss, it is no defence to say that you were not calling for assistance but simply singing a song. Alternatively, Austin points out, you will not escape a charge of bigamy by saying that you had all kinds of mental reservations when you uttered 'I thee wed' for the second time.

Like nearly all liguistic philosophers, Austin worked with *invented* examples, relying on his native intuition. Social scientists prefer to understand the complexities of naturally occurring talk. What they take from Austin is his concern with the activities performed in talk.

Because DA is so heterogeneous, it is difficult to arrive at a clear definition of it. Like CA, following Austin, it seeks to analyse the activities present in talk. Unlike CA, DA possesses the following three features:

1   It is concerned with a far broader range of activities, often related to more conventional social science concerns (e.g. gender relations, social control, etc.).
2   It does not always use analysis of ordinary conversation as a baseline for understanding talk in institutional settings.
3   DA works with far less precise transcripts than CA.

In order to show both the possibilities and limits of DA, I will use two examples. It should be understood that these examples are illustrative rather than representative of such work. Readers interested in further examples might consult the journal *Discourse and Society*.

Constituting Motherhood

Extract 6.2 is drawn from the clinics for young diabetics which I have discussed elsewhere (Silverman: 1987). Here is the start of a consultation between a mother of a diabetic child aged 16 and her paediatrician. It takes place when her daughter is in another room having her blood taken and the mother has asked specially if she can see the doctor. This extract comes a little way into the consultation.

Extract 6.2
(D = Doctor; M = Mother of June, aged 16)

M: She's going through a very languid stage (   ) she won't do anything
       unless you push her
D: so you're finding you're having to push her quite a lot?
M: mm no well I don't (.) I just leave her now

Now what I have done is to analyse this kind of case and other examples in terms of what I call a *charge–rebuttal* sequence. It seems to me there is evidence, in what the mother says, to suggest that she is hearing what the doctor is saying as a charge against her parenting. Notice how she withdraws from her initial depiction about 'pushing' her daughter when the doctor, through repeating it, makes it accountable.

Now why would she want to withdraw from this depiction? I think the charge available in the doctor's question involves a depiction of her as what is hearable as a 'nagging' mother. (It is interesting that only women can nag!) When the doctor topicalises 'pushing', the mother withdraws into an account which suggests that she respects her daughter's autonomy.

Shortly after, June's mother produces another worry about how her daughter is coping with her diabetes. This time her concern is her daughter's diet:

Extract 6.3
M: I don't think she's really sticking to her diet (.) I don't know the effects this
   will have on her (.) it's bound to alter her sugar if she's not got the right insulin
   isn't it? I mean I know what she eats at home but [outside
D: [so there's no real consistency to her diet? It's sort [of
M: [no well I keep it as consistent as I can at
   home

Now look at what the doctor says this time. What he makes topical here
is not that the mother may be illegitimately nagging her child. Instead, he
produces a hearable charge against her responsibility towards the child
(there 'is no real consistency to her diet').

In response, the mother now uses the very thing she denied earlier. She
is appealing to a discourse of parental responsibility in order to rebut what
she hears as the charge of 'irresponsibility' in what the doctor is saying.

This reveals a number of things. It goes back to the issue that people are
cleverer than they can say in so many words. The mother is skilfully
operating with two discourses that logically are quite contradictory. You
can't on the one hand say 'I watch everything my child does' and at the
same time 'I leave my child to do anything she wants to do'. However, by
using each discourse when situationally appropriate, the mother is able to
detect and rebut possible traps in the way the doctor is responding to what
she is saying.

There is both a methodological and a practical interest in all this. The
naturally occurring material reveals that this mother is not *intrinsically*
'nagging' or 'irresponsible'. Instead, both are depictions which are *locally*
available and *locally* resisted. Conversely, if we had interviewed mothers,
the temptation would have been to search for idealised conceptions of their
role.

The reader will note that the gain of this analysis is that, like many DA
studies, it addresses a conventional social science topic (conceptions of
gender and motherhood). Moreover, it seems to have an immediate
practical application. For instance, doctors were interested to learn about
the double-binds present in their attention to the autonomy of their young
patients. Likewise, parents' groups (largely mothers) of diabetic children
found it very helpful to go through material of this kind. It brought out the
way in which things they may feel personally guilty about in their
relationships with their teenage children are not something that relates to
their individual failings. Instead, such problems arise in our culture in the
double-binds built into the parent–adolescent relationship.

However, the analysis does not bring out how this talk in an institutional
setting (a medical clinic) derives from and departs from ordinary conversation. Consequently, it lays itself open to the charge of basing its analysis
upon taken-for-granted knowledge about the basic structures of talk (e.g.
how charges or accusations are hearable by conversationalists). The same
arguments can be made about my second example of DA.

Exercise 6.2

Below is a later extract drawn from the consultation presented in Extracts 6.2 and 6.3:

(D = Doctor, M = Mother)

1 D: It sounds as if generally you're having a difficult time
2 M: Her temper is vile
3 D: She with you and you with her
4 M: Yes. And her control of the diabetes is gone, her temper
5   then takes control of her

Using the analysis already given of Extracts 6.2 and 6.3, consider the following:

1 How is D's interpretation in line 3 of M's utterance in line 2 hearable as a charge?
2 How does M's utterance in lines 4–5 respond to D's interpretation? Is it hearable as a rebuttal?
3 Can we learn anything from this extract about:

   (a) M's attitude to her daughter
   (b) cultural assumptions about motherhood?

What Teachers Do

The dialogue in Extract 6.4 is drawn from a classroom (from a study by Edwards and Mercer: 1987, reported by Billig *et al*: 1988, 51–52). A teacher is introducing a group of 9-year-olds to the concept of pendulums. She is telling them a story about Galileo, attempting to elicit from them his use of his pulse to time the swings of incense burners in church:

Extract 6.4
(T = Teacher; ( ) = untimed pauses; *had* = vocal emphasis; concurrent behaviour is recorded to the right)

T: Now he didn't have a watch ( ) but he *had* on *him* something that was a very good timekeeper that he could to hand straight away ( )	T swinging her pendant
	T snaps her fingers on 'straight away' and looks invitingly at pupils
You've* got it. *I've* got it What is it? ( ) What could we use to count beats? What have *you* got? ( )	* T points
	T beats hand on table slowly, look around group of pupils, who smile and shrug

You can feel it *here*	T puts finger on her wrist pulse
Pupils: Pulse	(in near unison)
T: A pulse. Everybody see if you can find it	All imitate T, feeling for their wrist pulses

This extract is unusual in transcribing body movements as well as talk. CA uses a more complex system of transcription for gaze and body movements (see Heath: 1988, Peräkylä and Silverman: 1991a). The simple transcription used here shows how T's words are linked to her actions. Through both talk and gesture, T gets her pupils to produce the information she is seeking. The process is described by Billig *et al* as 'cued elicitation' (1988, 52).

Research like this is helpful in understanding the basic structures of classroom interaction which are presumed in normative accounts of teaching practice. It is highly likely that student teachers' complaints about the lack of relevance of educational theories in the classroom would be satisfied by concentrating teacher-education on such naturally-occurring examples.

However, as with the earlier analysis of mother-doctor interaction, no attempt is made to locate the activity described ('cued elicitation') in the context of practices observable in everyday talk. Elsewhere, for instance, Mehan (1979) has shown how the structure of classroom 'lessons' is a modified version of a question–answer 'chaining' procedure (Q–A–Q–A, etc.) found in ordinary conversation. The modification occurs through an additional element, teacher evaluation of the pupil's answer, so that the classroom sequence becomes Q–A–E–Q–A–E, etc.

However, it should not be assumed that DA is simply a worthless project. Undoubtedly, as we shall see, CA gains by mobilising information about the structures of ordinary conversation in the context of very detailed transcripts. However, DA-based research studies do provide important insights into institutional talk based on pressing sociological and practical concerns (like doctor–patient and teacher–pupil communication). Equally, like CA, it can be attentive to the sequential embeddedness of talk – as, for instance, in Extract 6.2, when the mother's changes of tack are interpreted in terms of the doctor's glosses on what she has just said.

Moreover, we cannot assume that transcripts which do not record such details as length of pauses (as in Extract 6.4) are necessarily imperfect. There cannot be a *perfect* transcript of a tape-recording. Everything depends upon what you are trying to do in the analysis, as well as upon practical considerations involving time and resources.

Conversation Analysis

I will begin by summarising Heritage's (1984, 241–244) account of three fundamental assumptions of CA:

The structural organisation of talk: Talk exhibits stable, organised patterns, demonstrably oriented to by the participants. These patterns 'stand independently of the psychological or other characteristics of particular speakers' (241). This has two important implications. First, the structural organisation of talk is to be treated as on a par with the structural organisation of any social institution, i.e. as a 'social fact', in Durkheim's terms. Second, it follows that it is illegitimate and unnecessary to explain that organisation by appealing to the presumed psychological or other characteristics of particular speakers.

Sequential organisation: 'A speaker's action is *context-shaped* in that its contribution to an on-going sequence of actions cannot adequately be understood except by reference to its context . . . in which it participates' (242). However, this context is addressed by CA largely in terms of the preceding sequence of talk: 'in this sense, the context of a next action is repeatedly renewed with every current action' (*ibid*).

The empirical grounding of analysis: The first two properties need to be identified in precise analyses of detailed transcripts. It is therefore necessary to avoid premature theory-construction and the 'idealisation' of research materials which use only general, non-detailed characterisations.
    Heritage sums up these assumptions as follows:

> Specifically, analysis is strongly 'data-driven' – developed from phenomena which are in various ways evidenced in the data of interaction. Correspondingly, there is a strong bias against *a priori* speculation about the orientations and motives of speakers and in favour of detailed examination of conversationalists' actual actions. Thus the empirical conduct of speakers is treated as the central resource out of which analysis may develop. (1984, 243)

In practice, Heritage adds, this means that it must be demonstrated that the regularities described 'are produced and oriented to by the participants as normatively oriented-to grounds for inference and action' (244). Further, deviant cases, in which such regularities are absent, must be identified and analysed (see Chapter 7 for a further discussion of the role of deviant case analysis in relation to the validity of field research).
    Lest it seem that CA is an esoteric kind of enterprise, it will be helpful, using the early work of Harvey Sacks, to show the links between CA and the analysis of descriptions that we have already discussed in Chapter 4.

Sacks: The Sequential Organisation of Talk

Although we might assume that analysis of 'descriptions' is concerned with 'content', while the sequencing of talk addresses 'forms', this assumption is mistaken. As his address of his data shows, Sacks' contribution to our understanding of description is not intended to stand apart from his account of the sequential organisation of talk. For instance 'recipient-design' is, for members, both a descriptive and sequential consideration.

Underlying both sets of concerns is a desire to unearth the apparatus or machinery that would reproduce whatever members do. As Sacks himself puts it:

> The kind of phenomena we are dealing with are always transcriptions of actual occurrences, in their actual sequence. And I take it our business is to try to construct the *machinery* that would produce those occurrences. That is, we find and name some objects, and find and name some rules for using those objects, where the rules for using those objects will produce those objects. (1992b, 113, my emphasis)

Among these objects, fundamental to conversation analysis, are: people talk one at a time; speaker change recurs at completion transition points while preserving one-party-at-a-time; current speaker can select next speaker or next speaker can self-select; current speaker can select a next action (e.g. an answer) (1992, Fall: 1968, Lecture 3).

Sacks notes how the obligation to *listen* is built into conversation since you may be selected as next speaker and, for instance, may need to produce the second part of an adjacency-pair. However, the requirements of recipient-design mean that a speaker may try to avoid 'springing' certain kinds of first parts, like invitations and requests, upon another. Thus, before giving an invitation, they can produce a 'pre-sequence' (cf. Schegloff: 1980) which 'can pre-signal "invitation to come" . . . Instead of saying "Would you like to come over to dinner tonight?" they can say "What are you doing tonight?" where the answer to that controls whether they're going to do the invitation' (1992b, 529).

The exchange of turns implies that co-operative work is required if a turn is to be extended through various possible completion points. For instance, to tell a story may involve a 'preface' (1992b, 10 and 18–19) which both provides for the multi-turn nature of the talk and allows its recipient to know when it is to be completed. But equally the recipient will need to offer minimal 'response-tokens' (such as 'mm') which serve to indicate that one is listening but passes one's turn and invites the other to continue. Moreover, as Sacks notes, response tokens can be subtly recipient-designed by anticipating a possible pause and ensuring no gap, no overlap between speakers. Equally, by declining a possible turn, response-tokens can require a speaker to produce more, even when they are not claiming an extension of their turn – think of 'mm mm's used by counsellors and the like (see Sacks 1992b, May 24, 1971).

However, not every story is equally tellable. Sacks notes how people work up a story to make it tellable. For instance, 'newsworthiness' is a consideration in story-telling. Hence hearers can cut you off by saying either that they already know that or that you already told them. Moreover, much will depend on the frequency of contact that is maintained. What has just happened is more tellable where the parties have frequent contact. So we have the paradox, noted by Sacks, that one has more to tell to someone one speaks to every day than to someone one hasn't talked to for some months (1992a, 16). Further features of story-telling are found in Sacks' discussion of the organisation of telephone calls. For instance, where 'bad news' is to be broken, a speaker will want to avoid a 'how are you?' sequence which might well elicit a response of 'fine'. Similarly, if someone calls you and you have a piece of news that constitutes a 'reason for a call', then you may want to get round the rule that says: 'caller raises first topic'. So, for instance, you may make yourself into the putative caller by saying something like: 'Wow! I was just about to call you' (1992b, 166).

Story-telling is not the only activity in which parties attune their talk to one another. Other attuning devices, noted by Sacks, include 'passwords', which for some group serve as 'correct' answers to a recognisable 'challenge' (1992b, 116), proverbs, which affirm social solidarity and usually work as pre-closing invitations (1992a, 24–25) and correction–invitation devices through which candidate answers are offered which the hearer is invited to correct (1992a, 22) – see the discussion below of Maynard (1991).

Having set out some basic issues in CA, I now will examine some of the features so far discovered in talk. I begin with an early paper by Schegloff and Sacks (1974).

Conversational Openings

Schegloff and Sacks' study is based on data drawn from the first five seconds of around 500 telephone calls to and from an American police station. They begin by noting that the basic rule for two-party conversation, that one party speaks at a time (i.e. providing for a sequence a-b-a-b-a-b where a and b are the parties), 'does not provide for the allocation of the roles "a" and "b"' (1974, 350). Telephone calls offer interesting data in this regard because non-verbal forms of communication – apart from the telephone bell – are absent. Somehow, despite the absence of visual cues, speakers manage an orderly sequence in which both parties know when to speak. How? 'A first rule of telephone conversations which might be called "a distribution rule for first utterances" is: *the answerer speaks first*' (*ibid*, 351, original emphasis). In order to see the force of the 'distribution rule', consider the confusion that occurs when a call is made and the phone is picked up, but nothing is said by the receiver of the call. Schegloff cites an anecdote by a woman who adopted this strategy of silence after she began receiving obscene telephone calls. Her friends were constantly irritated by this practice, thus indicating the force of the rule 'the answerer speaks first'. Moreover, her tactic was successful: 'However obscene her caller might be, he would not talk until she had said "hello", thereby obeying the requirements of the distribution rule' (*ibid*, 355).

Although answerers are expected to speak first, it is callers who are expected to provide the first topic. Answerers, after all, do not normally know who is making the call, whereas callers can usually identify answerers and answerers will assume that callers have initiated a call in order to raise a topic – hence the embarrassment we feel when somebody we have neglected to call calls us instead. Here we may convert ourselves from answerers to hypothetical callers by using some formula like: 'Oh, I'd been trying to reach you.' Having reallocated our roles, we are now free to introduce the first topic.

On examining their material further, Schegloff and Sacks discovered only one case (out of 500) which did not fit the rule: answerer speaks first. Using the method of analytic induction (see Chapter 7, pp. 160–162), they reworked all their data to find rules which would account for this apparently deviant case. They concluded that this could be done by seeing the distribution rule as 'a derivative of more general rules'(*ibid*: 356).

The person who responds to a telephone bell is not really answering a *question*, but responding to a *summons*. A summons is any attention-getting device (a telephone bell, a term of address – 'John?' – or a gesture, like a tap on the shoulder or raising your hand). A summons tends to produce answers. Schegloff suggests that summons–answer (SA) sequences have the following features which they share with a number of other linked turns (e.g. questions–answers, greetings) classed as 'adjacency pairs':

Non-terminality: They are preambles to some further activity; they cannot properly stand as final exchanges. Consequently, the summoner is obliged to talk again when the summoned completes the SA sequence.

Conditional relevance: Further interaction is conditional upon the successful completion of the SA sequence.

Obligations to answer: Answers to a summons have the character of questions (e.g. What? Yes? Hello?). This means that, as in question–answer (QA) sequences, the summoner must produce the answer to the question (s)he has elicited. Furthermore, the person who has asked the question is obliged to listen to the answer (s)he has obligated the other to produce. Each subsequent nod or 'uh huh' recommits the speaker to attend to the utterances that follow. Through this 'chaining', 'provision is made by an SA sequence not only for the coordinated entry in a conversation but also for its continued orderliness' (*ibid*, 378–379).

However, in referring to 'obligations', it should not be thought that participants have no choice in the matter. The kinds of rules discussed here operate by being oriented to by the participants. This means that rules can be broken but the rule-break can be made accountable.

Schegloff and Sacks are now able to explain their deviant case as follows: Summons (phone rings) – no answer; further summons (caller says

'Hello'). The normal form of a telephone call is: Summons (phone rings) – answer (recipient says 'Hello'). In the deviant case, the absence of an answer is treated as the absence of a reply to a summons. So the caller's use of 'Hello' replaces the summons of the telephone bell. The failure of the summoned person to speak first is heard as an uncompleted SA sequence. Consequently, the caller's speaking first makes sense within the 'conditional relevance' of SA sequences.

The power of these observations is suggested by two examples. The first is mentioned by Cuff and Payne (1979): 'The recipient of summons feels impelled to answer. (We note that in Northern Ireland, persons still open the door and get shot – despite their knowledge that such things happen)' (1979, 151).

The second example arises in Schegloff and Sacks' discussion of a child's utterance, first discussed by Sacks (1974): 'You know what, Mommy?' This establishes an SA sequence, where a proper answer to the summons is 'What?' This allows the child to say what it wanted to at the start, but as an obligation (because questions must produce answers). Consequently, this utterance is a powerful way in which children enter into conversations despite their usually restricted rights to speak.

Exercise 6.3

Examine Extracts 6.5 and 6.6 below (drawn from Atkinson and Drew: 1979, 52, and discussed in Heritage: 1984, 248–249):

Extract 6.5
1 A: Is there something bothering you or not?
2 (1.0)
3 A: Yes or no
4 (1.5)
5 A: Eh?
6 B: No.

Extract 6.6
1 Ch: Have to cut the:se Mummy.
2 (1.3)
3 Ch: Won't we Mummy
4 (1.5)
5 Ch: Won't we
6 M: Yes

1 Why does Heritage argue that these extracts demonstrate that 'questioners attend to the fact that their questions are framed within normative expectations which have sequential implications' (1984, 249)? Use the concept of 'adjacency pairs' in your answer.
2 What are the consequences of Ch. (in Extract 6.6) naming the person to whom his utterance is addressed? Why might children often engage in such naming? Use the concept of 'summons–answer'.

An Aside: Communication or Ritual?

Goffman (1981) argues that any inspection of naturally-occurring conversation should suggest that more is going on than an attempt at mutual understanding in the framework of a communication system. For instance, when one asks a stranger for the time, one has to guard against 'the potentially offensive consequence of encroaching on another with a demand' (*ibid*, 16). Consequently, a complex sequence is often enacted involving a 'remedy' (for a demand), 'relief' for potential offence, 'appreciation' for the service rendered and 'minimisation' of the effort involved. Hence:

   (i) A: 'Do you have the time?' (remedy)
   (ii) B: 'Sure. It's five o'clock' (relief)
   (iii) A: 'Thanks' (appreciation)
   (iv) B: '(Gesture) 'T's okay' (minimisation) (*ibid*)

Although the exchange can be reduced to a question–answer sequence (QA) (utterances (i) and (ii)) which allows the questioner to speak again, this conceals the essentially ritual practices within which QAs are enacted.

In what Goffman calls 'ritual interchanges', speakers not only convey information but attend to the 'social acceptance' of what they are conveying. Social acceptance involves whether what is being said is compatible with recipients' views of the speaker and of themselves. Goffman's 'ritual frame' thus allows analysts to account for what occurs in talk as a response to both communication and ritual constraints. Further, it encourages a move away from empty formalism to a recognition of cultural variety: 'Observe that although system constraints might be conceived of as pancultural, ritual concerns are patently dependent on cultural definition and can be expected to vary quite markedly from society to society' (Goffman: 1981, 17).

However, such cultural variance does not mean that we cannot generalise. Instead, Goffman claims to be offering a way of identifying those characteristics of social situations which have particular implications for the management of talk. For instance, restaurants and used car lots offer what Goffman calls different 'strategic environments'. The car salesman, unlike the waiter, will want to establish a selling relationship which allows for an extended period of salesmanship. Consequently, customer enquiries will not tend to produce the kind of truncated responses found in the restaurant.

Again, as Mehan (1979) points out, in classrooms conversational exchange will follow a different logic – usually of the form:

   teacher: question
   pupil: answer
   teacher: evaluation

Goffman insists that the constraints in these different settings are ritual and institutional (i.e. oriented to certain context-related tasks) and not simply conversational. For instance, an utterance by a pupil is not simply 'a turn at talk' but a display of an obligation 'to participate in this testing process' (*ibid*, 54).

Sacks was influenced by Goffman, who had been involved with his dissertation at Berkeley (not always constructively). Particularly in Sacks' early lectures, we see his interest in Goffman's (1961b) work on ritual and ceremonial orders. However, Sacks wants to understand 'ceremony' by reference to the sequential analysis of conversations. For instance, we know that the proper return to 'how are you feeling?' is 'fine'. This means that if you want to treat it as a question about your feelings you have to request permission (e.g. 'It's a long story' where the next party may say 'That's alright, I have time'). This means that 'everyone has to lie' because people attend to 'the procedural location of their answers' and, in part, produce answers by reference to 'the various uses that the answer may have for next actions that may be done' (565). Thus Goffman's (1981) attempt to separate 'ritual' and 'system' requirements would have been a nonstarter for Sacks.

We will see the relevance of this argument in my discussion of 'institutional talk' below. Before we leave Goffman, however, we should recognise a fruitful point that he makes.

As Goffman often emphasises, we need an understanding of both talk and non-verbal behaviour. CA's implicit recognition of this argument is shown by its early concentration on telephone conversations where (apart from the telephone bell) non-verbal communication is notably absent and so does not 'interfere' with an analysis of purely verbal sequencing rules. More recently, workers in this tradition, like Heath, have begun the difficult task of constructing an apparatus to describe the relationship between speech and body movements. Using the apparatus, Heath (1988) has shown how, in medical consultations, patients may encourage the doctor to re-establish eye-contact or to view a part of their body by means of both hesitations and physical gestures, such as hand movements. Similarly, Peräkylä and Silverman (1991b) demonstrate how the complex practice of 'family therapy' can depend on the organisation of gaze through which the addressee of a question is defined (see also Goodwin: 1981).

While the notation is at present far less developed than that used in the analysis of talk, such work offers an encouraging indication that the thrust of Goffman's argument is well taken by CA.

The Structure of Turn-taking

Schegloff's early work led to a systematic statement by Sacks, Schegloff and Jefferson (1974) of the structure of turn-taking. While Schegloff is concerned with the interactional consequences of initial turns at talk, these writers set out to provide a more general model of the sequencing of conversations. Turns, they argue, have three aspects. These involve:

1 How the speaker makes a turn relate to a previous turn (e.g. 'Yes', 'But', 'Uh huh').

2 What the turn interactionally accomplishes.
3 How the turn relates to a succeeding turn (e.g. by a question, request, summons, etc.).

Where turn-taking errors and violations occur, the authors note that 'repair mechanisms' will be used. For instance, where more than one party is speaking at a time, a speaker may stop speaking before a normally possible completion point of a turn. Again, when turn-transfer does not occur at the appropriate place, the current speaker may repair the failure of the sequence by speaking again. Finally, where repairs by other than the current speaker are required (for instance because another party has been misidentified), the next speaker typically waits until the completion of a turn. Thus the turn-taking system's allocation of rights to a turn is respected even when a repair is found necessary. Turn-taking and repair can now be seen to be embedded in each other:

> The compatibility of the model of turn-taking with the facts of repair is thus of a dual character: the turn-taking system lends itself to, and incorporates devices for, repair of its troubles; and the turn-taking system is a basic organisational device for the repair of any other troubles in conversation. The turn-taking system and the organisation of repair are thus 'made for each other' in a double sense. (Sacks *et al*: 1974, 723)

The authors conclude by stating three consequences of their model which are of general interest:

1 *Needing to listen*: The turn-taking system provides an 'intrinsic motivation' for listening to all utterances in a conversation. Interest or politeness alone is not sufficient to explain such attention. Rather, every participant must listen to and analyse each utterance in case (s)he is selected as next speaker.
2 *Understanding*: Turn-taking organisation controls some of the ways in which utterances are understood. So, for instance, it allows 'How are you?', as a first turn, to be usually understood not as an enquiry but as a greeting.
3 *Displaying understanding*: When someone offers the 'appropriate' form of reply (e.g. an answer to a question, or an apology to a complaint), (s)he displays an understanding of the interactional force of the first utterance. The turn-taking system is thus the means whereby actors display to one another that they are engaged in *social* action – action defined by Weber as involving taking account of others.

Thus CA is an empirically-oriented research activity, grounded in a basic theory of social action and generating significant implications from an analysis of previously unnoticed interactional forms.

As Heritage (1984) points out, this should not lead us to an over-mechanical view of conversation: 'conversation is not an endless series of interlocking adjacency pairs in which sharply constrained options confront the next speaker' (261).

Instead, the phenomenon of adjacency works according to two non-mechanistic assumptions:

1 An assumption that an utterance which is placed immediately after another one is to be understood as produced in response to or in relation to the preceding utterance.

2 This means that, if a speaker wishes some contribution to be heard as *unrelated* to an immediately prior utterance, he or she must do something special to lift assumption 1 – for instance by the use of a prefix (like 'by the way') designed to show that what follows is unrelated to the immediately prior turn at talk.

As Atkinson and Heritage put it, 'For conversational analysts, therefore, it is sequences and turns-within-sequences, rather than isolated utterances or sentences, which are the primary units of analysis' (Atkinson and Heritage: 1984, 3).

Institutional Talk

So far, we have been examining ordinary, or casual, conversation. However, much talk occurs in institutional settings. What contribution can CA make to the analysis of such settings?

As we saw in Chapter 3, observational data can contribute a great deal to understanding how institutions function. However, a problem of such ethnographic work is that its observations may be based upon a taken-for-granted version of the setting in question. For instance, Strong's (1979a) powerful analysis of the 'ceremonial order' of doctor–parent consultations undoubtedly depends, in part, upon our readiness to read his data-extracts in the context of our shared knowledge of what medical consultations look like.

Consequently, ethnographic work can only take us so far. It is able to show us how people respond to particular settings. It is unable to answer basic questions about how people are constituting that setting through their talk.

As Maynard and Clayman (1991) argue:

> Conversation analysts . . . [are] concerned that using terms such as 'doctor's office', 'courtroom', 'police department', 'school room', and the like, to characterise settings . . . can obscure much of what occurs within those settings . . . For this reason, conversation analysts rarely rely on ethnographic data and instead examine if and how interactants themselves reveal an orientation to institutional or other contexts. (406–407)

In the course of his published lectures, Sacks (1992a and 1992b) occasionally ponders what might specifically distinguish 'institutional' talk. For instance, using Schegloff (1968), he notes how a caller has to engage in considerable work to transform the directions of a called-defined 'business call' (1992b, 200–201). He also notes that a candidate-feature of institutional talk is the absence of 'second stories'. For instance: 'it is absolutely not the business of a psychiatrist, having had some experience reported to him, to say "My mother was just like that, too"' (1992b, 259).

However, in these lectures there is no systematic attention to institutional talk, although a crucial direction for its analysis was later provided in Sacks *et al* (1974) via the argument that ordinary conversation always provides a baseline from which any departures are organised. As Maynard and Clayman (1991) argue, subsequent work has gone on to examine how particular sequence types found in conversation 'become specialised, simplified, reduced, or otherwise structurally adapted for institutional purposes' (1991, 407).

CA uses the practices found in ordinary conversation as a baseline from which to analyse institutional talk. It can then examine how particular sequence types found in conversation 'become specialised, simplified, reduced, or otherwise structurally adapted for institutional purposes' (*ibid*, 407).

I now move to give examples of CA-inspired studies of institutional talk in three settings – paediatric clinics, courtrooms and counselling interviews.

Maynard: Perspective-Display Sequences in Clinics

Using data from paediatric settings, Maynard (1991) neatly demonstrates the previous point about the adaptation of ordinary conversational practices in institutional talk. One such practice is to elicit an opinion from someone else before making one's own statement. Maynard gives this example:

> *Extract 6.7*
> 1 Bob: Have you ever heard anything about wire wheels?
> 2 Al: They can be a real pain. They you know they go outta line
> 3   and—
> 4 Bob: Yeah the— if ya get a flat you hafta take it to a
> 5   special place ta get the flat repaired.
> 6 Al: Uh— why's that?
> (Maynard: 1991, 459)

Notice how Bob's report (lines 4–5) is preceded by an earlier sequence. At lines 1–3, Bob asks Al a question on the same topic and receives an answer. Why not launch straight into his report?

Maynard suggests a number of functions of this 'pre-sequence':

1 It allows Bob to monitor Al's opinions and knowledge on the topic before delivering his own views.
2 Bob can then modify his statement to take account of Al's opinions or even delay further such a statement by asking further questions of Al (using the 'chaining' rule).
3 Because Bob aligns himself with Al's proffered 'complaint' (about wire wheels), his statement is given in an 'hospitable environment' which implicates Al.

4 This means that it will be difficult (although not impossible) for Al subsequently to dispute Bob's statement.

Maynard calls such sequences a *perspective-display series* (or PDS). The PDS is 'a device by which one party can produce a report or opinion after first soliciting a recipient's perspective' (*ibid*, 464). Typically, a PDS will have three parts:

- a question from A
- an answer by B
- a statement by A.

However, 'the PDS can be expanded through use of the probe, a secondary query that prefigures the asker's subsequent report and occasions a more precise display of recipient's position' (*ibid*).

In the paediatric clinic for children referred for developmental difficulties, the use of PDS by doctors is common. Extract 6.8 below is one such example:

Extract 6.8
```
 1  Dr E:   What do you see? as— as his difficulty.
 2  Mrs C:  Mainly his uhm— the fact that he doesn't understand
 3          everything and also the fact that his speech is very
 4          hard to understand what he's saying, lots of time
 5  Dr E:   Right
 6  Dr E:   Do you have any ideas WHY it is? are you— do you?
 7  Mrs C:  No
 8  Dr E:   Okay I think you know I think we BASICALLY in some
 9          ways agree with you, insofar as we think that D's
10          MAIN problem, you know, DOES involve you know
11          LANGuage.
12  Mrs C:  Mm hmm
```
(Maynard: 1991, 468)

The basic three-part structure of the PDS works here as follows:

1 Question (line 1).
2 Answer (lines 2–4).
3 Statement (lines 8–11).

Notice, however, how Dr E expands the PDS at line 6 by asking a further question.

As Maynard points out, doctors are expected to deliver diagnoses. Often, however, when the diagnosis is bad, they may expect some resistance from their patients. This may be particularly true of paediatrics where mothers are accorded special knowledge and competence in assessing their child's condition. The function of the PDS in such an institutional context is that it seeks to align the mother to the upcoming diagnosis. Notice how Dr E's statement in lines 8–11 begins by expressing agreement with Mrs C's perspective but then reformulates it from 'speech' to 'language'. Mrs C has now been implicated in what will turn out to be the announcement of bad news.

Of course, as Maynard notes, things do not always work out so easily for the doctor. Sometimes parents display perspectives which are out of line with the forthcoming announcement, e.g. by saying that they are quite happy with their child's progress. In such circumstances, Maynard shows how the doctor typically pursues a statement from the parent which acknowledges *some* problem (e.g. a problem perceived by the child's teacher) and then delivers his diagnosis in terms of that.

Maynard concludes that the PDS has a special function in circumstances requiring *caution*. In ordinary conversations, this may explain why it is seen most frequently in conversations between strangers or acquaintances where the person about to deliver an opinion is unlikely to know about the other person's views. In the paediatric setting discussed, the functions of the PDS are obvious:

> By adducing a display of their recipients' knowledge or beliefs, clinicians can potentially deliver the news in a hospitable conversational environment, confirm the parents' understanding, coimplicate their perspective in the news delivery, and thereby present assessments in a publicly affirmative and nonconflicting manner. (Maynard: 1991, 484)

Maynard's work shows how medical encounters may, in part, involve the use of mechanisms, like the PDS, which occur in ordinary conversation. By using such conversation as a baseline, CA allows us to identify what is distinctive about institutional discourses.

In addition, a distinctive contribution of CA is to ask questions about the *functions* of any recurrent social process. So Maynard examines how his PDS sequences work in the context of the delivery of bad news. It also follows that his work achieves considerably more than out-of-context ideological critiques of medical practice which tend to cast doctors as mere tyrants or spokespersons for capitalist interests (see Waitzkin: 1979).

Atkinson: Pre-Allocated Turns in Courtrooms

Maynard's study of paediatric clinics largely deals with two-party conversations. What special features of talk may be found in institutional settings, like courtrooms, where multi-party talk is common?

Atkinson (1982) suggests that, in all multi-party conversations, practical solutions must be found to the problem of achieving and attaining shared attentiveness to turns at talk. The turn-taking system may be less effective for five reasons:

1 In a large group, there will be less opportunity for everybody to have a turn.
2 Any current speaker will find it more difficult to monitor the attentiveness of all recipients.
3 Without shared monitoring, more than one concurrent conversation is likely to occur.
4 Monitoring is limited by physical distance from the speaker, the

---

Exercise 6.4

Extract 6.9 is taken from Maynard's data in a clinic dealing with children referred for developmental disabilities:

Extract 6.9

```
 1 Dr E:    How's B doing?
 2 Mrs M:   Well he's doing uh pretty good you know especially
 3          in the school. I explained the teacher what you told
 4          me that he might be sent into a special class maybe,
 5          that I wasn't sure. And HE says you know I asks his
 6          opinion an' he says that was doing pretty good in
 7          the school, that he was responding you know in uhm
 8          everything that he tells them. Now he thinks that
 9          he's not gonna need to be sent to another
10 Dr E:    He doesn't think that he's gonna need to be sent
11 Mrs M:   Yeah that he was catching on a little bit uh more
12          you know like I said I— I— I— KNOW that he needs
13          a— you know I was 'splaining to her that I'm you
14          know that I know for sure that he needs some special
15          class or something
16 Dr E:    Wu' whatta you think his PROblem is
17 Mrs M:   Speech
18 Dr E:    Yeah, yeah his main problem is a— you know a
19          LANguage problem
20 Mrs M:   Yeah language
```

1 Identify the perspective-display series found here.
2 Account for the delay in Dr E's delivery of the diagnosis statement (it is not given until lines 18–19).
3 Given the course that the conversation takes, what are the likely conversational conditions for Mrs M agreeing with the doctor's diagnosis in line 20?

---

direction in which (s)he is looking and the presence of obstacles, whether people or objects.
5 Limited opportunities for speaking may diminish the chance of under-standing checks where difficulties of interpretation may arise (*ibid, passim*, 99–101).

How may these problems be overcome? Sacks *et al* (1974) offer a general solution. Instead of one turn-allocation at a time, as in natural conver-sation, all turns may be *pre-allocated* (as in debates) or chairpersons may pre-allocate turns and have the right to talk first (as in meetings). This suggests, for them, a continuum or 'linear array' of turn-taking systems:

> The linear array is one in which one polar type (exemplified by conversation) involves 'one-turn-at-a-time' allocation, i.e. the use of local allocational means; the other pole (exemplified by debate) involves pre-allocation of all turns; and

medial types (exemplified by meetings) involve various mixes of pre-allocation and allocational means. (1974, 729)

Atkinson takes up the pre-allocation of turns as a solution to the interactional problems of multi-party conversations. Using his study of courtroom procedures (Atkinson and Drew: 1979), he adds a further three solutions:

1   *Turn-type pre-allocation*: the pre-allocation of specific *types* of turns to different participants in a particular sequence (e.g. proposing and seconding, praying and responding).
2   *Turn mediation*: allocating special rights to decide the speaker and the topic to a particular person (e.g. a chairperson or judge).
3   *'Situated particulars'*: this (my term not Atkinson's) refers to his discussion of how the organisation of seating or the wearing of special garments may indicate specific speakers and their rights. Alternatively, speakers may claim the floor by standing up to speak.

Peräkylä and Silverman: Formats in HIV Counselling

All interactions within institutional contexts, however, do not show the qualities of strict turn and turn-type pre-allocation. Heritage and Great-batch (1989, 51–52) emphasise that in a number of less-formal forms of institutional interaction (occurring in e.g. medical, social service and business environments) turn-taking procedures are either conversational or 'quasi conversational'. As a result of this, there is room for considerable negotiation and stylistic variation. Consequently, they argue, the 'institutional' character of these interactions may be more difficult to tackle, especially if we expected it to be pervasively present in the participants' action.

In a current study of video- and audio-taped counselling session with persons coming for an HIV antibody test or diagnosed as HIV seroposit-ive, we have begun to view the flow of events in a counselling session as a chain of shifts between a small number of simple sets of locally managed conversational roles of questioner, answerer, speaker and recipient. We call the sets of these roles *communication formats*.

Two communication formats, or sets of alignments, appear in HIV counselling sessions:

1   *Interview*.
2   *Information delivery*.

In the *interview* (hereafter IW) format the counsellor (hereafter C) and the patient (hereafter P) are aligned as questioner and answerer. Typical examples of the IW format are the following:

Extract 6.10
C: has your partner ever used a condom with you?
(1.2)
P: no:
(1.2)

C: do yer know what a condom looks like?
P: no (   )
C: have you perhaps (1.0) a condom shown to you (.) at school or:
P: no

The basic structure of IW appears to be a very simple chain of questions and answers. The chain draws upon two conversational rules which have been laid bare in the early work of Sacks and his followers. First, until P has provided an answer, it would be difficult for C to ask a further question without making the absence of an answer accountable. This is because question–answer sequences are 'adjacency pairs', coupled activities in which the first part creates a strong moral expectation for the second to appear (Schegloff and Sacks: 1974). Second, a completed answer (particularly in a two-party conversation) gives the floor back to the questioner, who is thus free to ask a further question (Sacks: 1974).

In Extract 6.10, P does not produce an answer immediately after C's questions. P pauses for 1.2 sec before producing an answer to C's initial question. C, however, cannot produce further questions (or other kind of talk) before P has answered. As the question creates a constraint for P to answer, the continuation of the conversation is dependent on P. And concurrently, by confining him/herself to answering, P displays an understanding that the participants are in interview (IW) format.

In *information delivery* (hereafter ID) format, the P's contribution is not essential, for the C holds the floor. The C has the role of the speaker and the P confines him/herself to recipiency. We see this asymmetric division of labour particularly clearly in the following excerpt, where C tells the patient about the services the clinic can offer to infected people.

Extract 6.11
C: *This* clinic is:
(1.0)
C: geared up (.) to: (.3) give as much *help* and supp*ort* to that pe:rson, (.) and that pe:rson's friends (.) family: (.2) *lovers*
(1.2)
C: erm: (.2) as possible (.3) during (.3) es*p*ecially during these first three months when?
(.6)
C: erm:
(.8)
C: the (trouble) is (.) is (.2) ba:d (   ) and the anx*i*ety is great.
(.2)
C: .hhhh (.2) we: have: *thr*ee health advisers of whom I'm one,
(.9)
C: a clinical psychologist (.) whose job (.2) is: (.2) to *deal* with the anxiety:
(.3)
C: .hh and supp*o*rt groups
(.7)
C: to: help the families: (.4) erm: (.2) and the ((continues))

In ordinary conversations, if one party takes a long turn, stretching beyond the ordinary boundaries of turns of talk (called 'turn construction units' by Sacks *et al* 1974), he or she must engage in specific activities in order to secure holding the floor. One such is a 'story preface', an announcement for the co-participants about an interest of the current speaker to produce an extended turn of talk. The co-participants, correspondingly, are expected to display their agreement in the production of a long stretch of talk by producing 'continuers'. These are small response tokens usually taking the form of 'hm mm', 'yes', or the like which appear close to the potential slots of change in speakership. The continuers do the work of passing an opportunity to produce a full turn of talk, thus giving 'permission' for the current speaker to continue.

In Extract 6.11, we don't see any provisions for C's long turn. C does not produce any equivalent of a 'story preface' but simply begins her account of the clinical services at line 1. Neither does P pass the opportunity to get the floor by producing continuers; she is, instead, silently receiving the information.

However, this does not mean that P is not required to do any interactional work during the ID. First, as in any conversation, the silent party is expected to show recipiency by directing her gaze towards the speaker. Second, although the provisions typical for multi-unit turns in ordinary conversations are not necessarily needed, they nevertheless occur often in the counselling sessions.

Heritage and Greatbatch (1989) argue that the asymmetries often found in patterns of activities in 'non-formal' institutional encounters are apparently not the product of turn-taking procedures that are normatively sanctionable.

This seems to be what we have here. The stability of the interview (IW) format depends largely on the character of question–answer sequences discussed earlier. The strong obligation of the P to produce an answer to a question asked by the C, and the right of the questioner to ask a further question secure the maintenance of the format in most cases. The IW format seems also to be unproblematically set up in most cases: as soon as C holds the floor (which is the case at the outset of any consultation and at any stage of an ID sequence), a shift into IW can be made through simply asking a question.

In these features helping to maintain the IW format, there is then apparently nothing particularly institutionally determined. The adjacent relation between a question and an answer, and the 'chaining rule' are both devices originating in mundane conversation.

The information delivery (ID) format is equally stable. As noted earlier, the extended turns of talk by the C do not necessarily require such provisions as accompany long turns in an ordinary conversation. Devices sanctioning the production of multi-unit turns and continuers from the recipient are, however, usually used.

As a whole, then, the stability and persistence of the IW and ID formats seem not to be a result of particular institutionally shaped turn-taking procedures related to setting up and maintaining these two formats. They trade off the procedures of mundane conversation.

The focussed character of HIV counselling thus explains why the two professionally-structured formats predominate in our transcripts. Clearly, each, in its own way, is functional for the achievement of the task at hand. However, the fact that either format may be used as a home-base suggests that we need to examine the more specific functions each serves.

The interview format has the major advantage that, because of the nature of question–answer adjacency pairs, Ps are required to speak. This means that Cs can tailor the information they give to the P's expressed needs, thereby probably maximising its impact and, incidentally, avoiding the boredom of repetitively providing identical information packages to all Ps.

In comparison with the interview, the information delivery format is far less complicated for the C. The C is less dependent on the P's contribution to the conversation because only recipiency and little talk are required from the P. This has two advantages for the hard-pressed C. First, the C can deliver pre-designed information packages without much reflection. Second, a similar range of issues can be covered within a shorter period of time, particularly because the greater dependency of the interview format upon the P's contribution makes it more liable to the kind of communication difficulties we saw in Extract 6.10. This is not an irrelevant consideration given the pressures on Cs in many counselling centres.

The concept of 'communication formats' allows us to describe the local management of the turn-taking machinery. By considering sequential explanations of the stability of each format and contextual explanations of their functionality, we are able to describe and analyse counselling interviews in ways which are sensitive to the local organisation of communication but avoid reducing it to 'culture' or to the structure of adjacent turns-at-talk. The method allows the precise description of the special characteristics of counselling as a structure of communication in ways which are relevant to both sociologists and practitioners.

Summary

Sociologists concerned with describing the organisation of interaction have, until recently, been faced with two diverging options. They can focus either on local cultures or on the sequential order of conversation. Ethnography's emphasis on context underpins the first option; conversation analysis's concern with a context-free yet context-sensitive structure of turn-taking provides the rationale for the second. Analysis of transcripts of AIDS counselling suggests a middle way.

Table 6.2 below summarises the examples that we have been considering.

Table 6.2:   *Institutional Talk – Some Examples*

Institution	Author	Structures of talk	Function
Clinic	Maynard (1991)	Question–answer–diagnosis (PDS)	Aligning parent to the diagnosis
Courtroom	Atkinson and Drew (1979)	Turn and turn-type pre-allocation	Selecting next speaker
Counselling	Peräkylä and Silverman (1991a)	Communication formats	Stability; eliciting patient's view (IW); speed (ID)

By focussing on the turn-by-turn organisation of talk, CA has shown the distinctive turn-taking systems that organise institutional settings. It has also suggested the functions of these systems in each institutional context.

Conclusion

In this conclusion, I return to my theme of the basic simplicity of the assumptions underlying the analysis of naturally occurring talk. Sacks' lectures are a wonderful resource for appreciating this simplicity. Not only do they use riveting examples but they also include exchanges between Sacks and his students.

In an answer to a student's question which asked how you can use conversational data to address a traditional sociological problem, Sacks says: 'The first rule is to learn to be interested in what it is you've got. I take it that what you want to do is pose those problems that the data bears' (1992b, 471).

Schegloff sums up the two most crucial things which Sacks left us when 'posing those problems that the data bears':

1   A methodology: 'A most remarkable, inventive and productive account of how to study human sociality' (1992b, xii).
2   A topic: 'the distinctive and utterly critical recognition . . . that . . . talk can be examined in its own right, and not merely as a screen on which are projected other processes' (xviii).

Sacks aims for a cumulative science of conversation, offering 'stable accounts of human behaviour [through] producing accounts of the methods and procedures for producing it' (xxxi). As Schegloff puts it, the task then is driven by the observation of actual talk with actual outcomes. The question one poses is simply: how was this outcome accomplished?

The method is also straightforward: 'begin with some observations, then find the problem for which these observations could serve as . . . the solution' (1992b, xlviii).

Like Socrates, Sacks' aim was, in some sense, to remind us about things we already know. As Sacks remarks:

I take it that lots of the results I offer, people can see for themselves. And they needn't be afraid to. And they needn't figure that the results are wrong because they can see them . . . As if we found a new plant. It may have been a plant in your garden, but now you see its different than something else. And you can look at it to see how it's different, and whether it's different in the way that somebody has said. (1992b, 488)

Despite the battery of concepts contained in this chapter, Sacks' remark shows that the analysis of conversations does not require exceptional skills.

PART THREE

IMPLICATIONS

7

Validity and Reliability

Much of the textbook debate about the scientific status of sociology is somewhat fatuous. Few researchers would now dispute that the cultural world has different properties from the natural world. Again, only hard-core laboratory scientists would assume that the controlled experiment offers an appropriate or indeed useful model for social science.

It is an increasingly accepted view that work becomes scientific by adopting methods of study *appropriate* to its subject matter. Sociology is thus scientific to the extent that it uses appropriate methods and is rigorous, critical and objective in its handling of data. As Kirk and Miller argue:

> The assumptions underlying the search for objectivity are simple. There is a world of empirical reality out there. The way we perceive and understand that world is largely up to us, but the world does not tolerate all understandings of it equally. (Kirk and Miller: 1986, 11)

Kirk and Miller remind us of the need for 'objectivity' in scientific research. It is particularly important to remember this need in social research. The array of suggestive theories and contrasting methodologies, reviewed in Part Two of this book, may tempt us to believe that 'anything goes'. However, such anarchy is, I believe, bad for social research in at least two ways. First, it leads us to believe that the only important debates are conducted between 'armchair' theorists. Second, by downplaying the cumulative weight of evidence from social science research, it lowers our standing in the community.

The real issue is how our research can be *both* intellectually challenging and rigorous and critical. One way of being critical is, as Popper (1959) has suggested, to seek to refute assumed relations between phenomena. This means overcoming the temptation to jump to easy conclusions just because there is some evidence that seems to lead in an interesting direction. Instead, we must subject this evidence to every possible test. Then, only if we cannot refute the existence of a certain relationship, are we in a position to speak about 'objective' knowledge. Even then, however, our knowledge is always provisional, subject to a subsequent study which may come up with disconfirming evidence.

Popper puts it this way:

> What characterises the empirical method is its manner of exposing to falsification, in every conceivable way, the system to be tested. Its aim is not to save the lives of untenable systems but, on the contrary, to select the one which is by comparison the fittest, by exposing them all to the fiercest struggle for survival. (Popper: 1959, 42)

The two central concepts in any discussion of rigour in scientific research are 'reliability' and 'validity'. I will discuss each in turn, examining what each concept means in practice in both quantitative and field research.

Reliability

> [Reliability] refers to the degree of consistency with which instances are assigned to the same category by different observers or by the same observer on different occasions. (Hammersley: 1992a, 67)

What reliability involves and its relation to validity can be understood simply following Kirk and Miller's example of using a thermometer:

> A thermometer that shows the same reading of 82 degrees each time it is plunged into boiling water gives a reliable measurement. A second thermometer might give readings over a series of measurements that vary from around 100 degrees. The second thermometer would be unreliable but relatively valid, whereas the first would be invalid but perfectly reliable. (1986, 19)

Kirk and Miller usefully distinguish three kinds of reliability, as follows:

1 *Quixotic reliability*: 'the circumstances in which a single method of observation continually yields an unvarying measurement'; but this kind of reliability can be 'trivial and misleading'. For instance, just because an interview question always elicits a predictable response does not mean that it is analytically interesting or that the response necessarily relates to what people say and do in different contexts.

2 *Diachronic reliability*: 'the stability of an observation through time'. For instance, showing that ways of defining advice sequences work equally well with data drawn from different periods.

3 *Synchronic reliability*: 'the similarity of observations within the same time-period' (Kirk and Miller: 1986, 41–42). A standard way through which this is assessed is through triangulation of methods (e.g. the use of interviews as well as observation). As Kirk and Miller argue, paradoxically the value of such triangulation is that it 'forces the ethnographer to imagine how multiple, but somehow different, qualitative measures might simultaneously be true' (1986, 42).

Not a Problem?

Some social researchers argue that a concern for the reliability of observations arises only within the quantitative research tradition. Because such 'positivist' work sees no difference between the natural and social worlds, it is appropriately concerned to produce reliable measures of social life. Conversely, it is argued, once we treat social reality as always in flux, then it makes no sense to worry about whether our research instruments measure accurately.

This is an example of such an argument:

> Positivist notions of reliability assume an underlying universe where inquiry could, quite logically, be replicated. This assumption of an unchanging social world is in direct contrast to the qualitative/interpretative assumption that the social world is always changing and the concept of replication is itself problematic. (Marshall and Rossman: 1989, 147)

But is this so? It is one thing to argue that the world is processual; it is much more problematic to imply, as Marshall and Rossman seem to do, that the world is in infinite flux (appropriate to the pre-Socratic philosopher Heraclitus, perhaps, but not a comfortable position for social scientists).

Such a position would rule out any systematic research since it implies that we cannot assume any stable properties in the social world. However, if we concede the possible existence of such properties, why shouldn't other work replicate these properties? As Kirk and Miller argue:

> Qualitative researchers can no longer afford to beg the issue of reliability. While the forte of field research will always lie in its capability to sort out the validity of propositions, its results will (reasonably) go ignored minus attention to reliability. For reliability to be calculated, it is incumbent on the scientific investigator to document his or her procedure. (Kirk and Miller: 1986, 72)

Following Kirk and Miller, I consider below how reliability can be addressed in qualitative studies. I will look in turn at the four methodologies discussed in Part Two of this book: observation, textual analysis, the interview and the transcript of naturally-occurring talk.

Reliability and Observation

Observational studies rarely provide readers with anything other than brief, persuasive, data extracts. As Bryman (1988) notes about the typical ethnography: 'field notes or extended transcripts are rarely available; these would be very helpful in order to allow the reader to formulate his or her own hunches about the perspective of the people who have been studied' (Bryman: 1988, 77).

Although, as Bryman suggests, extended extracts from fieldnotes would be helpful, the reader also should require information on how fieldnotes were recorded and in what contexts. As Kirk and Miller argue: 'The contemporary search for reliability in qualitative observation revolves around detailing the relevant context of observation' (Kirk and Miller: 1986, 52).

Spradley (1979) suggests that observers keep four separate sets of notes:

1   Short notes made at the time.
2   Expanded notes made as soon as possible after each field session.

3   A fieldwork journal to record problems and ideas that arise during each stage of fieldwork.
4   A provisional running record of analysis and interpretation (discussed by Kirk and Miller: 1986, 53).

Spradley's suggestions help to systematise fieldnotes and thus improve their reliability. Implicit in them is the need to distinguish between *etic* analysis (based on the researcher's concepts) and *emic* analysis (deriving from the conceptual framework of those being studied). Such a distinction is employed in the set of fieldnote conventions set out in Table 7.1.

Table 7.1:   *Some Fieldnote Conventions*

Sign	Convention	Use
" "	double quotation marks	verbatim quotes
' '	single quotation marks	paraphrases
( )	parentheses	contextual data or fieldworker's interpretations
⟨ ⟩	angled brackets	*emic* concepts
/	slash	*etic* concepts
———	solid line	partitions time

Source: adapted from Kirk and Miller: 1986, 57

Exercise 7.1

This exercise asks you to use the fieldnote conventions set out in Table 7.1. You should gather observational data in any setting with which you are familiar and in which it is relatively easy to find a place to make notes (you may return to the setting you used for Exercise 3.2). Observe for about an hour. Ideally, you should carry out your observations with someone else who also is using the same conventions.

1   Record your notes using these fieldnote conventions. Compare your notes with your colleague's. Identify and explain any differences.
2   What conventions were difficult to use? Why was this so (e.g. because they are unclear or inappropriate to the setting)?
3   Can you think of other conventions that would improve the reliability of your fieldnotes?
4   What have you gained (or lost) compared to earlier observational exercises (e.g. Exercise 3.2)?
5   Which further fields of enquiry do your fieldnotes suggest?

Reliability and Texts

When you are dealing with a text, the data are already available, unfiltered through the researcher's fieldnotes. Issues of reliability now arise only through the *categories* you use to analyse each text. It is important that these categories should be used in a *standardised* way, so that any researcher would categorise in the same way.

A standard method of doing this is known as 'inter-rater reliability'. It involves giving the same data to a number of analysts (or raters) and asking them to analyse it according to an agreed set of categories. Their reports are then examined and any differences discussed and ironed out.

In order to see how this method works, you should find a colleague who worked on the same exercise in Chapter 4. Compare your analyses of the same data and see if you can iron out any differences.

Reliability and Interviews

The reliability of interview schedules is a central question in quantitative methods textbooks. According to these books, it is very important that each respondent understands the questions in the same way and that answers can be coded without the possibility of uncertainty. This is achieved through a number of means, including:

– thorough pre-testing of interview schedules
– thorough training of interviewers
– as much use as possible of fixed-choice answers
– inter-rater reliability checks on the coding of answers to open-ended questions.

Exercise 7.2

This exercise gives you the opportunity to assess the reliability of your analysis of the data used in earlier exercises, using the method of inter-rater agreement.

You should find a colleague who carried out the same data-analysis exercises in Chapters 4–6. Return to your answers to one of those exercises and now consider:

1 What are the major differences and similarities in the way in which you used concepts and categories in this exercise?
2 Which part of either person's analysis needs to be revised or abandoned?
3 Do similarities in your analyses mean that the concepts and categories you have used are good ones (distinguish issues of reliability and usefulness)?
4 Do any differences mean that the concepts and categories you have used are badly designed and/or that you have used them inappropriately?
5 What have you learned from this comparison? How would you redo your analysis in the light of it?

In Chapter 5, I argued that a concentration on such matters tended to deflect attention away from the theoretical assumptions underlying the meaning that we attach to interviewees' answers. Nonetheless, this does not mean that we can altogether ignore conventional issues of reliability, even if we deliberately avoid treating interview accounts as simple 'reports' on reality. For instance, even when our analytic concern is with narrative structure or membership categorisation, it is still helpful to pre-test an interview schedule and to compare how at least two researchers analyse the same data.

Reliability and Transcripts

Kirk and Miller's suggestion that the conventionalisation of methods for recording fieldnotes offers a useful method for addressing the issue of reliability can be applied to transcripts. For we need only depend upon fieldnotes in the absence of audio- or video-recordings. The availability of transcripts of such recordings, using standard conventions, satisfies Kirk and Miller's proper demand for the documentation of procedures.

In conversation analysis, as discussed in Chapter 6, a method similar to inter-rater comparison is used to ensure reliability. Wherever possible, group data-analysis sessions are held to listen to (or watch) audio- or video-recordings. It is important here that we do not delude ourselves into seeking a 'perfect' transcript. Transcripts can always be improved and the search for perfection is illusory and time-consuming. Rather the aim is to arrive at an agreed transcript, adequate for the task at hand. A further benefit arising from such group sessions is that they usually lead to suggestions about promising lines of analysis.

Validity

> By validity, I mean truth: interpreted as the extent to which an account accurately represents the social phenomena to which it refers. (Hammersley: 1990, 57)

Proposing a purportedly 'true' statement involves the possibility of two kinds of *error* which have been clearly defined by Kirk and Miller (1986, 29–30):

Type 1 error is believing a statement to be true when it is not (in statistical terms, this means rejecting the 'null hypothesis', i.e. the hypothesis that there is no relation between the variables).

Type 2 error is rejecting a statement which, in fact, is true (i.e. incorrectly supporting the 'null hypothesis').

Validity in Quantitative Research

In quantitative research, a common form of Type 1 error arises if we accept a 'spurious' correlation. For instance, just because X seems always to be followed by Y, this does not mean that X necessarily *causes* Y. There might be a third factor, Z, which produces both X and Y. Alternatively, Z might be an 'intervening variable' which is caused by X and then influences Y (see Selltiz *et al*: 1964, 424–431).

The quantitative researcher, however, can use sophisticated means to guard against the possibility of spurious correlations. For instance, Lipset *et al* (1962), were aware that a correlation between membership of a printers' club and stated activity in union elections might be spurious. Perhaps people who joined such clubs were more interested anyway in union politics and so already predisposed to participate more in elections than non-members. Consequently, Lipset compared the participation rates of members and non-members who had the *same* prior interest in union politics. The results are shown in Table 7.2.

Table 7.2:   *Club Membership and Voting in Union Elections*

	Political interest		
	High	Medium	Low
Club member	63%	41%	41%
Non-member	52%	28%	19%
	Percentage participating in elections		

Source: adapted from Lipset *et al*: 1962

Table 7.2 should be read vertically. It shows that, if you only compare people with the *same* political interest, club membership is associated with a larger percentage who participate in union elections. Consequently, the researchers had excluded one variable which might have rendered spurious the correlation between club membership and voting.

Following Popper's emphasis on attempts at refutation, Lipset *et al* could be reasonably confident that they had found a nonspurious correlation. However, since other factors could still be relevant in this correlation, as in any statistical finding, they could only talk about an *association* between phenomena not a *causal* relationship.

Lipset's attempt to control for spurious correlations was possible because of the quantitative style of his research. This had the disadvantage of being dependent upon survey methods with all their attendant difficulties. As Fielding and Fielding argue: 'the most advanced survey procedures themselves only manipulate data that had to be gained at some point by asking people' (Fielding and Fielding: 1986, 12).

As we saw in Chapter 5, what people say in answer to interview questions does not have a stable relationship to how they behave in naturally-occurring situations. Again, Fielding and Fielding make the relevant point: 'researchers who generalise from a sample survey to a larger population ignore the possible disparity between the discourse of actors about some topical issue and the way they respond to questions in a formal context' (*ibid*, 21).

Exercise 7.3

Table 7.3 is also drawn from the Lipset study. It relates voting in union politics to having friends who are also printers. Examine it carefully and then answer the questions beneath it.

Table 7.3

	Political interest		
	High	Medium	Low
Printer friends	61%	42%	26%
No printer friends	48%	22%	23%
	Percentage participating in elections		

Source: adapted from Lipset *et al*: 1962

1 Does Table 7.3 show that there is an association between having a printing friend and participating in union elections? Explain carefully, referring to the table.
2 Can we be confident that the degree of political interest of a printer does not make any correlation between friendships and participation into a spurious one?
3 Compare Table 7.3 with Table 7.2. Among what levels of political interest is any association between voting and (a) printer friends and (b) club membership most marked?
4 What might explain the differences between the two tables in the groups with shared political interest who are most influenced by variables (a) and (b) above?
5 How might you test this explanation?

Let me summarise what I have been saying so far. First, the criterion of *refutability* is an excellent way to test the validity of any research finding. Second, *quantitative* researchers have a sophisticated armoury of weapons to assess the validity of the correlations which they generate. Third, we should not assume that techniques used in quantitative research are the *only* way of establishing the validity of findings from qualitative or field research.

This third point means that a number of practices which originate from quantitative studies may be *inappropriate* to field research. The following assumptions are highly dubious in qualitative research:

1 All social science research can only be valid if based on experimental data, official statistics or the random sampling of populations.
2 Quantified data are the only valid or generalisable social facts.

3   Having a cumulative view of data drawn from different contexts allows
    us, as in trigonometry, to triangulate the 'true' state of affairs by
    examining where the different data intersect.

Each of these assumptions has a number of defects, many of which are
discussed (and some displayed) in a number of texts concerned with
qualitative research methodology, from Cicourel (1964) through Denzin
(1970) to Schwartz and Jacobs (1979), Hammersley and Atkinson (1983)
and Gubrium (1988).

Following the same order as in the list above, I note that:

1   Experiments, official statistics and survey data may simply be inappro-
    priate to some of the tasks of social science. For instance, they exclude
    the observation of 'naturally-occurring' data by ethnographic case-
    studies (see Chapter 3) or by conversation and discourse analysis (see
    Chapter 6).
2   While quantification may *sometimes* be useful, it can both conceal as
    well as reveal basic social processes. Consider the problem of counting
    attitudes in surveys. Do we all have coherent attitudes on any topics
    which await the researcher's questions? And how do 'attitudes' relate
    to what we actually do – our practices? Or think of official statistics on
    cause of death compared to studies of the officially organised 'death
    work' of nurses and orderlies (Sudnow: 1968a) and of pathologists
    (Prior: 1987). Note that this is *not* to argue that such statistics may be
    biased. Instead, it is to suggest that there are areas of social reality
    which such statistics cannot measure.
3   Triangulation of data seeks to overcome the context-boundedness of
    our materials at the cost of analysing their sense in context. For
    purposes of social research, it may simply not be useful to conceive of
    an over-arching reality to which data, gathered in different contexts,
    approximates.

So my support for critical field research which takes seriously issues of
validity is not based on an uncritical acceptance of the standard recipes of
conventional methodology texts ·or the standard practices of purely
quantitative research. In any event, quantitative measures offer no simple
solution to the question of validity:

> ultimately all methods of data collection are analysed 'qualitatively', in so far as
> the act of analysis is an interpretation, and therefore of necessity a selective
> rendering. Whether the data collected are quantifiable or qualitative, the issue
> of the *warrant* for their inferences must be confronted. (Fielding and Fielding:
> 1986, 12, my emphasis)

Shortly, we will examine how qualitative or field researchers may claim,
in Fielding and Fielding's terms, that they have a 'warrant for their
inferences'. For the moment, however, I want to deal briefly with the
argument that validity is not an issue in field research.

Validity as Unnecessary

Agar (1986) criticises 'the received view' of science, a view that centres on the systematic test of explicit hypotheses (11). This view, he argues, is inappropriate to research problems concerned with 'What is going on here?' (12) which involve learning about a world first-hand.

The implication, according to Agar, is a rejection of the standard issues of reliability and validity in favour of: 'an intensive personal involvement, an abandonment of traditional scientific control, an improvisational style to meet situations not of the researcher's making, and an ability to learn from a long series of mistakes' (12).

However, this too readily abandons any reference to the validity of the ethnographer's statements. It simply will not do to accept any account simply on the basis of the researcher's claims to 'an intensive personal involvement'. Immediacy and authenticity may be a good basis for certain kinds of journalism but ethnography must make different claims if we are to take it seriously.

Nonetheless, even a brief perusal of published articles using qualitative methods can be profoundly disturbing. When I reviewed recent volumes of two social science journals (Silverman: 1989a), I was struck by the 'anecdotal' quality of much of what I was reading. Much too frequently, the authors had fallen foul of two problems identified by Fielding and Fielding (1986):

- a tendency to select field data to fit an ideal conception (preconception) of the phenomenon
- a tendency to select field data which are conspicuous because they are exotic, at the expense of less dramatic (but possibly indicative) data (32)

As Bryman argues:

> There is a tendency towards an anecdotal approach to the use of 'data' in relation to conclusions or explanations in qualitative research. Brief conversations, snippets from unstructured interviews, or examples of a particular activity are used to provide evidence for a particular contention. There are grounds for disquiet in that the *representativeness* or generality of these fragments is rarely addressed. (Bryman: 1988, 77, my emphasis)

As already noted (in Chapter 3), another way in which field researchers have sidestepped the issue of validity is by stressing a concern to generate rather than to test theories. For instance, Glaser and Strauss' concept of 'grounded theory' (1967) seeks to generate and develop categories in order to produce delimited theories grounded in the data. While Glaser and Strauss' emphasis on 'the constant comparative method' is helpful, others have rightly criticised their apparent lack of interest in *testing* hypotheses (e.g. Fielding: 1988, 8), although, in a later work, Strauss (1987) does claim that his approach is 'designed especially for generating and testing theory' (xi).

If some field researchers sidestep the issue of validity, others reject it altogether as an appropriate issue for social research. For instance, from a feminist position, Stanley and Wise describe 'objectivity' as:

> an excuse for a power relationship every bit as obscene as the power relationship that leads women to be sexually assaulted, murdered and otherwise treated as mere objects. The assault on our minds, the removal from existence of our experiences as valid and true, is every bit as questionable. (1983, 169)

Like many feminist sociologists, Stanley and Wise argue that the validity of 'experiences' should replace supposedly male-dominated versions of 'objectivity'. Thus, although qualitative methods are held to be most appropriate for understanding women's experience, such experiences are valid or 'true' in themselves. In any event, it is argued, the goal of research is not to accumulate knowledge but to serve in the emancipation of women.

For purposes of exposition, I have chosen an extreme position – readers wanting a less dogmatic feminist approach might turn to Cain (1986). However, Stanley and Wise's argument has the merit that it reveals methodological assumptions which many feminists share.

Each assumption can be questioned as follows (for another relevant critique, see Hammersley: 1992a):

1 The assumption that 'experience' is paramount is not at all new. Indeed, it was a primary feature of nineteenth-century romantic thought (see Silverman: 1989b). As I have argued in this book (especially in Chapter 5), to focus on 'experience' alone undermines what we know about the cultural and linguistic forms which structure what we count as 'experience'.

2 Rather than being a male standard, the attempt to generate valid knowledge lies at the basis of *any* dialogue. Without the ability to choose between the truth-claims of any statement, we would be reduced to name-calling along the lines of 'you would say that, wouldn't you?'. Against certain current fashions, we ought to recognise how, when eighteenth century 'Enlightenment' thinkers pursued objectivity, they were seeking just such a way out from prejudice and unreason.

3 To assume that emancipation is the goal of research conflates yet again 'fact' and 'value'. How research is used is a value-laden, political question. The first goal of scientific research is valid knowledge. To claim otherwise is to make an alliance with an awful dynasty that includes 'Aryan science' under the Nazis, and 'Socialist science' under Stalin.

Stanley and Wise do share a common assumption with some (male) sociologists with whom they might otherwise disagree. Many qualitative researchers assume that there is a huge gulf not only between natural science and social science but between qualitative and quantitative social research. However, we must not make too much of the differences between field research and other research styles. For instance, as Hammersley (1990) points out, although replication of an ethnographic study in the same setting may be difficult, we need to understand that replication is not always a straightforward process even in the natural sciences. Hence where research findings are not replicated this is often put down to variation in laboratory conditions and procedures (this relates to the reliability of the research instruments used – see below).

However, if social science statements are simply accounts, with no claims to validity, why should we read them? Moreover, it is paradoxical to assert that social scientists should be the only group that cannot *check* their statements: 'This is a paradoxical conclusion. While culture members freely and legitimately engage in checking claims against facts . . . the social scientist [claims to be] . . . disbarred from this on the grounds that it would "distort reality" ' (Hammersley and Atkinson: 1983, 13).

Hammersley (1990, and 1992a) has suggested that qualitative researchers *can* address issues of validity by adopting what he calls a 'subtle form of realism'. This has the following three elements:

1 Validity is identified with confidence in our knowledge but not certainty.
2 Reality is assumed to be independent of the claims that researchers make about it.
3 Reality is always viewed through particular perspectives; hence our accounts *represent* reality they do *not* reproduce it (Hammersley: 1992a, 50–51).

This is very close to Popper's account of *falsifiability* rather than verifiability as the distinguishing criterion of a scientific statement. Like Popper, Hammersley also argues that claims to validity, based on attempts at refutation, are sustained by a scientific community prepared 'to resolve disagreements by seeking common grounds of agreement' (1990, 63).

If we recognise that 'no knowledge is certain', how can we go about judging 'knowledge claims . . . in terms of their likely truth' (Hammersley: 1990, 61)? Hammersley suggests three steps:

1 The *plausibility* of the claim, given our existing knowledge.
2 The *credibility* of the claim, given the nature of the phenomena, circumstances of the research and characteristics of the researcher.
3 Where we have doubt about either 1 or 2, then we need to be convinced by the plausibility and credibility of the *evidence* (1990, 61–62).

In practice, Hammersley's points 1 and 2 create many problems. First, they exemplify the conservatism of the scientific community and the practice of 'normal science' described by Kuhn (1970). If we only accept as valid those accounts which are plausible and credible, then we are unable to be surprised and condemned to reproduce existing models of the world. Second, as we saw in the discussion of 'scientism' in Chapter 1 (p. 5) researchers' claims may sometimes be credible merely because they rely on common-sense knowledge which stands in need of explication rather than passive acceptance.

I will, therefore, stick with Hammersley's point 3. How can we be convinced by the plausibility and credibility of the evidence produced by field research? Let us review the standards by which such researchers claims to be judged.

Claims to Validity in Field Research

As I have argued, the issue of validity is appropriate whatever one's theoretical orientation or use of quantitative or qualitative data. Few contemporary social scientists have any stomach for any remaining field researchers who might maintain that our only methodological imperative is to 'hang out' and to return with 'authentic' accounts of the field.

However, I shall not discuss here many standard criteria of assessing validity, either because they are available in other methodology texts or because they are commonsensical and/or inappropriate to the theoretical logic of field research as normatively defined in Chapter 2. These criteria include:

- the impact of the researcher on the setting (the so-called 'halo' or 'Hawthorne' effect) (see Hammersley: 1990, 80–82, Landsberger: 1958)
- the values of the researcher (see Weber: 1949, and this volume, Chapter 8)
- the truth-status of a respondent's account (see this volume, Chapter 5).

Two forms of validation have been suggested as particularly appropriate to the logic of qualitative research:

1 Comparing different kinds of data (e.g. quantitative and qualitative) and different methods (e.g. observation and interviews) to see whether they corroborate one another. As already noted, this form of comparison, called *triangulation*, derives from navigation, where different bearings give the correct position of an object.
2 Taking one's findings back to the subjects being studied. Where these people verify one's findings, it is argued, one can be more confident of their validity. This method is known as *respondent validation*.

Each of these methods is discussed below where I show why I believe these methods are usually inappropriate to qualitative research.

Triangulating Data and Methods

A major early advocate of the method of triangulation is Norman Denzin (1970). This arises in the context of Denzin's discussion of the advantages and limitations of observational work. Unlike survey research, Denzin points out: 'the participant observer is not bound in his field work by pre-judgements about the nature of his problem, by rigid data-gathering devices, or by hypotheses' (*ibid*, 216).

However, Denzin also notes that participant observation is not without its own difficulties. First, its focus on the present may blind the observer to important events that occurred before his entry on the scene. Second, as Dalton (1959) points out, confidants or informants in a social setting may be entirely unrepresentative of the less open participants. Third, observers may change the situation just by their presence and so the decision about what role to adopt will be fateful. Finally, the observer may 'go native', identifying so much with participants that, like a child learning to talk, (s)he cannot remember how (s)he found out or articulate the principles underlying what (s)he is doing.

Given these difficulties, Denzin offers two related solutions. The first is non-contentious. It involves using multiple sources of data-collection, as part of the methodology. Thus Denzin defines participant observation: 'as a field strategy that simultaneously combines document analysis, respondent and informant interviewing, direct participation and observation and introspection' (*ibid*, 186).

Now, as an assembly of reminders about the partiality of any one context of data-collection, such a 'field strategy' makes a great deal of sense. However, it seems that Denzin wants to go beyond a recognition of the partiality of data, for his second solution to the difficulties of participant observation is to suggest that a more general practice of 'method triangulation' can serve to overcome partial views and present something like a complete picture.

As Denzin elsewhere notes, actions and accounts are 'situated'. This implies, contrary to what Denzin argues about triangulation, that methods, often drawn from different theories, cannot give us an 'objective' truth (33). So:

> multiple theories and multiple methods are . . . worth pursuing, but not for the reasons Denzin cites . . . The accuracy of a method comes from its systematic application, but rarely does the inaccuracy of one approach to the data complement the accuracies of another. (Fielding and Fielding: 1986, 35)

To counter what Fielding and Fielding rightly call Denzin's 'eclecticism' (34), they suggest that the use of triangulation should operate according to ground rules (*ibid*). Basically, these seem to operate as follows:

– begin from a theoretical perspective (e.g. interactionism)
– choose methods and data which will give you an account of structure and meaning from within that perspective (e.g. by showing the structural contexts of the interactions studied).

Even when we use a single theoretical perspective, we cannot simply aggregate data in order to arrive at an overall 'truth'. As Hammersley and Atkinson point out: 'one should not adopt a naively "optimistic" view that the aggregation of data from different sources will unproblematically add up to produce a more complete picture' (1983, 199).

The sociologist's role is not, as Dingwall (1981) reminds us, 'to adjudicate between participants' competing versions' but to understand the situated work that they do.

Of course, this does not imply that the sociologist should avoid generating data in multiple ways. As already noted, this can serve as an assembly of reminders about the situated character of action. The 'mistake' only arises in using data to adjudicate between accounts. For this reduces the role of the researcher to what Garfinkel (1967) calls an 'ironist', using one account to undercut another, while remaining blind to the sense of each account in the context in which it arises.

To conclude: the major problem with triangulation as a test of validity is that, by counterposing different contexts, it ignores the context-bound and skilful character of social interaction and assumes that members are 'cultural dopes', who need a sociologist to dispel their illusions (see Garfinkel: 1967, Bloor: 1978).

A better solution may be to distinguish 'how' from 'why' questions and to triangulate methods and data only at the 'why' stage (see Chapter 8). Equally, Dingwall (personal correspondence) has suggested that triangulation has some value where, for instance, it reveals the existence of public and private accounts of an agency's work. Here 'interview and field data can be combined . . . to make better sense of the other'. I entirely accept Dingwall's point. His example shows triangulation being used to address the *situated work* of accounts rather than, as in Denzin's case, to do *ironies*.

Exercise 7.4

This exercise is concerned with method triangulation. You should select any TWO of the methods discussed in Chapters 3–6 (i.e. observation, texts, interviews and transcripts). Then you should choose a research topic where these two methods can be applied. For example, you might want to compare your observations of a library with interviews with library-users and staff. Alternatively, you could obtain official documents about the academic aims of your university and compare these to your observations, interviews or audio-recordings of a teaching session (subject to everyone's agreement).

Now do the following:

1 Briefly analyse each of your two sources of data. What does each source tell you about your topic?
2 Identify different themes emerging in the two data sources. How far are these differences relevant for an overall understanding of the topic?
3 Using your data, assess the argument that evidence is only relevant in the context of the situation in which it arises.
4 In the light of the above, explain whether, if you had to pursue your topic further, you would use multiple methods.

Respondent Validation

Reason and Rowan (1981) criticise researchers who are fearful of contaminating their data with the experience of the subject. On the contrary, they argue, good research goes back to the subjects with the tentative results, and refines them in the light of the subjects' reactions.

This is just what Michael Bloor (1978, 1983) attempted in his research on doctors' decision-making. Bloor (1978) discusses three procedures which attempt respondent validation:

1 The researcher seeks to predict participants' classifications in actual situations of their use (see Frake: 1964).
2 The researcher prepares hypothetical cases and predicts respondents' responses to them (see also Frake: 1964).
3 The researcher provides respondents with a research report and records their reactions to it.

In his study of doctors' decision-making in adeno-tonsillectomy cases, Bloor used the third method, hoping for 'a sort of self-recognition effect' (1978, 549). Although Bloor reports that he was able to make some useful modifications as a result of the surgeons' comments, he reports many reservations. These centre around whether respondents are able to follow a report written for a sociological audience and, even if it is presented intelligibly, whether they will (or should) have any interest in it (*ibid*, 550). A further problem, noted by Abrams (1984), is that: 'overt respondent validation is only possible if the results on the analysis are compatible with the self-image of the respondents' (8).

However, Bloor concludes, this need not mean that attempts at respondents' validation have *no* value. They do generate further data which, while not validating the research report, often suggest interesting paths for further analysis (Bloor:1983, 172).

Bloor's point has been very effectively taken up by Fielding and Fielding (1986) (respondent validation is also criticised by Bryman: 1988, 78–79). The Fieldings concede that subjects being studied may have additional knowledge, especially about the context of their actions. However:

> there is no reason to assume that members have privileged status as commentators on their actions . . . such feedback cannot be taken as direct validation or refutation of the observer's inferences. Rather such processes of so-called 'validation' should be treated as yet another source of data and insight. (43)

Of course, this leaves on one side the ethics, politics and practicalities of the researcher's relation with subjects in the field (see Chapter 8). Nonetheless, these latter issues should not be *confused* with the validation of research findings.

If we reject triangulation and members' validation, how, then, are we to overcome the anecdotal quality of much field research? To answer this question, I will review what I believe to be more appropriate methods for validating studies based largely or entirely upon qualitative data.

Choosing Cases

Field research studies are usually based on one or more cases. It is unlikely that these cases will have been selected on a random basis. More likely, a case will be chosen because it allows access.

This give rise to a problem, familiar to users of quantitative methods: 'How do we know . . . how representative case study findings are of all members of the population from which the case was selected?' (Bryman: 1988, 88).

The problem of 'representativeness' is a perennial worry of case-study researchers. Let me outline a number of ways that we can address it:

Inferring from one case to a larger population: Hammersley (1992a) suggests three methods through which we can attempt to generalise from the analysis of a single case:

- obtaining information about relevant aspects of the population of cases and comparing our case to them
- using survey research on a random sample of cases
- co-ordinating several ethnographic studies.

Through such comparisons with a larger sample, we may be able to establish some sense of the representativeness of our single case.

Generalisations in terms of theories: It is important to recognise that generalising from cases to populations does not follow a purely statistical logic in field research. Quoting Mitchell (1983), Bryman thus argues that: 'the issue should be couched in terms of the generalisability of cases to *theoretical* propositions rather than to *populations* or universes' (1988, 90, my emphasis).

As an example, Bryman uses Glaser and Strauss' discussion of 'awareness contexts' in relation to dying in hospital:

> The issue of whether the particular hospital studied is 'typical' is not the critical issue; what is important is whether the experiences of dying patients are typical of the broad class of phenomena . . . to which the theory refers. Subsequent research would then focus on the validity of the proposition in other milieux (e.g. doctors' surgeries). (1988, 91)

As our understanding of social processes improves, we are increasingly able to choose cases on theoretical grounds – for instance, because the case offers a crucial test of a theory. This leads directly to the issue of how we can test hypotheses in field research.

Testing Hypotheses

Analytic Induction (AI)

The standard method of testing a hypothesis in field research is AI. Fielding (1988) notes that we should begin by defining a phenomenon and generating some hypothesis. Then we take a small body of data (a 'case') and examine it as follows:

'[O]ne case is . . . studied to see whether the hypothesis relates to it'. If not, the hypothesis is reformulated (or the phenomenon redefined to exclude the case). While a small number of cases support 'practical certainty, negative cases disprove the explanation, which is then reformulated. Examination of cases, redefinition of the phenomenon and re-formulation of hypotheses is repeated until a universal relationship is shown' (7–8).

So AI is the equivalent to the statistical testing of quantitative associations to see if they are greater than might be expected at random (random error). However: 'in qualitative analysis . . . there is no random error variance. All exceptions are eliminated by revising hypotheses until all the data fit. The result of this procedure is that statistical tests are actually *unnecessary* once the negative cases are removed' (Fielding and Fielding: 1986, 89).

An example of AI being used in a field research study will be helpful. In Bloor's study of surgeons, already discussed, he tried: 'to inductively reconstruct each specialist's own standard "decision rules" which he normally used to decide on a disposal' (Bloor: 1978, 545). These rules were then compared to each doctor's procedures for searching through relevant information.

Bloor draws upon the distinction between 'necessary' and 'sufficient' conditions for an outcome. 'Necessary' conditions are conditions without which a particular outcome is impossible. 'Sufficient' conditions are conditions which totally explain the outcome in question. For instance, a necessary condition for me to give a lecture is that I should be present at a particular time and place. Sufficient conditions may include me knowing about the subject, having my notes with me, finding an audience awaiting me, and so on. This is how Bloor reports his inductive method:

1 For each specialist separately, cases were provisionally classified according to the disposal-category into which they fell.
2 The data on all a specialist's cases in a particular disposal-category were scrutinised in order to attempt a provisional list of those case-features common to the cases in that category.
3 The 'deviant cases' (i.e. those cases where features common to many of the cases in the disposal-category were lacking) were scrutinised in order to ascertain whether (a) the provisional list of case-features common to a particular category could be modified as to allow the inclusion of the deviant cases; or, (b) the classificatory system could be so modified as to allow the inclusion of the deviant cases within a modified category.
4 Having thus produced a list of case-features common to all cases in a particular category, cases in alternative categories were scrutinised to discover which case-features were shared with cases outside the first category considered. Such shared case-features were thus judged *necessary* rather than *sufficient* for the achievement of a particular disposal.

5 From the necessary and sufficient case-features associated with a particular category of cases sharing a common disposal, the specialist's relevant decision rules were derived. (Bloor: 1978, 546, my emphasis)

This is a shortened version of Bloor's list. He adds two further stages where cases are rescrutinised for each decision rule and then the whole process is re-enacted in order to account for the disposals obtained by all the specialists in the study.

Bloor recognises that his procedure was not *wholly* inductive. Before beginning the analysis, he already had general impressions, gained from contact in the field (*ibid*, 547). We might also add that no hypothesis-testing can or should be theory-free. Necessarily, then, analytic induction depends upon both a model of how social life works (e.g. interactionism, CA, etc.) and a set of concepts specific to that model (e.g. 'frames', 'recipient-design' and, as we discuss below, the environment around 'advice-reception').

For further discussion of AI, using Bloor's study as an exemplar, see Abrams (1984).

AI may appear to be rather complicated. However, it boils down to two simple techniques:

- the search for deviant cases
- the use of the constant comparative method.

Both techniques are susceptible to simple methods of counting.

Counting in Qualitative Research

By our pragmatic view, qualitative research does imply a commitment to field activities. It does not imply a commitment to innumeracy. (Kirk and Miller: 1986, 10)

In this part of the chapter I want to make some practical suggestions about how quantitative data can be incorporated into qualitative research. These suggestions flow from my own recent research experience in a number of studies, two of which are briefly discussed shortly.

Since the 1960s, a story has got about that no good sociologists should dirty their hands with numbers. Sometimes this story has been supported by sound critiques of the rationale underlying some quantitative analyses (Blumer: 1956, Cicourel: 1964). Even here, however, the story has been better on critique than on the development of positive, alternative strategies.

The various forms of ethnography, through which attempts are made to describe social processes, share a single defect. The critical reader is forced to ponder whether the researcher has selected only those fragments of data which support his argument. Where deviant cases are cited and explained (cf. Strong: 1979a, Heath: 1981), the reader feels more confident about the analysis. But doubts should still remain about the persuasiveness of claims made on the basis of a few selected examples.

I do not attempt here to defend quantitative or positivistic research *per se*. I am not concerned with research designs which centre on quantitative methods and/or are indifferent to the interpretivist problem of meaning. Instead, I want to try to demonstrate some uses of quantification in research which is qualitative and interpretive in design.

I shall try to show that simple counting techniques can offer a means to survey the whole corpus of data ordinarily lost in intensive, qualitative research. Instead of taking the researcher's word for it, the reader has a chance to gain a sense of the flavour of the data as a whole. In turn, researchers are able to test and to revise their generalisations, removing nagging doubts about the accuracy of their impressions about the data.

As Cicourel (1964) noted thirty years ago, in a bureaucratic-technological society, numbers talk. Today, with sociology on trial, we cannot afford to live like hermits, blinded by global, theoretical critiques to the possible analytical and practical uses of quantification. In the mid-1990s I believe this case holds just as strongly.

In a study of oncology clinics (Silverman: 1984), I used some simple quantitative measures in order to respond to some of these problems. The aim was to demonstrate that the qualitative analysis was reasonably representative of the data as a whole. Occasionally, however, the figures revealed that the reality was not in line with my overall impressions. Consequently, the analysis was tightened and the characterisations of clinic behaviour were specified more carefully.

A major aim was to compare what, following Strong (1979a), I called the 'ceremonial order' observed in the two British National Health Service (NHS) clinics with a clinic in the private sector. My method of analysis was largely qualitative and, like him, I used extracts of what patients and doctors had said as well as offering a brief ethnography of the setting and of certain behavioural data. In addition, however, I constructed a coding form which enabled me to collate a number of crude measures of doctor and patient interactions.

My impression was that the private clinic encouraged a more 'personalised' service and allowed patients to orchestrate their care, control the agenda and obtain some 'territorial' control of the setting. In my discussion of the data, like Strong, I cite extracts from consultations to support these points, while referring to deviant cases and to the continuum of forms found in the NHS clinics.

The crude quantitative data I had recorded did not allow any real test of the major thrust of this argument. Nonetheless, it did offer a summary measure of the characteristics of the total sample which allowed closer specification of features of private and NHS clinics. In order to illustrate this, I shall briefly look at the data on consultation length, patient participation and widening of the scope of the consultation.

My overall impression was that private consultations lasted considerably longer than those held in the NHS clinics. When examined, the data indeed did show that the former were almost twice as long as the latter (20 minutes as against 11 minutes) and that the difference was statistically highly significant. However, I recalled that, for special reasons, one of the NHS clinics had abnormally short consultations. I felt a fairer comparison of consultations in the two sectors should exclude this clinic and should only compare consultations taken by a single doctor in both sectors. This sub-sample of cases revealed that the difference in length between NHS and private consultations was now reduced to an average of under 3 minutes. This was still statistically significant, although the significance was reduced. Finally, however, if I compared only *new* patients seen by the same doctor, NHS patients got 4 minutes more on average – 34 minutes as against 30 minutes in the private clinic. This last finding was not suspected and had interesting implications for the overall assessment of the individual's costs and benefits from 'going private'. It is possible, for instance, that the tighter scheduling of appointments at the private clinic may limit the amount of time that can be given to new patients.

As a further aid to comparative analysis, I measured patient partici-pation in the form of questions and unelicited statements. Once again, a highly significant difference was found: on this measure, private patients participated much more in the consultation. However, once more taking only patients seen by the same doctor, the difference between the clinics became very small and was *not* significant. Finally, no significant difference was found in the degree to which non-medical matters (e.g. patient's work or home circumstances) were discussed in the clinics.

These quantitative data were a useful check on over-enthusiastic claims about the degree of difference between the NHS and private clinics. However, it must be remembered that my major concern was with the 'ceremonial order' of the three clinics. I had amassed a considerable number of exchanges in which doctors and patients appeared to behave in the private clinic in a manner deviant from what we know about NHS hospital consultations. The question was: would the quantitative data offer any support to my observations?

The answer was, to some extent, positive. Two quantitative measures were helpful in relation to the ceremonial order. One dealt with the extent to which the doctor fixed treatment or attendance at the patient's convenience. The second measured whether patients or doctor engaged in polite small-talk with one another about their personal or professional lives. (I called this 'social elicitation'.) As Table 7.4 shows, both these measures revealed significant differences, in the expected direction, according to the mode of payment.

Now, of course, such data could not offer proof of my claims about the different interactional forms. However, coupled with the qualitative data, they provided strong evidence of the direction of difference, as well as giving me a simple measure of the sample as a whole which contexted the few extracts of talk I was able to use. I do not deny that counting can be as

Table 7.4: *Private and NHS Clinics: Ceremonial Orders*

	Private clinic (n = 42)	NHS clinics (n = 104)
Treatment or attendance fixed at patients' convenience	15 (36%)	10 (10%)
Social elicitation	25 (60%)	31 (30%)

arbitrary as qualitative interpretation of a few fragments of data. However, providing the researcher resists the temptation to try to count everything, and bases his analysis on a sound conceptual basis linked to actors' own methods of ordering the world, then both types of data can inform the analysis of the other.

Exercise 7.5

This exercise is meant to accustom you to the advantages and limitations of simple tabulations. You should return to one of the settings which you have observed in a previous exercise.
  Now follow these steps:

1 Count whatever seems to be countable in this setting (e.g. the number of people entering and leaving or engaging in certain activities).
2 Assess what this quantitative data tells you about social life in this setting. How far can what you have counted be related to any *one* social science theory or concept with which you are familiar?
3 Beginning from the theory or concept selected in step 2, indicate how you might count in terms of it rather than in terms of common-sense categories.
4 Attempt to count again on this basis. What associations can you establish?
5 Identify deviant cases (i.e. items that do not support the associations that you have established). How might you further analyse these deviant cases, using either quantitative or qualitative techniques? What light might that throw on the associations which you have identified?

Summary

I have suggested that both reliability and validity are important issues in field research. I went on to suggest that reliability can be addressed by using standardised methods to write fieldnotes and prepare transcripts. In the case of interview and textual studies, I also argued that reliability can be improved by comparing the analyses of the same data by several researchers.

I further suggested that data triangulation and member validation are usually inappropriate to validate field research. Instead, I suggested three ways of validating such research:

1 Methods of generalising to a larger population.
2 Methods of testing hypotheses.
3 The use of simple counting procedures.

I now want to conclude this chapter by an account of one further case study which illustrates several of these issues.

An Example: Analysing Advice Sequences

Heritage and Sefi (1992) (henceforth H&S) have analysed 70 instances of advice-giving sequences drawn from 8 first visits to first-time mothers by 5 different health visitors. H&S found that most advice was initiated by the professional, often prior to any clear indication that it was desired by the client.

Health visitor (HV) initiated advice took four forms:

1 Stepwise entry in the sequence below:

    (a) HV enquiry
    (b) problem-indicative response by client
    (c) request for specification by HV ('a focussing enquiry')
    (d) a specification by the client
    (e) advice-giving.

2 The same sequence but with no request for specification because the client volunteers how she dealt with the problem.
3 No client statement of how she dealt with the problem and no HV request for specification – thus stages (c) and (d) are omitted.
4 HV-initiated advice without the client giving a problem indicative response, i.e. stage (a) is followed directly by stage (e).

The majority of advice initiations analysed by H&S were of form 4. Indeed, in many cases, even the HV's enquiry was not problem-oriented but was more concerned to topicalise the issue for which advice was subsequently delivered.

The reception of advice by mothers took three forms:

1 A marked acknowledgment (MA) (e.g. 'oh right' or repeats of key components of the advice); H&S say such utterances acknowledge the informativeness and appropriateness of the advice.
2 An unmarked acknowledgment (UA) (e.g. 'mm', 'yeah', 'right' without an 'oh'). These are minimal response tokens which, H&S argue, have a primarily continuative function; they do *not* (a) acknowledge the advice-giving as newsworthy to the recipient or (b) constitute an

undertaking to follow the advice and (c) can be heard as a form of resistance in themselves because, implicitly, such responses are refusing to treat the talk as advice.

3 Assertions of knowledge or competence by the mother. These indicate that the advice is redundant – hence they also may be taken as resistance.

This underlines H&S's argument about the advantages of stepwise entry into advice-giving (form 1 above). In this form of advice-giving, they find less resistance and more uptake displayed by mothers' use of marked acknowledgments. Here the HV's request for her client to specify a problem means that the advice can be recipient-designed, non-adversarial and not attribute blame.

Like H&S, in a study of AIDS counselling (Silverman *et al*: 1992), we focussed on the link between the form in which advice is delivered and its reception. Nearly all advice sequences were C-initiated and many were truncated. As in H&S's study, step-by-step sequences were more likely to produce MAs, truncated sequences usually produced UAs. The data on uptake are shown in Table 7.5.

Table 7.5: *Form of Advice and Degree of Uptake*

Advice format	Number	Type of acknowledgement[1]	
		Unmarked	Marked
P-initiated	2	0	2
C-initiated			
Step by step: full-sequence	11	1	10
Shortened	5	3	2
Truncated: no P problem elicited	32	29	3
	Based on 50 advice sequences		

[1] 'Unmarked' means *only* unmarked acknowledgments were given in the advice sequence; 'marked' means that at least *one* marked acknowledgment was given.

Table 7.5 shows a very clear correlation between the way in which an advice sequence is set up and the response that it elicits from the patient. In the total of 32 cases where the counsellor delivers advice without attempting to generate a perceived problem from the patient, there are only 3 cases where the patient shows any sign of uptake. Conversely, in the other 18 cases, where the advice emerges either at the request of the patient or in a step-by-step sequence, there are only 4 cases where the patient does *not* show uptake.

Table 7.5 thus shows how simple tabulations can offer a valuable means of validating impressions obtained from qualitative data-analysis.

Following the discussion above of deviant-case analysis (in Bloor's work), I now will show how the analysis of these gross findings was developed by the examination of two deviant cases. In one case a truncated sequence of generalised advice was, unusually, associated with marked acknowledgments (MAs). This is shown as Extract 7.1 below.

Extract 7.1
(C = counsellor; P = patient; C is talking about contracting full-blown AIDS)
```
 1 C: But we can't tell you know whether uh one individual is
 2     going to or whether they're [no:t.
 3 P:                              [(It's just on proportions).=
 4 C: That's ri:[ght.
 5 P:           [(            )
 6 C: .hhhh A:nd obviously if someone looks after themselves they
 7     stand a better chance you know keeping fit and healthy.
 8 P: Ye:s.
 9 C: .hhhh The advice we give is common sense really if you think
10     about it.=To keep fit and healthy, (.)      eat a
11       [well) a balanced di:et,
12 P:    [For your natural resistance.=
13 C:  =That's [right.
14 P:          [Ye:s.
15 C: .hh Plenty of exerci:[se:
16 P:                      [Right.
17 C: [Uh::m  or  enough  exercise.
18 P: [(I already get that) hheh .hhh [hhh .hhhh Too=
19 C:                                 [Yeah.
20 P:  =much of it. hhuh=
21 C:  =Enough slee:p.
22 P: Y[es.
23 C:  [You know. All the things we should normally
24     do[: to keep healthy,
25 P:    [Right. Rather than let yourself get run down.=
26 C:  =That's ri:ght.
```

Extract 7.1 is remarkable for the large number of marked acknowledgments given by the client (lines 12, 18 and 25). How can we account for this unusual reception of truncated advice? A part of the answer seems to lie in the content of the advice given. Extract 7.1 is largely concerned with what the counsellor tells people who have a positive test-result. This leaves it open to the patient to treat what he is being told not as advice but as *information delivery* (about the advice C would give if P turned out to be seropositive).

It follows that such uptake obviously need have no direct implication for what the patient does (as opposed to what he thinks) – unlike the uptake of advice. Hence, as in Extract 7.1, P may choose to offer marked acknowledgments to what C says. But, in so doing, he may be simply showing uptake of a sequence that is hearable as information rather than personalised advice.

So when Cs formulate their talk as 'advice' but offer a generalised message (e.g. 'what we tell people who test positive'), they depart from many of the constraints of personalised advice-giving. This is because information delivery is compatible with a wide range of response (from simple continuers to newsworthiness-tokens). Whatever the patient says will normally be heard as a receipt of information rather than, as in personalised advice sequences, bearing on the uptake of advice. Consequently, when MAs are found in such truncated advice sequences they function as strong information receipts rather than as positive uptakes of advice.

In the second deviant case, a series of questions from the counsellor led to MAs of advice even though no advice was actually tendered. Here we found that a series of hypothetical questions, increasingly specified in terms of the patient's answers, eventually led the patient to formulate the direction in which the questions were leading.

In both cases, the problematic features of response to personalised advice-giving were avoided. In the latter case, this was associated with advice-uptake but at the cost of the resources involved in the long interviews required to lead the patient in the direction desired by the counsellor. Conversely, although generalised advice sequences were not receipted as advice but as information delivery, they saved in resources by being far quicker.

I have tried to show how simple tabulations, combined with the constant comparative method and deviant case analysis, allow us to generate and to test hypotheses. However, case-study research can rarely make any claims about the representativeness of its samples. How far does this undermine its validity?

Following my earlier discussion (and the work of Mitchell: 1983), I would argue that case-study work derives its validity not from the representativeness of its samples but from the thoroughness of its analysis. For instance, while survey researchers may be satisfied with explaining 99 per cent of the variance in their samples, case-study researchers must pursue every single instance in order to refine their analysis. This I have demonstrated in my discussion of our analysis of deviant cases.

Furthermore, although we did not select a random sample, we chose our data-sets for analytical reasons in a way which tested a theoretically-derived hypothesis. So, although the HIV counselling setting differs in important respects from Heritage and Sefi's study of health visitors (see Silverman *et al*: 1992), nonetheless it provided a comparable body of advice sequences drawn from professional–client interaction. Using concepts drawn from CA, like Heritage and Sefi, we were able to support and to refine the analysis of the processes surrounding advice-reception.

Conclusion

I have concluded this chapter on rigorous field research by focussing upon the uses of simple methods of counting in largely qualitative studies. The 'advice' study uses purely descriptive statistics; the study of private practice consultations introduces some straightforward correlations. This concentration on description is not coincidental.

The kind of interpretive sociology which I have been discussing is doubly interested in description. First, like all scientific work, it is concerned with the problem of how to generate adequate descriptions of what it observes. Second, however, unlike other kinds of sociology; it is especially interested in how ordinary people observe and describe their world. Many of the procedures I have discussed here aim to offer adequate (sociological) descriptions of (lay) descriptions. Once this is recognised as the central problematic of much field research, then these procedures can be extended to what people say and write in a far broader range of contexts than the medical settings on which I have concentrated in this chapter.

More than thirty years ago, Becker and Geer (1960) recognised that adequate sociological description of social processes needs to look beyond purely qualitative methods. Everything depends, however, on the relation between the quantitative measures being used and the analytic issue being addressed: 'The usefulness of . . . statistics is a function of the theoretical problematic in which they are to be used and of the use to which they are to be put within it' (Hindess: 1973, 45).

However, I have also shown that quantitative measures are not the only way to test the validity of our propositions. Analytic induction, based upon deviant-case analysis and the constant comparative method, offers a powerful tool through which to overcome the danger of purely 'anecdotal' field research.

The time for wholesale critiques of quantitative research has passed. What we need to do now is to show the ways in which field research is every bit as rigorous as the best quantitative work.

8

The Practical Relevance of Qualitative Research

There are several claims we might like to make about the value of ethnography in policy-making. Here is one recent list, suggested by Janet Finch:

- it is relatively flexible
- it studies what people are doing in their natural context
- it is well placed to study processes as well as outcomes
- it studies meanings as well as causes (cited by Hammersley: 1992a, 125).

Together with other ethnographers, I have made similar claims both to practitioners and to research funding bodies. Unfortunately, things are not quite as easy as this list might suggest.

First, as we have already seen (especially in Chapter 2), the status of ethnography or field research as a naturalistic enterprise, concerned with meanings, is disputable. Second, as Hammersley (1992c) points out, non-ethnographic approaches can study some of these features (e.g. questionnaire panel studies can examine change over time and thus social processes). Third, as I argued in Chapter 7, the issue of the validity of qualitative research (its generalisability to larger populations, and the possible anecdotal basis of its claims) is a real one which does not exist just in the minds of policy-makers.

In responding to these problems about the practical relevance of field research, my underlying theme is simple: the relevance to practice of rigorous fieldwork informed by analytical issues rather than by social problems.

This means that it is usually necessary to refuse to allow our research topics to be defined in terms of the conceptions of 'social problems' as recognised by either professional or community groups. Ironically, by beginning from a clearly defined sociological perspective, we can later address such social problems with, I believe, considerable force and persuasiveness.

These are claims in need of demonstration. I will attempt this shortly. For the moment, however, I want to move away from the specifics of field research to review the wider debate about how all forms of sociological research stand in relation to social problems. In doing so, I shall re-state some of the arguments found in my earlier text (Silverman: 1985).

Three Roles for the Sociologist

> The question is not whether we should take sides, since we inevitably will,
> but rather whose side are we on? (Becker: 1967a, 239)

Not all sociologists would agree with Becker's call for moral or political partisanship. Perhaps responding to state apparatuses which are at best suspicious of the purposes of social science, many would go on the defensive. They might find it easier or more acceptable to argue that their concern is simply with the establishment of facts through the judicious testing of competing hypotheses and theories. Their only slogan, they would say, is the pursuit of knowledge. They would claim to reject political partisanship, at least in their academic work; they are only, they would say, partisans for truth.

I am not, for the moment, concerned to make a detailed assessment of either Becker's statement or the defensive response to it which I have just depicted. I believe both contain dangerous simplifications. As I shall later show, the partisans for truth are mistaken about the purity of knowledge, while Becker's rhetoric of 'sides' is often associated with a style of research which is unable to discover anything because of its prior commitment to a revealed truth (the plight of the underdog, the inevitable course of human history, etc.). Curiously, both positions can be élitist, establishing themselves apart from and above the people they study.

For the moment, however, I want to stress a more positive feature of both arguments. Both recognise that no simply neutral or value-free position is possible in social science (or, indeed, elsewhere). The partisans for truth just as much as the partisans of the 'underdog' are committed to an absolute value for which there can be no purely factual foundation. As Weber pointed out in the early years of this century, all research is contaminated to some extent by the values of the researcher. Only through those values do certain problems get identified and studied in particular ways. Even the commitment to scientific (or rigorous) method is itself, as Weber emphasises, a value. Finally, the conclusions and implications to be drawn from a study are, Weber stresses, largely grounded in the moral and political beliefs of the researcher.

More than thirty years ago, Gouldner (1962) pointed out how Weber had been grossly misinterpreted by positivist sociologists. Because Weber had suggested that purely scientific standards could govern the *study* of a sociological problem, they had used him as the standard-bearer for a value-free sociology. They had conveniently forgotten that Weber had argued that the initial choice and conceptualisation of a problem, as well as the subsequent attempt to seek practical implications from its study, were highly 'value-relevant' (to use Weber's term).

The 'Minotaur' of a value-free sociology which positivists had conjured up from misreading Weber is effectively destroyed by Gouldner. As Denzin (1970) shows, the myth of value-freedom is shattered not only by the researcher's own commitments but by the social and political environment in which research is carried out. Grant-giving bodies will seek to channel research in particular directions: there is no *neutral* money whether one is speaking about the well-meaning 'initiatives' of research councils or the more sinister funding schemes of the tobacco industry or the war-machine (Horowitz 1965). Moreover, organisations that are studied are likely to want some kind of return in terms of 'facts' (assumed to be theory-free and always quantifiable) as well as support for their current political strategy. Finally, as Dingwall (personal correspondence) has pointed out, governments may sponsor 'window-dressing' research to buy time and to legitimate inaction; while, as Denzin points out, the researcher may desire nothing more than a publishable paper, this pressure-group activity is bound to have an impact on the work.

Given the constraints under which research takes place, how may the researcher respond? To answer this question, in an earlier text (Silverman: 1985) I sought to characterise three different research roles which have been prescribed or adopted. These are presented in summary form in Table 8.1.

Table 8.1:   *Whose Side Are We On?*

Role	Politics	Commitment	Examples
Scholar	Liberal	Knowledge for knowledge's sake – protected by scholar's conscience	Weber, Denzin
State counsellor	Bureaucratic	Social engineering or enlightenment for policy-makers	Popper, Bulmer
Partisan	Marxist or conservative	Knowlege to support both a political theory and a political practice	Marx, Habermas, political research centres

It will probably be helpful if I now give a summary presentation of each of these three positions (a longer version is to be found in Silverman: 1985).

Scholar

In his two famous lectures 'Science as a Vocation' and 'Politics as a Vocation' (Weber: 1946), Weber enunciated basic liberal principles to a student audience in 1917. Despite the patriotic fervour of the First World War, he insisted on the primacy of the individual's own conscience as a basis for action. Taking the classic Kantian position, Weber argued that values could not be derived from facts. However, this was not because values were less important than facts (as logical positivists were soon to argue). Rather, precisely because 'ultimate evaluations' (or value choices) were so important, they were not to be reduced to purely factual judgments. The facts could only tell you about the likely consequences of given actions but they could not tell you which action to choose.

For Weber, the very commitment to science was an example of an ultimate evaluation, exemplifying a personal belief in standards of logic and rationality and in the value of factual knowledge. Ironically echoing certain aspects of the 'Protestant ethic' whose historical emergence he himself had traced, Weber appealed to the scholar's conscience as the sole basis for conferring meaning and significance upon events.

Weber's appeal to Protestantism's and liberalism's 'free individual' is fully shared, fifty years on, by Norman Denzin. Denzin (1970) rejects any fixed moral standards as the basis for research. He will not accept, for instance, that sociologists cannot conceal themselves or use disguised research techniques. Nor is he prepared to recognise that research must necessarily contribute to society's own self-understanding. Both standards are, for him, examples of 'ethical absolutism' which fail to respect the scholar's appeal to his own conscience in the varying contexts of research. Denzin's stand is distinctively liberal and individualist: 'One mandate governs sociological activity – the absolute freedom to pursue one's activities as one sees fit' (Denzin: 1970, 332). What 'one sees [as] fit' will take into account that no method of sociological research is intrinsically any more unethical than any other. Citing Goffman, Denzin argues that, since the researcher always wears some mask, covert observation is merely one mask among others.

Denzin does suggest that the pursuit of research in terms of one's own standards should have certain safeguards. For instance, subjects should be told of the researcher's own value judgments and biases, and should be warned about the kinds of interpretation the research may generate within the community. But he is insistent that the ultimate arbiter of proper conduct remains the conscience of the individual sociologist.

Weber's and Denzin's liberal position seems rather unrealistic. Curiously, as sociologists they fail to see the power of social organisation as it shapes the practice of research. For while Denzin acknowledges the role of pressure-groups, he remains silent about the privileged authority of the 'scientist' in society and about the deployment of scientific theories by agents of social control as mobilising forms of power/knowledge.

State Counsellor

Even liberal individualists may occasionally move away from their 'hands-off' attitude towards others. Denzin, for instance, considers the value of the information that sociologists may offer to participants: 'The investigator may open new avenues of action and perception among those studied. Organisational leaders may be ignorant of the dysfunctional aspects of certain programs, and an exposure to the sociologist's findings may correct their misconceptions' (*ibid*, 338).

Notice how Denzin uses 'organisational leaders' as his example of 'those studied'. Just as many sociologists automatically side with the underdog, so also there is a considerable weight of sociological work which identifies with the problems and interests of the 'leaders' or 'top dogs'. Another contemporary example is provided by Bulmer (1982). Despite having a general title, *The Uses of Social Research*, his book turns out to be solely a discussion of how social research may be used by 'policy-makers'. It will thus serve as an example of what I have called, in Table 8.1, *bureaucratic* politics where the researcher adopts the role of state counsellor.

It is at once clear, however, that Bulmer's bureaucrat-cum-researcher is intended to work at arm's length from the administration, offering no simple solutions and preferring to provide knowledge rather than to recommend policies. This is Bulmer's 'enlightenment model' of social research. It is based on a rejection of two other versions of the uses of research – 'empiricism' and the 'engineering model'.

I have set out below Bulmer's depictions of each of the three models:

Empiricism: This assumes that facts somehow speak for themselves. It reflects the administrative view that research is a neutral tool for the collection of facts for the use of policy-makers. Failing to take account of the post-Weberian consensus that facts can only be recognised in terms of theoretically derived categories, its 'bucket theory of mind' (Popper) is, Bulmer suggests, wholly inadequate. This is not merely a methodological quibble, because Bulmer demonstrates that empiricism fails because it offers no way of '[bringing] to bear the insights of social science – rather than merely the factual products of social research' (Bulmer: 1982, 42).

The engineering model: This seems to be based on Popper's (1959) own version of the contribution of research to 'piecemeal social engineering'. Derived from Popper's rejection of attempts at revolutionary social changes, the engineering model takes off from the definition, presumably by the bureaucracy, of a social problem. It then proceeds, in Bulmer's version, through a sequence of four stages: (i) the identification of the knowledge that is required; (ii) the acquisition of social research data; (iii) the interpretation of the data in the light of the problem; and (iv) a change in the policy.

Bulmer implies that the proponents of the engineering model are politically naive. Bureaucrats often know precisely what policy changes they wish to make and commission research in such a way that the end-product is likely to legitimate their thinking. He also points out that, in large organisations, it is often action rather than research that is needed. Moreover, where problems need to be analysed, the application of common sense is often quite sufficient.

The enlightenment model: This is Bulmer's preferred model. He sees the function of applied research as the provision of knowledge of alternative possibilities. Its role is to enlighten bureaucrats, and not to recommend policies or to choose between administrative options. This means that it *rejects* a number of research aims (Bulmer: 1982, 153–154) including: (i) the provision of authoritative facts (because facts are only authoritative in the context of theories); (ii) supplying political ammunition (because this is based, Bulmer points out, on the 'sterile' assumption that there are 'left-wing' facts as opposed to 'right-wing' facts); (iii) doing tactical research, as in government think-tanks (because this reduces the social scientist to a mere technician); and (iv) evaluating policies (because this is based on the rejected engineering model of applied social research).

Instead, Bulmer *proposes* two research aims which are consistent with his enlightenment model:

- interaction – offering mutual contact between researchers and policy-makers
- conceptualisation – creation of new problems for policy-makers to think about through the development of new concepts.

The weaknesses of Bulmer's enlightenment model are already implied by my labelling his approach the 'state counsellor'. In Silverman (1985), I argued that it offers an attractive version of how researchers who are already employed as functionaries of the state can preserve a degree of professional freedom. Pursuing 'enlightenment', they are relatively freer to define problems in terms of their own interests rather than to have them imposed on them by their political bosses (as empiricism or the engineering model implies). However, this 'professional' freedom is, to some extent, a fraud, for in Bulmer's discussion the enlightenment model never brings into question the role of research as the supplier of concepts and information to the powers-that-be. Precisely because it represents applied research as the hand-maiden of the state, 'enlightenment' offers a purely bureaucratic version of politics: as such, it totally fails to address the political and moral issues of research which is at anything other than arm's length from the state.

A case in point is the famous Project Camelot (Horowitz: 1965). This was a research project funded in 1963 by the Pentagon with a budget of 6 million dollars. Its purported aim was to gather data on the causes of revolutions in the Third World. However, when it became clear that such research was to be used as a basis for counter-insurgency techniques, it created a storm of protest and the project was withdrawn.

Horowitz points out that many social scientists had been prepared to overlook the source of the money when offered such big research funding. Presumably, they might have defended themselves as seeking merely to spread 'enlightenment' rather than to engage in political or social engineering.

However, this in no way settles the moral issue over whether social scientists should have this kind of relationship to such a government agency. Stewart Clegg (personal correspondence), for instance, suggests that we may need to call upon the organisational capacities of the state in order to produce real changes. His point reveals the dilemma that worthy ends may depend upon élitist means.

Partisan

If the state counsellor is co-opted by administrative interests and scholars delude themselves that they can stand apart from a socially-organised world, then the partisan's role would seem to be altogether more defensible. Unlike scholars, partisans do not shy away from their accountability to the world. Unlike the state counsellor, however, they hold the ruling bureaucracy at arm's length. Instead, the partisan seeks to provide the theoretical and factual resources for a political struggle aimed at transforming the assumptions through which both political and administrative games are played.

In Silverman (1985), I used Howard Waitzkin's, 'Medicine, Superstructure and Micropolitics' (1979) as an example of partisanship. Waitzkin has the laudable aim of relating 'the everyday micro-level interaction of individuals' to 'macro-level structures of domination' (Waitzkin: 1979, 601). Unfortunately, as Rayner and Stimson (1979) point out, he uses a mechanistic version of Marxism based on notions of the material base and the superstructure, which reduce the doctor–patient relationship simply to an ideological apparatus of the capitalist state. Knowing what he is going to find, Waitzkin treats his data largely as illustrative of a preconceived theory. Two things never seem to strike him:

- that what he finds is true but not necessarily caused by the factors in his theory (for instance, Strong: 1979a suggests that doctors' use of the machine analogy in describing the body may be a feature of medical consultations in all industrialised social systems and not, as Waitzkin suggests, specific to capitalism)
- that contrary evidence should be hunted down and followed up (for instance, Waitzkin notes – but makes nothing of – his own apparently contrary findings that women patients receive more information, while 'doctors from working-class backgrounds tend to communicate less information than doctors from upper-class backgrounds' (*ibid*, 604)).

Just as the partisan does not seek to be surprised by his/her data, (s)he tends to be élitist in regard to political change. Not surprisingly, Waitzkin seeks to encourage 'patient education' to invite the questioning of professional advice (*ibid*, 608). At the same time, as we have seen, he makes nothing of patients' self-generated attempts to challenge professional dominance. Marx's question 'who educates the educator?' seems entirely apposite.

Waitzkin's paper illustrates some of the more unfortunate consequences of the researcher adopting the role of the partisan. In the same way as the Bible advises 'look and ye shall find', so partisans (Marxists, feminists, conservatives) look and inevitably find examples which can be used to support their theories.

Dingwall (1980) has noted how such work 'undoubtedly furnishes an element of romance, radical chic even, to liven the humdrum routine of academic inquiry'. He then goes on to note that a concern to champion the 'underdog': 'is inimical to the serious practice of ethnography, whose claims to be distinguished from polemic or investigative journalism must rest on its ability to comprehend the perspectives of top dogs, bottom dogs and, indeed, lap dogs' (1980, 874).

Dingwall concludes that social research, whatever its methods, must seek to produce valid generalisations rather than 'synthetic moral outrage' (*ibid*). This leads him into a discussion of the ethics of ethnography which, although beyond the scope of this chapter, are valuable reading for any fieldworker.

Exercise 8.1

This exercise gives you an opportunity to think through the various ways sociologists have answered Becker's question: 'Whose side are we on?' You are asked to imagine that research funding is available for whatever topic and research design you prefer.

1   Suggest a research topic and outline a methodology using one or more of the methods set out in Chapters 3–6.
2   Justify the topic and methodology from the point of view of: (a) the scholar, (b) the state counsellor and (c) the partisan.
3   Now select any one article which reports research findings in a social science journal. Which of the positions referred to in 2 does it adopt?
4   Set out how this position might be criticised from the point of view of (a) the other positions and (b) your own views on the relevance of social science research.

Finding a Place for Sociology

Having taken up Becker's question 'whose side are we on?' and depicted three roles adopted by sociologists (scholar, state counsellor and partisan), I have found major problems in how these roles have been exercised. We would thus seem to be back at square one. Shortly, I shall try to be more positive and indicate the scope for what I believe to be a fruitful relation between sociology and society. However, before doing so, I want to continue a little further on this pessimistic tack, for if we can understand better the social and moral roots of sociology's failure to find a defensible role for itself, we shall be in a better position to come up with an acceptable alternative.

The Self-Righteousness of Sociology

A common theme in my depiction of how sociologists have practised their chosen role is the element of self-righteousness that seems to have been present. The scholar pretends to be apart from the world and claims special rights for conscience. State counsellors makes no bones about their worldly involvement, but seek to escape definitions of themselves as mere technicians. Finally, the partisan makes claims to know how things really are while all too often ignoring what people are actually saying and doing.

If there is anything in the charge of self-righteousness, then it would indeed put sociology in a curious situation. After all, as Berger and Kellner (1981, 12) have argued, sociologists depict themselves in terms of their special ability to unmask delusions. Yet, if sociologists are themselves possessed of delusions of grandeur, expressed in a self-righteous style, then the boot is on the other foot with a vengeance. Perhaps, as Strong (1979b) implies, sociologists should have conducted a sociology-of-knowledge-style investigation into their own unmasking, debunking, sceptical motif. For:

> Scepticism has considerable dramatic rewards. In writing in this fashion sociologists both formulate themselves as members of some insightful and incorruptible élite and, at the same time, gain considerable pleasure by the exposure and thus potential overthrow of those whom they dislike. (Strong: 1979b, 201)

For Strong, sociology has used a basic strategy of any professional group as a means to attack another:

> Given the relatively open trade in ideas, every profession is free to compete with every other to provide formulations and solutions for contemporary social issues. 'Discovering' social problems and, more especially, cashing them in such terms that one has exclusive rights to them, is the basic strategy of every bourgeois profession. (*ibid*, 202)

In pursuit of its vested, professional interest, sociology has shown an ability to define its product in a flexible, acceptable way: 'According to the times, it can threaten capitalists either with consumers or with workers and in both cases offers its services as interpreter, mediator, and ultimately, perhaps, planner' (*ibid*, 203).

This means that sociology can conceal its professional interest behind quite genuine convictions about the emancipatory role of social science. However, as Foucault (1977, 1979) has shown, defining everyday matters as 'social' has been a major route through which public institutions come to survey and monitor every aspect of our lives.

So far we have been dealing with criticisms internal to the sociological community. What about its vehement critics in society?

Sociology's Critics

> Where the social sciences are concerned, public hostility – or, perhaps, scepticism – derives in large measure from the general anti-philosophical spirit that prevails in this island of pragmatists.

> What need is there, the British ask, for all that theorising about issues which require only common sense? And why do scientists have to use such dreadful, obfuscating jargon in doing so? (*The Independent*, August 22, 1990)

The Independent, a British daily newspaper, raises issues which are, I believe, of general importance. They underline the ways in which people can become critical of social science in certain kinds of political and economic climates.

There are two sorts of charges present in this editorial. To what extent are we, as social scientists, theorising issues which only require common sense and, to a lesser extent, why do we have to use jargon in the way we do?

This calls for sociologists to reflect on the relationship between sociology and the community. By community, I include the state and professional workers as well as their clients.

In many Western societies, the social sciences are highly regarded. In France, Scandinavia and the U.S.A., for instance, sociologists are, by and large, respected professionals listened to by government and the media. In Britain, our no doubt healthy scepticism about theoretical thinking finds its clearest expression in the low status of sociology. A sociology degree from the London School of Economics condemned one party candidate to scorned oblivion in one Boulting Brothers movie of the late 1950s. More recently, Malcolm Bradbury's novel *The History Man* is most remembered for the image of Howard Kirk, the despicable and amoral university sociologist.

However, the status of any occupation is based on a two-way process. We do our subject no service if we assume that our low status is simply the result of a cruel world. If, in Britain, sociologists are often little more than figures of fun, then the activities of sociologists themselves may have something to do with this – as I shall later try to demonstrate.

In some ways, then, the situation is even worse than *The Independent* editorial suggests. Through a whole series of intellectual and historical factors, the relationship between sociology and the community in Britain is dangerously delicate. If the situation is rosier in other countries, the British situation points to underlying concerns that are voiced everywhere.

Let me list some points that concern people:

Social structures:　Well-informed people wonder about sociologists' public reputation for talking about the impact on behaviour of large-scale social structures (like structures of class, structures of ethnicity, structures of gender-relations and structures of power). Quite rightly, they might think that there is little that can be done about these structures at least in the short term. So why should they pay us to speculate about them or even to study them?

Validity:　We do not always convince others about the validity of our findings on social structures. We may sometimes give the impression that we know already about what these structures are like and just look at our data for confirming instances. I think, unfortunately, one only has to open a sociology journal to see at least one article where you are pretty sure that before the person did their research they knew what they were going to find and they were looking for examples to support whatever it is they wanted to say.

Relativism: A more general feature of the sociological culture, affecting its public esteem, is its addiction to relativist forms of discourse. Understandably, if you are looking at the ways in which things operate differently in different milieux, you tend to get to the position where it is difficult to take a stand on anything because everything is relative to its particular context. Although our stress on the infinite variability of cultures is a useful critique of absolutist notions, if pushed too far, it can be disabling in terms of our relationships to the wider community. For instance, in my own work (Silverman: 1987), I have been forced to question favourite liberal or progressive ideas such as 'patient-centred medicine' – doctors paying more attention to their patient's needs and language rather than looking at everything in a purely organic way. My research suggests that there are traps and power-plays present even within apparently patient-centred medicine. Such a relativist sociology needs to think about how it can present its findings in a way that will seem relevant to people who turn to social science with a naive belief in progress and an absolutist version of the role of science.

Common sense dressed up in jargon: Remember the charges made by *The Independent* – that sociology is just telling us what we know already commonsensically but is using unnecessary jargon? Perhaps, there is, indeed, something in the charge of common sense.

Subjectivist approaches imply that feelings or experiences are the most authentic data about the social world. Such an assumption is problematic because, as Durkheim showed us at the turn of the century, experience is never unmediated but is always structured by particular cultures and by settings. Often, perhaps when we think we are expressing our true selves, we are merely reproducing a script that everybody works to. After all, it was Michael Moerman (1974), an ethnomethodologist, who reminded us, nearly two decades ago, not to confuse actors' accounts with sociological analysis (see Chapter 3).

Responding to the Critics

The previous chapters show how field research can deal with the 'micro' structures of interaction which are de-emphasised by social scientists concerned with large-scale social institutions. Moreover, as I argued in Chapter 6, studies of institutional talk hold out the possibility of showing how social structures are 'talked into being'.

The question of validity is a serious one for all social scientists. In Chapter 7, I showed how field researchers can produce valid and reliable knowledge. However, the issue of the relativistic character of social science is very difficult and I will postpone addressing it until later in this chapter. For the moment, let me turn to the charges that social science is commonsensical and full of jargon.

Sociology and Common Sense

There are two ways to respond to this charge, depending on the social science approach you favour. For ethnomethodologists, common sense constitutes the *topic* which we study. Thus, although it is unavoidable that common sense will be used as an initial resource to understand interaction, we strongly differ from everyday thinking in making that common sense into a problem to be investigated.

Such an activity is hardly commonsensical. Using the example of my research on job selection procedures (Silverman and Jones: 1976), it is impossible to select people for jobs while, at the same time, making problematic how one is inevitably fitting decisions to rules rather than the other way round (see Chapter 4).

The second way of responding to this charge is to argue that social science often refutes common-sense ideas. We saw a crude example of this in Exercise 3.1 which was based on a sociologist claiming that laboratory investigation could show which common-sense maxims were incorrect. This approach can be labelled naively positivistic because it fails to understand how common-sense usage is amazingly sophisticated and therefore, implausibly, desires to replace common sense with science.

Nonetheless, even non-positivistic social scientists, who respect the power of common sense, often end up with contra-intuitive findings. For instance, Moerman (1974) shows how the Lue of Thailand only became a 'tribe' in certain circumstances. Again, Molotch and Boden (1985) demonstrate how just 'sticking to the facts' in quasi-legal enquiries can end up by producing meaningless answers (see Chapter 4).

Sometimes, in my own research, without any intellectual intent, I have revealed things opposed to what common sense might tell us. In work I was doing in a paediatric cardiology unit, in the early 1980s, we interviewed parents of children (about their experiences!). Parents told us that one of the things that made their first outpatient consultations so difficult was that there were so many people in the room. This was a very serious occasion which, to many parents, would give their child a sentence of life or death. And it was confusing and intimidating, they said, because of the many doctors, nurses and sociologists present.

We found this quite convincing but used a problematic kind of measure to look at this further. We looked through our tape-recorded consultations where there were different numbers of people in the room and then we counted the number of questions asked by parents. Table 8.2 presents our findings.

Table 8.2:   *Questions asked by Parents and Medical Staff Present*

	Number of consultations	Total questions	Average questions
1–4 medical staff	17	48	2.8
5+ medical staff	23	99	4.3
	Difference significant at .05, x = 5.83, 1 d.f.		

As you can see, our findings went against the common sense expectation that the more people in the room, the fewer questions would be asked. Based on its crude measures, Table 8.2 shows that, in our sample, parents asked more questions when there were five or more people in the room. I won't go into detail about what we made of this. But let me reassure you that we did not say that this meant that parents were wrong. On the contrary, there was evidence that parents were trying to behave responsibly and were appealing to the number of people present at the consultation as one way of depicting the pressures which they were under. The numbers present thus worked not as a *causal* factor in determining parents' behaviour but as something which could subsequently be used to make sense of that behaviour. In a more technical sense, parents' accounts were viewed as situated narratives which worked as moral tales rather than as scientific accounts of their experiences (see Chapter 5, pp. 108–114).

We started to develop policy interventions in relationship to what the parents were telling us. For instance, how could a context be created where parents could display their responsibility to medical staff who, unlike sociologists, could not visit them in their own homes? In due course, at our suggestion, the hospital created an additional clinic which was held some weeks after the first hospital interview. Here children were not examined and parents were free to interview doctors. The intervention was liked by both parents and doctors. Doctors liked it because it provided a good opportunity to get to know families before they were admitted to the ward. Parents said that they felt under less time-pressure because their child did not need to be examined and because, in the weeks that had passed since their first hospital visit, they had time to work out what they wanted to know. Moreover, many mothers commented that they felt that their children had benefited as well because, while their parents spoke to the doctor, they could spend time in the hospital children's play-room. Consequently, the hospital now seemed a less frightening place to these children.

So this is an example of a situation in which sociological research, by resisting common sense, has come up with a practical solution to an everyday problem. I think these kinds of matters have an important implication for social scientific work.

The way I would put it is that we are all cleverer than we can say in so many words. That is, the kinds of skills we are using in everyday settings, like medical consultations, are much more complicated and require much more analysis than we can actually tell the researcher in an interview study. Yet, by working with naturally-occurring material we can make the skills used by all parties more available for analysis.

By analysing 'common sense' in fine detail, research can often make a direct contribution to professional practice. Moreover, the transcripts alone are an excellent resource which professionals can use to examine their own and each other's practice.

I think such research also has an implication for how phenomena can be made available for sociological analysis. Researchers too readily assume that some topics, like sexuality, are private matters to which we cannot get direct access – for instance without putting a tape-recorder under every-body's bed or video camera above it. However, this is an example of unclear thinking.

This assumes that sexuality is a unitary phenomenon that only takes place in a certain kind of setting. Instead, I would argue that most phenomena take place in a multiplicity of settings. Why can't we find sexuality present in soap-operas, in cartoons or, indeed, in how clients and professionals present versions of themselves and descriptions of their partners and activities (see the discussion of Gubrium's work in Chapter 3)?

As I point out in Chapter 9, the problem arises from the use by researchers of essentialist conceptions of social phenomena. Once we are freed from this common-sense assumption, we can proceed to explicate common-sense practices in order to reveal their fine detail.

My favourite philosopher, Ludwig Wittgenstein, made this point for me. He writes: 'The aspects of things that are most important for us are hidden because of their simplicity and familiarity' (Wittgenstein, *Philosophical Investigations*, 1968 para. 129). Now Wittgenstein, of course, is referring to what is hidden from philosophers. But the same issue often arises for social scientists – to whom things can be 'hidden because of their simplicity and familiarity'.

This means that it is often unhelpful for researchers to begin their work on a basis of a 'social problem' identified by either practitioners or managers. It is a commonplace that such definitions of 'problems' often may serve vested interests. My point, however, is that if field research has anything to offer, its theoretical imperatives drive it in a direction which can offer participants new perspectives on their problems. Paradoxically, by refusing to begin from a common conception of what is 'wrong' in a setting, we may be most able to contribute to the identification both of what is going on and, thereby, how it may be modified in the pursuit of desired ends.

Strangely, what we are concerned with in social science is what is closest to hand. However, because it is so close to hand, both participants *and* researchers may often forget about it. Our common-sense knowledge about the way in which the world is organised is being used all the time by us in the everyday world and also to understand our research findings. But rarely do we topicalise that common-sense knowledge. Wittgenstein draws our attention to this paradox.

Sociology and Jargon

To summarise: I have been arguing that the task of social science is not to replicate common sense but to explicate common sense. This gives us a workable response to *The Independent*'s criticism of our work being common sense. Now, if you agree with me, and if the community agrees with me, this provides a defence of the criticism of using 'jargon'. Why shouldn't we be permitted our theoretical perspective, with its associated technical terms, just like any other discipline, provided that we can demonstrate a practical pay-off?

At the same time, I think we need to recognise that the use of technical language confers a responsibility upon us to make sure that the community can see the value of our approach to it. This has been a problem in British sociology. Certainly, during the 1970s, we engaged too much in empty system building, in which grand theories competed with one another but had virtually nothing to say to the community. The unfortunate consequence was that the same community stopped listening to sociology and turned to other disciplines – because they seemed either more practical (social policy) or more prestigious (economics).

In the 1970s, we learned the danger of generating a theoretical machinery which did not actually apply anywhere to the world, but just ground on in its own internal workings. I still worry very much about sociology courses for undergraduates where people are taught a version of sociological theory as purely a history of ideas, turning the subject into simply an intellectual exercise.

By contrast, I tell my students that the only way which you can really understand a theory is if you can apply the theory to explain phenomena other than those with which that theory was concerned. So if you can use Weber, say, not on rationalisation or bureaucracy or capitalism or religion but on (say) counselling, then you may have understood him. As we saw in the Preface (p. x) Wittgenstein suggests that we must throw away the ladder once we have climbed up it.

I think that must be the point of all theory – to throw away the ladder. Ironically, the greatest compliment one can pay theorists is to use their ideas in a different context.

Exercise 8.2

This exercise gives you an opportunity to assess the relevance of the charges made by the critics of social science, namely:

- that it deals with structures which are difficult to change
- that it is often invalid
- that it is relativistic
- that it is commonsensical
- that it uses unnecessary jargon.

1 Select any one article which reports research findings in a social science journal (you may use the same article that you used in Exercise 8.1).
2 Review the article in terms of each of the charges above. Are they appropriate to it? Do the authors recognise such issues? If so, how do they respond to them?
3 In the light of 2, what contribution, if any, does the article make to recognising or handling social problems?
4 How could the study have been reshaped to make a more effective contribution to such problems?

Social Science's Contribution

I said earlier that I would postpone addressing the question of relativism. I want now to tackle it, but not head-on because this would deflect us into a philosophical minefield. Instead, I want to show how social science (and, in particular, field research) can overcome relativism simply by making three contributions to society, namely:

1 Participating in debates about public policy.
2 Providing new opportunities for people to make their own choices.
3 Offering a new perspective to practitioners and clients.

Let me consider each contribution in turn:

Debating Public Policy

The first task, as I see it, is to participate in debates about public policy. Let me take an example which returns us to the issue of patient-centred medicine. In the same cardiology unit which we have already discussed, we also looked at how doctors talked to parents about the decision to have a small diagnostic test on their children. In most cases, the doctor would say something like: 'What we propose to do, if you agree, is a small test.' No parent disagreed with an offer which appeared to be purely formal – like the formal right (never exercised) of the Queen not to sign legislation passed by the British Parliament.

For a sub-sample of children, however, the parents' right to choose was far from formal. The doctor would say things to them like the following:

I think what we would do now depends a little bit on parents' feelings.

Now it depends a little bit on what you think.

It depends very much on your own personal views as to whether we should proceed.

Moreover, these consultations were longer and apparently more democratic than elsewhere. A view of the patient in a family context was encouraged and parents were given every opportunity to voice their concerns and to participate in decision-making.

In this sub-sample, unlike the larger sample, when given a real choice, parents refused the test – with only one exception. Yet this served to reinforce rather than to challenge the medical policy in the unit concerned.

It turns out that this smaller sample was composed of Down's Syndrome children, with an additional mental and physical handicap in addition to their suspected heart disease. Moreover, the policy of the consultant at this unit was to discourage surgery, all things being equal, on such children. So the democratic form coexisted with (and was indeed sustained by) the maintenance of an autocratic policy.

The research thus discovered the mechanics whereby a particular medical policy was enacted. The availability of tape-recordings of large numbers of consultations, together with a research method that sought to develop hypotheses inductively, meant that we were able to discover a phenomenon for which we had not originally been looking. More importantly, from the point of view of our present concerns, the research underlined how power can work just as much by encouraging people to speak as by silencing them (see Foucault: 1977, 1979).

'Democratic' decision-making and 'whole-patient medicine' are thus revealed as discourses with no intrinsic meaning. Instead, their consequences depend upon their deployment and articulation in particular contexts.

So even democracy is not something that we must appeal to in all circumstances. In contexts like this, democratic forms can be part of a power-play. On the one hand, this helps me with this debate with the community because it shows the ways in which sociology doesn't always support common sense.

On the other hand, I am still faced with the charge of relativism because I am treating what many of us would hold to be an absolute value (democracy) as having a variable meaning. However, even the findings of relativistic studies can have a practical relevance.

Two such practical issues arose from the study of Down's Syndrome consultations. First, we asked the doctor concerned to rethink his policy or at least reveal his hidden agenda to parents. We did not dispute that there are many grounds to treat such children differently from others in relation to surgery. For instance, they have a poorer post-surgical survival rate and most parents are reluctant to contemplate surgery. However, there is a danger of stereotyping the needs of such children and their parents. By 'coming clean' about his policy, the doctor would enable parents to make a more informed choice.

The second practical point, revealed by this research, has already been mentioned. Its relativistic stance about 'patient-centred' medicine rightly serves to discomfit liberal doctors wedded to this fashionable orthodoxy. For, as good practitioners realise, no style of communication is intrinsically superior to another. Everything depends upon its context.

The work I was doing in the paediatric cardiology clinic on the Down's parents already suggests one direction in which that debate could take place. Another example, already used in Chapter 7, arose from my research on three cancer clinics in which I looked at the practice of a doctor in the British National Health Service and compared it to his private practice (Silverman: 1984).

This study was relevant to a lively debate about the National Health Service and whether there should be more private medicine. I was able to show that, despite these 'ceremonial' gains, patients overall got a better deal when they didn't pay than when they did pay. So this serves as a further example of how field researchers can participate in debates about public policy.

Increasing People's Options

Field research can, I believe, provide new opportunities which allow people to make their own choices. Our work in the paediatric cardiology unit revealed two aspects of this. First, the study of doctors' decision-making highlighted the need for parents to make their own choices without feeling guilty. Second, the extra clinic that was offered to parents after a first outpatient consultation removed some constraints which allowed all parties to innovate in ways which we could not have predicted.

A further relevant example was the research on the mother talking to a doctor about her worries regarding her diabetic daughter (already discussed in Chapter 4, pp. 121–123). The naturally-occurring material revealed that this mother is not *intrinsically* 'nagging' or 'irresponsible'. Instead, both are depictions which are *locally* available and *locally* resisted. Conversely, if we had interviewed mothers, the temptation would have been to search for idealised conceptions of their role.

Doctors were interested to learn about the double-binds present in their attention to the autonomy of their young patients. Likewise, parents' groups (largely mothers) of diabetic children found it very helpful to go through material of this kind. It brought out the way in which things they may feel personally guilty about in their relationships with their teenage children are not something that relates to their individual failings. Instead, such problems arise in our culture in the double-binds built into the parent–adolescent relationship.

In all these cases, we contributed to practical matters without imposing any élitist form of social engineering. By attending to the fine detail of interactions, we come to respect the practical skills of the participants. The role of the social scientist is not to be more knowledgable than laypeople but, instead, to put an analytic method at their disposal.

Offering a New Perspective

I will take one further example from my own research to illustrate the new perspectives that field research can offer. This allows me to return to the practical implications of the study of advice sequences in HIV counselling already discussed in Chapter 7. As we saw, advice sequences are more effective when they either are requested by the client or derive from a specified client 'problem' (see also Byrne and Long: 1976).

How far can we advance from this barely newsworthy observation? In principle, the practical pay-off of research grounded in the understanding of locally organised practices should be considerably more than work based simply on 'fact-sheet' data (e.g. statistical tables showing correlations between pre-defined variables) and experimental studies based on idealised conceptions of the phenomena in question. But how can we show that our findings on advice-reception go beyond the somewhat trite recommendations for 'better professional communication'?

I will attempt to show how this can be done by moving beyond *how* professionals and clients communicate to *why* they do so in the ways we have discovered. This leads us on to a more conventional address of the constraints on professional–client communication. In doing so, we return to the issue of the social contexts of interaction (already discussed in Chapter 6). Now, however, we will be concerned about the policy pay-off of one way of settling this debate.

In my analysis of advice sequences in Chapter 7 I stayed at the level of verbal interaction. The only social context I was interested in was that locally produced by the participants. Thus I stuck closely to Schegloff's (1991) injunction about the need to identify context in observable features of the participants' activities.

I shall now argue that an understanding of the institutional contexts of talk allows us to move on from such 'how' questions to certain kinds of 'why' questions. As Maynard (1989) argues: 'the structure of the interaction, while being a local production, simultaneously enacts matters whose origins are externally initiated' (139). Maynard goes on to suggest 'combining discourse study with ethnography'. Elsewhere Maynard (1985) has demonstrated how such work can raise questions about the *functions* of communication patterns.

Closely following Maynard, gathering ethnographic data on the clinics where these counsellors work allowed me to address the functions of counsellors' behaviour and, thereby, made possible a constructive input into policy debates.

In short, my argument will be that we can develop the practical pay-off of such research by avoiding the language of 'communication problems' (which imply that professionals are bad at their job) and instead examine the *functions* of communication sequences in a particular institutional context (see also Chapter 1, pp. 17–19).

Let us look at a relevant extract from my HIV counselling data:

Extract 8.1

```
 1 C: so you know it's not hh dead set on ten years hh now there
 2     are other people who could be HIV positive but not actually
 3     develop AIDS as such hh so they could be (.) carriers they
 4     could (.) stay well hh but pass the virus to people that they
 5     have sex with hh this is why we say hh if you don't know the
 6     person that you're with (0.6) and you're going to have sex
 7     with them hh it's important that you tell them to (0.3) use a
 8     condom (0.8) or to practise safe sex that's what using a
 9     condom means.
10 (1.5)
11 C: okay?
12 (0.3)
13 P: uhum
14 (2.4)
15 C: has your pa:rtner ever used a condom with you?
16 (1.0)
17 P: n:o
18 (1.5)
19 C: do yer know what a condom looks like?
20 (0.5)
21 P: (I don't)
22 (0.3)
23 C:(Did you–) (0.3) have you perhaps– (1.0) a condom shown to
24     you (.) at school?= or:?
25 P: no:
26 C: yer didn't alright, =okay hhh
27 (2.0)
28 C: is there anything that yer worried about in terms of yer
29     test if it's done today? (.) would you like the test first of
30     all to be done today?
31 (0.8)
32 P: yeah
33 C: yer would (1.0) ri::ght hh (.) if we do the test today
34     (information follows on how the results of test are given)
```

Here, in lines 1–9, C offers an advice-package which, as in the majority of counselling interviews we have examined, has not been based on a prior specification of P's problem (see Silverman *et al*: 1992). When, at line 10, she gets no acknowledgment of any kind, she pursues one (line 11) and finally gets a minimal acknowledgment at line 13. C now moves into questions about P's knowledge of condoms (lines 15 and 19) which produce material that underlines the irrelevance to P of C's earlier advice. Now C swiftly exits from the whole topic (at line 28).

Extract 8.1 thus shows the potential instability of advice-giving when patients produce material that suggests the irrelevance of the advice to them. Since professionals presumably desire clients to take up their advice, the lack of such uptake would appear to indicate bad methods of communication. So we must pose the question: why do many counsellors organise their advice in this way rather than first eliciting their patients' own concerns and knowledge?

As I have already noted, it is no part of my argument to suggest that these counsellors are short-sighted in avoiding recipient-designed advice. It does not make sense to imply that experienced professionals do not know what they are doing (even if they cannot be aware of all the consequences of their actions). Instead, we might ask, what are the *functions* of giving very generalised advice, without first eliciting clients' perceptions of their problems? We can start to look at this by examining the potential *dysfunctions* of more recipient-designed advice based on careful questioning.

Throughout our corpus of examples, counsellors exit quickly from recipient-designed advice when patients offer only minimal response-tokens or when they display overt resistance. A fascinating example of such resistance is found in two of our Trinidad extracts where patients overtly resist question–answer sequences about 'safer sex' by asserting that the counsellor should not be asking about their behaviour and knowledge but, as the expert, telling them directly.

In this context, we can begin to see the function of how C constructs her advice in this extract. On the surface, it may appear strange that the advice is given (in lines 5–9) in an apparently 'depersonalised' way. Instead of saying something like:

* I suggest to you Sarah that you use a condom with your boyfriend

C, in fact, introduces her advice as follows:

C: this is why we say hh if you don't know the person that you're with

Notice the alternative readings that C thereby creates for the people who are to be regarded as the sender and receiver of the advice: who are 'we'?; are 'you' Sarah or just anybody?; who is 'the person'? These different readings create the possibility that the client can opt to hear what is being said either as advice directed at her or as simply information-about-the-kinds-of-things-we-tell-people-in-this-clinic.

In Chapter 7, I argued that, by constructing advice sequences that can be heard as information delivery, counsellors manage to stabilise advice-giving. A function of maintaining an ambiguous communication format is that the counsellor does not have to cope with the difficult interactional problems of the failure of the patient to mark that what she is hearing is personalised advice and hence to offer more than a mere response-token in reply. For, as we have shown elsewhere, information delivery can be co-operatively maintained simply by the client offering occasional response-tokens, like 'mm hmm' (Peräkylä and Silverman: 1991a). Indeed, C's prompt at line 11 makes remarkable the absence of such a response-token from P despite the 1.5 second slot at line 10.

A second function of offering advice in this way is that it neatly handles many of the issues of delicacy that can arise in discussing sexual behaviour. First, the counsellor can be heard as making reference to what she tells 'anyone' so that this particular patient need not feel singled out for attention about her private life. Second, because there is no step-by-step method of questioning, patients are not required to expand on their sexual practices with the kinds of hesitations we saw above. Third, setting up advice sequences that can be heard as information delivery shields the counsellor from some of the interactional difficulties of appearing to tell strangers what they should be doing in the most intimate aspects of their behaviour.

Exercise 8.3

This exercise offers you an opportunity to address the practical relevance of field research in the context of the conversation analysis skills you learned in Chapter 6. It is based on Extract 8.1.

1 Using any of the concepts mentioned in Chapter 6, attempt a further analysis of Extract 8.1.
2 What does your analysis show that is different from or adds to the analysis given above?
3 Imagine you are talking to counsellors about their work. What kinds of practical implications could you suggest in relation to how they communicate with their clients?
4 Imagine you are talking to people coming for HIV counselling. What kinds of practical implications could your analysis have for them?

So far I seem to be arguing that counsellors are right to use communication methods quite different from those recommended in the textbooks. However, this is not my point. Rather, I am suggesting the following:

1 Researchers ought *not* to begin from normative standards of 'good' and 'bad' communication.
2 Instead the aim should be to understand the *skills* that participants deploy and the *functions* of the communication patterns that are discovered.
3 Communication patterns are only functional within a particular institutional context. Therefore, the researcher's next task is to understand the social context in which the observed patterns operate.
4 The practical import of the research can then be discussed with participants in the light of the relationship between communication and context.

This means that there is no point in suggesting reforms in how practitioners communicate when the social context pressures them in a particular direction. Such an intervention can only be irrelevant and even élitist.

Instead, by appreciating the skills of practitioners, in the context of the demands made upon them, we can open up a fruitful debate about *both* communication and the social and economic constraints on communication.

I will conclude this chapter by an examination of how, by addressing such constraints, field research can make a significant impact upon practical matters. Once again, I will use the example of our counselling research.

Context as Social Structure: Policy and 'Why' Questions

Counselling prior to the HIV-antibody test occurs within at least two major constraints. First, it is dependent upon patient-flow. This produces sudden periods of demand (usually immediately after the latest media advertising campaigns), interspersed with relatively quiet periods. The uneven flow of patients makes it difficult to design an effective use of clinic resources.

The second problem is that pre-test counselling is expected to cover a huge number of topics – from the difference between HIV and AIDS, to the meaning of positive and negative test results, to issues of insurance-cover and confidentiality and to 'safer sex'. The consequence is that, in most English testing-sites, such counselling consists of largely stereotyped 'information packages' and is completed within fifteen minutes (see Peräkylä and Silverman: 1991a). The lack of patient uptake (Silverman *et al*: 1992) suggests that this is not very useful for clients. It is certainly a dull and repetitive task for the counsellors.

The analysis of the transcripts shows both that advice-giving is unstable and that, if advice is given in a personalised manner, it takes a long time. Truncated, non-personalised advice sequences are usually far shorter – an important consideration for hard-pressed counsellors.

I suggest, therefore, that the character of HIV counselling as a focussed conversation on mostly delicate topics explains why ambiguous, truncated advice sequences (like that seen in Extract 8.1) predominate in our transcripts. Clearly, such sequences are functional for *both* local and institutional contexts.

I return to my point about the need to locate 'communication problems' in a broader structural context. Our research has much to say about how counsellors can organise their talk in order to maximise patient uptake (Silverman *et al*: 1992). However, without organisational change, the impact of such communication techniques alone might be minimal or even harmful. For instance, encouraging patient uptake will usually involve longer counselling sessions. Experienced counsellors will tell you that, if they take so long with one client that the waiting period for others increases, some clients will simply walk out – and hence may continue their risky behaviour without learning their HIV status.

Three simple organisational changes might allow counsellors to adopt new, more effective but time-consuming styles of communication. First, central government could keep testing centres better informed of new media AIDS campaigns so that local structures can be more responsive to sudden surges of client demand. Second, testing centres might use an appointment system rather than seeing clients on a walk-in basis. Third, certain of the topics now cursorily covered in pre-test counselling might be just as well addressed by leaflets or, still better, by videos shown to patients while they are waiting to see a counsellor. AIDS counselling might then look more like a service encounter, where the client is encouraged to ask questions of the professional, rather than a sermon.

As our own recent work shows, professionals respond to research which seeks to document the fine detail of their practice, while acknowledging the structural constraints to which they must respond. Put in another way, this means that we should aim to identify the interactional skills of the participants rather than their failings. Although the researcher cannot tell practitioners how they should behave, understanding the intended and unintended consequences of actions can provide the basis for a fruitful dialogue.

Conclusion

Throughout this chapter, I have been arguing that field researchers contribute most by seeking to understand the local functions of talk rather than by directly entering into normative debates about communication styles. Put in another way, this means that we should aim to identify the interactional skills of the participants rather than their failings.

Earlier, I referred to an editorial in the London *The Independent*. I will conclude by a brief discussion of a dialogue in David Lodge's novel *Nice Work*. This novel is about the relationship between Robyn, a lecturer (at the same university as in all Lodge's books), and Vic, a manager in an engineering firm. She has spent some time with him in order to understand the world of industry. This is, of course, very much a document of the 1980s where one version of 'free market' economics suggested that the value of academic institutions is to be judged in terms of their contribution to the needs of industry.

Just before the extract below, Robyn, the cultural studies lecturer, had given a highly risqué reading of the cultural symbolism of a cigarette advertisement. Robyn's semiotic analysis of the advertisement is treated by Vic as a display of unnecessary jargon.

Here is the extract, with Vic, the manager, speaking first:

'Why can't you people take things at their face value?'
'What people are you referring to?'
'Highbrows. Intellectuals. You're always trying to find hidden meanings in things. Why? A cigarette is a cigarette. A piece of silk is a piece of silk. Why not leave it at that?'
'When they're represented they acquire additional meanings,' said Robyn. 'Signs are never innocent. Semiotics teaches us that.'

'Semi-what?'
'Semiotics. The study of signs.'
'It teaches us to have dirty minds, if you ask me.' (Lodge: 1989, 221)

It seems that Vic and Robyn talk past one another. He does not understand what an earth she is doing. And to her, the world of industry seems to be a world with no morality and little sense. However, at the end of the book they do achieve a dialogue between the world of academia and the everyday world. I think such a dialogue, though hard to achieve, should be our aim. In practice, this probably means that both sides will have to give a little. Policy-makers will have to give up their suspicion of research which is not based on statistics and refuses to define its research topic in terms of any obvious social problem. In turn, qualitative researchers will have to demonstrate how their work can be both insightful and valid.

As part of this dialogue, positivistic sociologists will have to give up their belief in the stupidity of common sense ways of acting. But, equally, interpretivist sociologists and some feminists will have to abandon their commitment to the transcendent character of 'experience' – a commitment that I have described elsewhere (Silverman: 1989b) as little short of 'romantic'.

PART FOUR

SUMMARY

9

Six Rules of Qualitative Research

In any text on social research methodology, there is a danger of reducing analytical questions to technical issues to be resolved by cookbook means. I attempt here, with a very broad brush, to raise some of the concealed analytic issues that lurk behind some apparently technical questions like observing 'private' encounters or interpreting interview data. Following Wittgenstein, to whom I return later, a touch of 'hygiene' may be useful in clearing our minds about the nature of the phenomena that qualitative researchers attempt to study.

An interesting case in point is Moerman's (1974) study of the Lue tribe in Thailand. As you may recall from earlier chapters, Moerman began with the anthropologist's conventional appetite to locate a people in a classificatory scheme. To satisfy this appetite, he started to ask tribespeople questions like, 'How do you recognise a member of your tribe?'

He reports that his respondents quickly became adept at providing a whole list of traits which constituted their tribe and distinguished them from their neighbours. At the same time, Moerman realised that such a list was, in purely logical terms, endless. Perhaps if you wanted to understand this people, it was not particularly useful to elicit an abstract account of their characteristics.

So Moerman stopped asking, 'Who are the Lue?' Clearly, such ethnic identification devices were not used all the time by these people any more than we use them to refer to ourselves in a Western culture. Instead, Moerman started to examine what went on in everyday situations.

Looked at this way, the issue is no longer who the Lue essentially are but when, among people living in these Thai villages, ethnic identification labels are invoked and the consequences of invoking them. Curiously enough, Moerman concluded that, when you looked at the matter this way, the apparent differences between the Lue and ourselves were

This chapter is a revised version of a paper entitled 'Six Rules of Qualitative Research: A Post-Romantic Argument' that originally appeared in *Symbolic Interaction*, 12, 2, Fall 1989, 215–230.

considerably reduced. Only an ethnocentric Westerner might have assumed otherwise, behaving like a tourist craving for out-of-the-way sights.

Moerman draws our attention to the nature of representation: its forms and, perhaps, its politics. This means that qualitative research can no longer concern itself with discovering truths which are unmediated by the situated use of forms of representation.

Yet British and American fieldwork still tends to respond, almost instinctively, to two older impulses (Silverman: 1989b). The Enlightenment urge to categorise and count is found in attempts to locate 'tribes' and cultures in classificatory schemes. Conversely, the desire to understand raw 'experience' (usually via in-depth interviews) harks back to the romantic movement of the nineteenth century.

In this chapter, I summarise the main argument of this book in the context of what remains of Romanticism in qualitative sociology. Admittedly, the crasser forms of this perspective are restricted to student essays and to some of the speeches of the British ex-Prime Minister Margaret Thatcher ('there is no such thing as society', she once commented). Nevertheless, professional social science often still responds to the Romantic impulse, particularly in fieldworkers' commitment to the sanctity of what respondents say in open-ended interviews. As we saw in Chapter 5, we are thus sometimes left with the unappetising choice between treating accounts as privileged data or as 'perspectival' and subject to check via the method of 'triangulation' with other observations.

To talk about 'rules' invites charges of simplification, over-generalisation and so on. While much has had to be crammed into a small space, I hope a common thread will emerge which will tie together the preceding chapters. Throughout, I return to the situated character of accounts and other practices and to the dangers of seeking to identify phenomena apart from these practices and the forms of representation which they embody.

Rule 1: Don't Mistake a Critique for a Reasoned Alternative

One of the bad things that happens to some students who take courses in social theory is that they end up being convinced that a whole series of theorists are little more than congenital idiots. Durkheim is a good example of the kind of 'straw man' figure that emerged in some people's imagination. How could anybody seriously assume, for instance, that such an individual act as suicide is a consequence of social structure? Surely, such students feel, no account of suicide is adequate when it depends on the 'distortions' of official statistics and fails to refer to the motives of the actor.

Disconcertingly, however, there are curious kinds of similarities between Durkheim's account of suicide and research by Atkinson (1978) which draws on an apparently opposed theoretical perspective. Like

Durkheim, Atkinson was not interested in psychological accounts of suicide which involve reference to the meaning of the act to the actor. Both Durkheim and Atkinson are concerned with the social organisation in which suicide is embedded – although Atkinson's ethnomethodological perspective locates that organisation in the practical reasoning of coroners rather than in forms of social integration. Curiously, also, neither sociologist would question suicide statistics, although, once again, their reasons would differ. In Durkheim's case, rates of suicide provide him with the social facts that need explanation and official statistics are the only record of such rates. For Atkinson, to question such statistics would imply that you had a *better* way of measuring suicide. This would only make an irony of real social practices (defining the nature of unexpected deaths, collating local and national statistics, recommending policies to reduce rates of suicide, etc.). Such practices should be topics for sociological investigation. So, although Atkinson considerably redefines Durkheim's problematic, he is, in some ways, quite close to his position, certainly in a common opposition to the student critique (see Silverman: 1985, 32–33).

It is also useful to recognise the limited nature of many of the claims of (I suppose we have to say) the 'Founding Fathers' of the discipline. For instance, again taking the despised Durkheim, it is important to note that Durkheim's polemical characterisations of 'society' have primarily a methodological status. We should read him as telling us how it is *useful* to view society, not what society *essentially* is.

Thus, just as psychologists would generally resist turning 'psychological' phenomena into purely neurological processes, so sociologists would usually not want to reduce social phenomena to the psychological dispositions of the people concerned (Durkheim: 1974, 24–25). In both cases, the problem is an uncritical reductionist form of thinking which fruitlessly searches for some more 'basic' level of analysis. Durkheim's solution, with which I fully concur, is to stay at one level of analysis and to see what you can say about data at that level, without seeking to resolve philosophical, or occasionally participants', questions about the 'essential' character of 'reality'. This may seem an obvious point but, judging by what is written in undergraduate examination answers, it does not usually lodge in students' consciousness. A further feature of such answers, at least in Great Britain, is students' general horror of what they call 'positivism'. Now, of course, this term may sometimes refer to certain practices, such as crude quantified 'variable analysis', which still go on and, in certain terms, should be criticised (Blumer: 1956, Cicourel: 1964). But usually students (and some qualitative sociologists) use 'positivism' as a 'catch-all' term which seems to encompass anything they don't like in social science. The problem that then arises is that it does not seem to have a referent, since I cannot think of any contemporary sociologist or indeed philosopher of science who adopts the label 'positivist' (although, ironically, I recently did – Silverman: 1989a).

'Positivism', then, now serves as a term of abuse and perhaps conceals that its critics have no coherent alternative. The status of 'positivism' as a rhetorical device is underlined when beginning graduate students find that they lack the resources to translate their critique into a reasoned research proposal.

Rule 2: Avoid Treating the Actor's Point of View as an Explanation

How could anybody have thought this was the case in social science? How could anybody think that what we ought to do is to go out into the field to report people's exciting, gruesome or intimate experiences?

Yet, judging by the prevalence of what I will call 'naive' interview studies in qualitative research, this indeed seems to be the case. Naive interviewers believe that the supposed limits of structural sociology are overcome by an open-ended interview schedule and a desire to catch 'authentic' experience. They fail to recognise what they have in common with media interviewers (whose perennial question is 'How do you/does it feel?') and with tourists (who, in their search for the 'authentic' or 'different', invariably end up with more of the same). They also totally fail to recognise the problematic analytic status of interview data which are never simply raw but are both situated and textual (Mishler: 1986). Such analytic issues, moreover, are not even touched upon in the elegant methodological 'remedies' of survey research.

If we reduce micro-sociology to the naive interview, we lose much of the thrust of the tradition from which it emerged. As I noted in Chapter 3, you only have to look at interactionist work from the Chicago School in the 1930s and 1940s to see the presence of a much more vital approach.

Using their eyes as well as listening to what people were saying, these sociologists invariably located 'consciousness' in specific patterns of social organisation. As we saw, Whyte (1949) showed how the behaviour of barmen and waitresses was a response to the imperatives of status and the organisation of work routines. The experiences of such staff needed to be contexted by knowledge of such features and by precise observation of the territorial organisation of restaurants.

This issue of the situated nature of people's accounts directly arose in our study of a paediatric cardiology unit (Silverman: 1987). As just noted in Chapter 8, when we interviewed parents after their child's first clinic visit, most said that they had a problem taking anything in. They reported that one of their major problems in concentrating properly was caused by the crowded room in which the consultation took place – as it was a teaching hospital, several other doctors as well as nurses and researchers were present.

Although we could empathise with the parents' response, we thought it worthwhile to go back to our tapes of the encounters they were discussing. As I reported in Chapter 8, it turned out that the number of questions parents asked was directly related to the number of staff present (not inversely related as their interview answers would have suggested).

As is often the case after such a counter-intuitive finding, we found quite a simple explanation. Perhaps when the senior doctor broke off the consultation to ask questions of the junior doctors present, quite unintentionally, this created a space for parents to think about what they had been told so far and to formulate their questions without being 'on stage' in direct eye contact with the doctor. This explanation was supported in another unit where parents also asked many questions after they had had some time on their own while the doctor studied clinical data (Silverman: 1987, 91–94).

This took us back to our interview material with the parents. We were not prepared to treat what they had told us ironically, i.e. as self-evidently mistaken in the light of the objective data. Such simple-minded 'triangulation' of data fails to do justice to the embedded, situated nature of accounts. Instead, we came to see parents' accounts as 'moral tales' (Baruch: 1982, Voysey: 1975). Our respondents struggled to present their actions in the context of moral versions of responsible parenthood in a situation where the dice were loaded against them (because of the risks to life and the high-technology means of diagnosis and treatment).

Parents' reference to the problems of the crowded consultation room were now treated not as an explanation of their behaviour at the time but as a situated appeal to the rationality and moral appropriateness of that behaviour. Similarly, in a study of fifty British general practice consultations, Webb and Stimson (1976) noted how the subsequent accounts of patients took on a dramatic quality in which the researcher was encouraged to empathise with the patient's difficulties in the consultation. A story was told in which a highly rational patient had behaved actively and sensibly. By contrast, doctors were routinely portrayed as acting insensitively or with poor judgment. By telling 'atrocity stories', Webb and Stimson suggest that patients were able to give vent to thoughts which had gone unvoiced at the time of the consultation, to redress a real or perceived inequality between doctor and patient and to highlight the teller's own rationality. Equally, atrocity stories have a dramatic form which captures the hearer's attention – a point which field researchers become aware of when asked to give brief accounts of their findings.

In a certain sense, once again we see how field researchers have come back, in a full circle, to a Durkheimian position. Like Durkheim, Stimson and Webb are rejecting the assumption that lay accounts can do the work of sociological explanations. Neither wants to take the actor's point of view as an explanation because this would be to equate common sense with sociology – a recipe for the lazy field researcher. Only when such a researcher moves beyond the gaze of the tourist, bemused with a sense of bizarre cultural practices ('Goodness, you do things differently here'), do the interesting analytic questions begin.

A parallel issue arose in a study by Gilbert and Mulkay (1983) of scientists' accounts of scientific practice. As they point out, one way of hearing what scientists say is as hard data which bears on debates in the philosophy of science about the character of scientific practice. It is then tempting to treat such accounts as 'inside' evidence ('from the horse's mouth', as it were) about whether scientists are actually influenced by paradigms and community affiliations more than by sober attempts to refute possible explanations.

Confusingly, Gilbert and Mulkay's scientists used both quasi-Kuhnian and quasi-Popperian explanations of scientific practice. Understandably, however, they were much keener to invoke the Popperian ('sober refutation') account of how they worked and the Kuhnian ('community context') account of how certain other scientists worked.

Were these accounts to be treated as a direct insight into how scientists do their work or how they experience things in the laboratory? Not at all, at least in any direct sense. Instead, this interview data gave Gilbert and Mulkay access to the *vocabularies* that scientists use. These vocabularies were located in two very different discourses:

- a 'contingent' discourse, in which people were very much influenced by political considerations, such as institutional affiliations, ability or inability to get big research contracts, etc.
- an 'empiricist' discourse, where science was a response to data 'out there' in the world.

Neither discourse conveyed the 'true' sense of science – there is no more an essential form of scientific practice than there is a single reality standing behind 'atrocity stories'. Everything is situated in particular contexts. Scientists, for instance, Gilbert and Mulkay note, are much more likely to use a 'contingent' discourse in a discussion at a bar than in a scientific paper. So the issue ceases to be 'What is science?' and becomes 'How is a particular scientific discourse invoked? When is it invoked? How does it stand in relation to other discourses?'

Rule 3: Recognise that the Phenomenon Always Escapes

Webb and Stimson, like Gilbert and Mulkay, remind us of the occasioned, situated nature of lay and sociological seeing, saying and doing. In this sense, the link with Durkheim is clearly broken. Given patients' and scientists' skilful invocation of discourses in appropriate social contexts, Durkheim's faith in a stable reality, separate from somebody's seeing, saying and doing, is misplaced. Clearly, the botanist classifying a plant is engaged in a less problematic activity than an anthropologist classifying a tribe.

In both the studies I have been discussing, the researchers disabused us of our common-sense assumptions about the stable realities of particular collectivities. So patients, conceived as a stable phenomenon, escaped the

Webb and Stimson study and scientists, treated as a collectivity having stable goals and practices, also escaped in Gilbert and Mulkay's work.

A paper by Woolgar (1985), in the main concerned with 'artificial intelligence', notes how participants themselves may be reluctant to treat their own activities as instances of particular idealised phenomena. Like Gilbert and Mulkay, Woolgar was interested in the sociology of science. Yet he reports that, when he tried to get access to laboratories to study scientists at work, each laboratory team would uniformly respond that, if he was interested in science, this really was not the best place to investigate it. For whatever reason, what was going on in this laboratory did not really fit what scientific work really should be. On the other hand, the work being done at some other place was much more truly scientific.

Curiously, Woolgar tells us that he has yet to find a laboratory where people are prepared to accept that whatever they do is 'real' science. He was perpetually being referred to some other site as the home of 'hard' science.

Like 'science', Woolgar also found that 'artificial intelligence' (AI), conceived as an indisputably 'real' phenomenon, was also perceived to be 'elsewhere'. As each new test of what might constitute 'real' AI appeared, grounds were cited to find it inadequate. The famous Türing test is now largely rejected because even if a hearer cannot tell the difference between human reasoning and AI, a machine may only be 'simulating intelligence' without being 'intelligent'. Even machines which successfully switch off televisions during commercials will not be recognised as an example of AI since, it is held, this is a response to changes in the broadcast signal rather than in programme content. Hence the search for 'genuine' AI, Woolgar argues, has generated a seemingly endless research programme in which the phenomenon always escapes.

These kinds of studies point to the way in which idealised conceptions of phenomena become like a will-o'-the-wisp on the basis of systematic field research, dissolving into sets of practices embedded in particular milieux. Nowhere is this clearer than in the field of studies of 'the family' (see also Chapter 3, pp. 56–58). As Gubrium and Holstein (1987) note, researchers have unnecessarily worried about getting 'authentic' reports of family life given the privacy of the household. But this implies an idealised reality – as if there were some authentic site of family life which could be isolated and put under the researcher's microscope. Instead, discourses of family life are applied in varying ways in a range of contexts, many of which, like courts of law, clinics and radio call-in programmes, are public and readily available for research investigation.

If 'the family' is present wherever it is invoked, then the worry of some qualitative researchers about observing 'real' family life looks to be misplaced. Their assumption that the family has an essential reality looks more like a common-sense way of approaching the phenomenon with little analytic basis. Finding the family is no problem at all for laypeople. In our everyday life, we can always locate and understand 'real' families by using the documentary method of interpretation (Garfinkel: 1967) to search beneath appearances to locate the 'true' reality. In this regard, think of how social workers or lawyers in juvenile or divorce courts 'discover' the essential features of a particular family. Yet, for sociologists, *how* we invoke the family, *when* we invoke the family and *where* we invoke the family become central analytic concerns. Because we cannot assume, as laypeople must, that families are 'available' for analysis in some kind of unexplicated way, 'the family', conceived as a self-evident phenomenon, always escapes.

The phenomenon that *always* escapes is the 'essential' reality pursued in such work. The phenomenon that can be made to *reappear* is the practical activity of participants in establishing a phenonomenon-in-context.

Rule 4: Avoid Choosing between All Polar Oppositions

The philosopher of science Thomas Kuhn (1970) has described sociology as lacking a single, agreed set of concepts. In Kuhn's terms, this makes sociology 'pre-paradigmatic' and in a state of competing paradigms. As I have already implied, the problem is that this has generated a whole series of sociology courses which pose different sociological approaches in terms of either/or questions.

Such courses are much appreciated by students. They learn about the paradigmatic oppositions in question, choose A rather than B and report back, parrot fashion, all the advantages of A and the drawbacks of B. It is hardly surprising that such courses produce very little evidence that students have ever thought about anything – even their choice of A is likely to be based on their teacher's implicit or explicit preferences. This may, in part, explain why so many undergraduate sociology courses actually provide a learned incapacity to go out and do research.

Learning about rival 'armed camps' in no way allows you to confront field data. In the field, material is much more messy than the different camps would suggest. Perhaps there is something to be learned from both sides, or, more constructively, perhaps we start to ask interesting questions when we reject the polarities that such a course markets.

In my discussion of Rule 3, and in Chapters 3 and 4, we saw how the opposition between 'structure' and 'meaning' is not very instructive in a range of settings including families, tribes, laboratories and coroners' courts.

As I argued in Chapter 5, the same might be said about the analysis of interview data. Does this tell us simply about people's experiences (and thus about 'meaning')? Or are interview responses instances of collective phenomena, such as moral forms and structures of narration? In the latter case, as Durkheimian 'collective representations', interview data tell us about structures. So the field researcher necessarily is concerned with both structure and meaning. Here, as elsewhere, attempts to place fieldwork on one side or another of competing paradigms are misplaced.

Another area in which the 'purity' of particular models may be invoked arises in the decision to use or to avoid quantitative methods. In the British sociology of the 1970s, the word got about that no good qualitative researcher would want to dirty her or his hands with any techniques of quantification. Yet, although many of the criticisms of survey methods in the 1960s were well placed (Cicourel: 1964), so were some of the survey researchers' suspicions about field research. As I argued in Chapter 7, we are all familiar with the case-study report that advances its argument on the basis of 'a good example of this is . . . ' or 'X's comment was typical'. Of course, these are 'good' or 'typical' examples because the researcher has selected them to underline the argument.

Just choosing examples of phenomena stands in the way of both rigorous and lateral thinking. Yet, if you are trying to get some feel about your data as a whole or are actively pursuing deviant cases, it may sometimes be very useful to use certain quantitative measures, however crude they may be. For instance, in the study of a paediatric cardiology clinic mentioned in Chapter 8, I observed that consultations with parents of Down's Syndrome children seemed very different in character to other consultations with parents of children who also had suspected congenital heart disease. To pursue my hunch, I examined closely the form of the doctor's initial question to the parents about whether they saw any symptoms in their child. Simple counting then revealed very nicely the way in which the usual doctor's question ('A well child?' or 'Is s/he well?') was transformed ('How is s/he?') with parents of Down's Syndrome children (Silverman: 1981).

This apparently trivial finding proved to be crucial in an analysis of how primarily 'social' rather than 'clinical' categories came to be central to the formulation of Down's Syndrome children with heart disease. This also tied into the doctor's policy of surgical non-intervention. Moreover, not only was I happier because I could account for all my data, instead of using selected examples, but I was able to do this by counting in terms of the language used by the participants rather than imposing my own categories on to the data prior to counting.

Categories abstracted from the business of daily life usually impose a set of polarities (or continuums) with an unknown relationship to that business. One obvious example of such *a priori* polarised theorising is in the abstract models of decision-making found in the polarity of rational/ non-rational action.

As Anderson, Hughes and Sharrock point out, such models, whether Weberian or social-psychological (e.g. Cyert and March: 1963) fail to address: 'the essentially socially organized character of the discovery, recognition, determination and solution of problems' (Anderson *et al*: 1987, 144).

Using materials from audio-tapes of business negotiations, Anderson *et al* show that the parties focus on problems and their provision of candidate solutions is embedded in how they play with the sequencing rules of natural language. For instance, a transition point to a next speaker or a next topic may not be accepted and so a party can avoid a commitment until more is known of the other party's game. Equally, requests for clarification both buy time and give the ball back to the first speaker in a three-part sequence (clarification request/clarification response).

In turn, these sequencing rules are enacted in the context of a set of 'business' relevances which, as Anderson *et al* show, depend on the display of 'competitiveness' coupled with a form of 'urbane affability' which takes for granted the reciprocity of personal and commercial relevances. Anderson *et al*'s analysis reveals 'what adopting a businesslike attitude to the solution of routine problems means as an observable, interactional feature of daily life' (*ibid*, 155). In doing so, it emphasises our Rules 3 and 4: not only does it reject prior polar oppositions (say, between rational and nonrational elements in negotiation) but it also shows how 'business' disappears as a unitary phenomenon. As Anderson *et al* note, 'business life' is interwoven with social life: the purely 'rational' cannot be filtered out from the social.

Rule 5: Never Appeal to a Single Element as an Explanation

A further parallel beteen qualitative and quantitative work is that multi-factorial explanation is likely to be more satisfactory than explanations which appeal to what I have called a 'single element'. Just because one is doing a case-study, limited to a particular set of interactions, does not mean that one cannot examine how particular sayings and doings are embedded in particular patterns of social organisation. Despite their very different theoretical frameworks, this is the distinctive quality shared by, say, Whyte (1949) and Moerman (1974). A classic case of this is found in Mary Douglas' (1975) work on a central African tribe, the Lele.

Douglas noticed that an anteater, which Western zoologists call a 'pangolin', was very important to the Lele's ritual life. For the Lele, the pangolin was both a cult animal and an anomaly. It was perceived to have both animal and human characteristics – for instance, it tended only to have one offspring at a time, unlike most other animals. It also did not readily fit into the Lele's classification of land and water creatures, spending some of its time on land and some time in the water. Curiously, among animals that were hunted, the pangolin seemed to the Lele to be unique in not trying to escape but almost offering itself up to its hunter.

Fortunately, Douglas resisted what I called earlier the 'tourist' response, moving beyond curiosity to systematic analysis. She noted that many groups who perceive anomalous entities in their environment reject them out of hand. To take an anomalous entity seriously might cast doubt on the 'natural' status of your group's system of classification.

The classic example of the rejection of anomaly is found in the Old Testament. Douglas points out that the reason why the pig is unclean, according to the Old Testament, is that it is anomalous. It has a cloven hoof which, following the classification system, makes it clean but it does not chew the cud – which makes it dirty. So it turns out that the pig is particularly unclean precisely because it is anomalous. Similarly, the Old Testament teachings on intermarriage work in relation to anomaly. Although you are not expected to marry somebody of another tribe, to marry the offspring of a marriage between a member of your tribe and an outsider is even more frowned upon. In both examples, anomaly is shunned.

However, the Lele are an exception: they celebrate the anomalous pangolin. What this suggests to Douglas is that there may be no *universal* propensity to frown upon anomaly. If there is variability from community to community, then this must say something about their social organisation.

Sure enough, there is something special about the Lele's social life. Their experience of relations with other tribes has been very successful. They exchange goods with them and have little experience of war.

What is involved in relating well with other tribes? It means successfully crossing a frontier or boundary. But what do anomalous entities do? They cut across boundaries. Here is the answer to the puzzle about why the Lele are different. Douglas is suggesting that the Lele's response to anomaly derives from experiences grounded in their social organisation. They perceive the pangolin favourably because it cuts across boundaries just as they themselves do. Conversely, the Ancient Israelites regard anomalies unfavourably because their own experience of crossings boundaries was profoundly unfavourable. Indeed, the Old Testament reads as a series of disastrous exchanges between the Israelites and other tribes.

Douglas' account of the relation between responses to anomaly and experiences of boundary-crossing answers the 'why' questions that I discussed in Chapter 8. It can also be applied elsewhere. Perhaps bad experiences of exchanges with other groups (particularly the state and the media) explains why British sociologists for many years divided themselves between warring 'armed camps' (so shunning anomaly)? And again, the less apparent doctrinal battles in North American sociology suggest a more peaceful relation wlth the outside world.

Douglas' study of the Lele exemplifies the need to locate how individual elements are embedded in forms of social organisation. In her case, this is done in an explicitly Durkheimian manner which sees behaviour as the expression of a 'society' which works as a 'hidden hand' constraining and forming human action. Alternatively, Atkinson's and Anderson *et al*'s work indicates how one can follow Rule 5 and avoid single-element explanations by pursuing answers to 'how' questions, without treating social organisation as a purely external force. In the latter case, people cease to be 'cultural dopes' (Garfinkel: 1967) and skilfully reproduce the moral order.

Durkheim's contemporary, Saussure, provides a message appropriate to both these traditions when he reminds us that no meaning ever resides in a single term (see the discussion of Saussure in Chapter 4, pp. 71–73). This is an instruction equally relevant to Douglas' structural anthropology as to Atkinson's (1982) interest in the sequencing of conversation in 'formal' settings. So we can take Saussure's message out of context from the kind of linguistics that Saussure himself was doing and use it as a very general methodological principle in qualitative research. What we are concerned with, as Saussure (1974) showed us, is not individual elements but their relations. As Saussure points out, these relations may be organised in terms of paradigmatic oppositions (Ancient Israelites, British sociologists, etc.) or in terms of systems of relations which are organised in terms of what precedes and what follows each item.

An example that Saussure himself gives shows the importance of organisation and sequence in social phenomena. The 8.15 train from Zurich to Geneva remains the 8.15 train even if it does not depart till 8.45. The meaning of the train – its identity – only arises within the oppositions and relationships set out in the railway timetable.

Let me illustrate the significance of this with an example drawn from a further case-study. Dingwall and Murray (1983) were concerned with how medical staff responded to patients presenting themselves at a British 'casualty' or emergency hospital unit. They note that Jeffery (1979) suggests that patients are typified by staff as either 'good' and 'interesting' or 'bad' and 'rubbish'. The former might be patients who tested the specialised competences of staff; the latter might be patients with trivial complaints and/or responsible for their own illnesses.

Dingwall and Murray argue that Jeffery's polarity inadequately spells out the system of relations in which these labels are embedded. They note, for instance, that children often have trivial complaints for which they themselves are responsible and yet are not usually defined by staff as 'bad' or 'rubbish' patients. Drawing upon McHugh's (1970) treatment of deviance, Dingwall and Murray suggest that casualty staff assign such labels only after assessing whether the patient is 'theoretic' (i.e. perceived to be able to make choices) and the situation is 'conventional' (i.e. that it offers a choice for the patient to make).

On this basis, Dingwall and Murray offer a 2 x 2 table which reveals the staff's decision-making rules. This is set out in Table 9.1.

Table 9.1: *Casualty Department Rules*

	Situation	
Actor	Conventional	Non-conventional
'Theoretic'	'Bad' patients	'Inappropriate' patients
'Non-theoretic'	Children	'Naive' patients

Source: adapted from Dingwall and Murray: 1983

So, in a conventional situation, a patient who does not cooperate with staff is normally defined as 'bad'. Children, however, because they may be perceived as non-theoretic, will not find that such behaviour leads to this label. Similarly, in a situation offering no choice (i.e. 'non-conventional'), patients will be labelled as 'inappropriate' ('theoretic') or 'naive' ('non-theoretic').

Indeed, as Dingwall and Murray show, the attribution of deviance to a patient arises only within one of three 'frames' which shape the perceived clinical priority of a presenting patient as set out below:

1   A 'special' frame sorts out patients according to their perceived moral worth (e.g. as 'bad', 'inappropriate', 'naive' or simply a child).
2   A 'clinical' frame judges patients simply by whether they constitute what staff perceive to be an 'interesting' case.
3   A 'bureaucratic' frame operates in terms of a conception of 'routine' patients, without perceived deviant characteristics or special clinical interest. Such patients get routine treatment.

Just as Douglas discovered that the pangolin's anomalous characteristics were the key to unravelling the social organisation of the Lele, so the anomaly created by children who break rules and yet are not treated as 'bad' patients shows the complexity of decision-making in a hospital setting. In both cases, the importance is revealed of avoiding single-element explanations and of focussing upon the processes through which the relations between elements are articulated.

Rule 6: Understand the Cultural Forms through Which 'Truths' Are Accomplished

In the Preface to this book, I referred to my preference for working with 'naturally-occurring' data. This seems logical if your interest is in the practices through which phenomena like 'families', 'tribes' or 'laboratory science' are constructed or assembled. Despite this, however, many ethnographers move relatively easily between observational data and data that are an artifact of a research setting, usually an interview. In Chapters 5 and 7, I pointed out the difficulties this can create, especially where 'triangulation' is used to compare findings from different settings and to assemble the context-free 'truth'.

However, there are two dangers in pushing this argument very far. First, we can become smug about the status of 'naturally-occurring' data. I have already referred to Hammersley and Atkinson's (1983) observation that there are no 'pure' data; all data are mediated by our own reasoning as well as that of participants. So to assume that 'naturally-occurring' data are unmediated data is, self-evidently, a fiction of the same kind as put about by survey researchers who argue that techniques and controls suffice to produce data which are not an artifact of the research setting.

The second danger implicit in the purist response is that it can blind us to the really powerful, compelling nature of interview accounts. Consider, for instance, the striking 'atrocity stories' told by mothers of handicapped children and their appeal to listeners to hear them as 'coping splendidly' (see my discussion, in Chapter 5, of Baruch: 1981, Voysey: 1975).

There are powerful cultural forms at work in such 'moral tales'. Consequently, the last thing you want to do is to treat them as simple statements of events to be triangulated with other people's accounts or observations. For the fact is that, as societal members, we can see the 'good sense' of such tales. In many respects, an 'atrocity story' is no less powerful because there is no corroborating evidence. It reveals the 'moral work' involved in displays of 'responsible' parenthood, particularly, as in Baruch's study, where that responsibility had to be demonstrated in the context of potentially unintelligible, high-technology cardiac medicine.

Such a perspective derives from two very different but equally neglected sources. Wittgenstein (1968) implies that we should not treat people's utterances as standing for their unmediated inner experiences. This is particularly striking in his discussion of statements about pain (paras. 244–246, 448–449). Wittgenstein asks: what does it mean when I say I'm in pain? And why is it that we feel unable to deny this assertion when someone makes it? In our community, it seems, we talk about pain as if it belongs to individuals. So, in understanding the meaning of someone saying 'I'm in pain' we reveal what our community takes for granted about private experience (but not private experience itself). So Wittgenstein makes the point that, in analysing another's activities, we are always describing what is appropriate to a communal 'language-game'. Just as I have argued that 'the phenomenon always escapes', so, for Wittgenstein, there is no direct route to what we might choose to call 'inner experience'.

A second source for understanding the public sense of interview accounts is to be found in Mills' (1940) discussion of 'vocabularies of motive'. Mills reminds us that, for sociological purposes, nothing lies 'behind' people's accounts. So when people describe their own or others' motives, the appropriate questions to ask are: when does such talk get done, what motives are available and what work does 'motive talk' do in the context in which it arises? As Gilbert and Mulkay (1983) were to argue, many years later: 'the goal of the analyst no longer parallels that of the participants, who are concerned to find out what they and others did or thought but becomes that of reflecting upon the patterned character of participants' portrayals of action' (1983, 24).

Conceived in this sort of way, interview data become a fascinating topic for analytically sensitive case-study work. As I argued in Chapter 8, with a little lateral thinking, it is also possible to derive from this approach practical as well as analytic insights. For instance, given the cultural compunction for parents, particularly mothers, to display their 'responsible parenthood', can this be incorporated into medical consultations?

In the study of the paediatric cardiology unit (PCU), it would have been tempting to follow other researchers (e.g. Byrne and Long: 1976) and to suggest that parents' reported problems derive from doctors' inadequate communication skills. Our analysis suggested, however, that the constraints of the setting and of the task at hand (speedy diagnosis and treatment) meant that the first outpatients clinic had no space for some parental concerns and that, in any event, many parents needed time to come to terms with what they were being told. If time was allowed to pass (when, for instance, parents had faced the questions of other anxious relatives and had consulted popular medical manuals or the family physician) and the family was invited to revisit the hospital, things might turn out differently.

Such a clinic was indeed established at the PCU and the constraints further altered by informlng parents in advance that their child would not be examined this time. An evaluation study indicated that, in the eyes of the participants, this was a successful innovation (Silverman: 1987, 86–103).

Yet at no point had we set out to teach doctors communication skills. So the sociological truism 'change the constraints of the setting and people will behave differently' had paid off in ways that we had not foreseen. People responded to the new setting by innovating themselves, parents bringing their children along to see the playroom and to discover that the ward was not such a frightening place after all.

Conclusion

I hope that the discussion of the policy input of one qualitative study has introduced a positive note into these observations. Reviewing my first five rules, I could not fail to notice the uniformly *negative* form in which they are couched – as if research were all a matter of what you must not do. Of course, I intended throughout to convey a sense of the good things that research can do. I tried to convey this in the examples of successful case-studies and, above all, in my implicit appeal to lateral thinking. If, as I heard somebody say the other day, the world is divided into two sorts of people – those who make such a statement and those who don't – then I am firmly with the latter group.

Perhaps, as Douglas implies, we have something to learn from the Lele. Part of what we might learn is living with uncertainty. Curiously, the critics of such apparently disparate theorists as Garfinkel and Saussure and his heirs have one argument in common. If everything derives from forms of representation, how can we find any secure ground from which to speak? Are we not inevitably led to an infinite regress where ultimate truths are unavailable (see Bury: 1986)?

Three responses suggest themselves. First, isn't it a little surprising that such possibilities should be found threatening when the natural sciences, particularly quantum physics, seem to live with them all the time and adapt accordingly, even ingeniously? Second, instead of throwing up our hands in horror at the context-boundedness of accounts, why not marvel at the elegant solutions that societal members use to remedy this? For practical actors, the regress becomes no problem at all. Finally, like societal members, why not use practical solutions to practical problems? For instance, as I argued in Chapter 7, even sophisticated qualitative analysis can find practical solutions to the problem of validity (counting where it makes sense to count, using the constant comparative method, and so on).

The worst thing that contemporary qualitative research can imply is that, in this post-modern age, anything goes. The trick is to produce intelligent, disciplined work on the very edge of the abyss.

References

Abrams, P. (1984) 'Evaluating soft findings: some problems of measuring informal care', *Research Policy and Planning*, 2, 2, 1–8

Agar, M. (1986) *Speaking of Ethnography*, Qualitative Research Methods Series No. 2, London: Sage

Anderson, R., Hughes, J. and Sharrock, W.L. (1987) 'Executive problem finding: some material and initial observations', *Social Psychology Quarterly*, 50, 2, 143–159

Atkinson, J.M. (1978) *Discovering Suicide*, London: Macmillan

Atkinson, J.M. (1982) 'Understanding formality', *British Journal of Sociology*, 33, 1, 86–117

Atkinson, J.M. and Drew, P. (1979) *Order in Court: The Organization of Verbal Interaction and Judicial Settings*, London: Macmillan

Atkinson J.M. and Heritage, J.C. (eds) (1984) *Structures of Social Action*, Cambridge: Cambridge University Press

Atkinson, P. (1992) 'The ethnography of a medical setting: reading, writing and rhetoric', *Qualitative Health Research*, 2, 4, 451–474

Austin, J.L. (1962) *How to Do Things with Words*, Oxford: Clarendon Press

Baker, C.D. (1982) 'Adolescent–adult talk as a practical interpretive problem'. In G. Payne and E. Cuff (eds), *Doing Teaching: The Practical Management of Classrooms*, London: Batsford, 104–125

Baker, C.D. (1984) 'The search for adultness: membership work in adolescent–adult talk', *Human Studies*, 7, 301–323

Barthes, R. (1967) *Elements of Semiology*, London: Cape

Barthes, R. (1972) *Mythologies*, London: Cape

Baruch, G. (1981) 'Moral tales: parents' stories of encounters with the health profession', *Sociology of Health and Illness*, 3, 3, 275–296

Baruch, G. (1982) 'Moral tales: interviewing parents of congenitally ill children', unpublished Ph.D. thesis, University of London

Basso, C. (1972) ' "To give up on words": silence in western Apache culture'. In Giglioli (ed.), *op. cit.*

Becker, H.S. (1953) 'Becoming a marihuana user', *American Journal of Sociology*, 59, 235–242

Becker, H.S. (1967a) 'Whose side are we on?', *Social Problems*, 14, 239–248

Becker, H.S. (ed.) (1967b) *Introduction to Social Problems: A Modern Approach*, New York: John Wiley

Becker, H.S. and Geer, B. (1960) 'Participant observation: the analysis of qualitative field data'. In R. Adams and J. Preiss (eds), *Human Organization Research: Field Relations and Techniques*, Homewood, Ill.: Dorsey

Berelson, B. (1952) *Content Analysis in Communicative Research*, New York: Free Press

Berger, P. and Kellner, H. (1981) *Sociology Re-interpreted*, Harmondsworth: Penguin

Billig, M., Condor, S., Edwards, D., Gane, M., Middleton, D. and Radley, A. (1988) *Ideological Dilemmas: A Social Psychology of Everyday Thinking*, London: Sage

Blau, P. and Schoenherr, R. (1971) *The Structure of Organizations*, New York: Basic Books

Blissett, M. (1972) *Politics in Science*, Boston: Little, Brown

Bloor, M. (1976) 'Bishop Berkeley and the adenotonsillectomy dilemma', *Sociology*, 10, 1, 43–61

Bloor, M. (1978) 'On the analysis of observational data: a discussion of the worth and uses of inductive techniques and respondent validation', *Sociology*, 12, 3, 545–557

Bloor, M. (1983) 'Notes on member validation'. In R. Emerson (ed.), *Contemporary Field Research: A Collection of Readings*, Boston: Little, Brown

Bloor, M., Leyland A., Barnard, M. and McKeganey, N. (1991) 'Estimating hidden populations: a new method of calculating the prevalence of drug-injecting and non-injecting female street prostitution', *British Journal of Addiction*, 86, XX

Blumer, H. (1956) 'Sociological analysis and the "variable" ', *American Sociological Review*, 21, 633–660

Blumer, H. (1968) *Symbolic Interactionism*, New York: Prentice-Hall

Bourdieu, P. (1977) *Outline of a Theory of Practice*, Cambridge: Cambridge University Press

Brenner, M. (ed.) (1981) *Social Method and Social Life*, London: Academic Press

Brown, J. and Sime, J. (1981) 'A methodology for accounts'. In Brenner (ed.), *op. cit.*

Bryman, A. (1988) *Quantity and Quality in Social Research*, London: Unwin Hyman

Bulmer, M. (1982) *The Uses of Social Research*, London: Allen & Unwin

Burgess, R. (ed.) (1980) *Field Research: A Sourcebook and Field Manual*, London: Allen & Unwin

Burton, L. (1975) *The Family Life of Sick Children*, London: Routledge

Bury, M. (1986) 'Social constructionism and the development of medical sociology', *Sociology of Health and Illness*, 8, 137–169

Byrne, P. and Long, B. (1976) *Doctors Talking to Patients*, London: Her Majesty's Stationery Office

Cain, M. (1986) 'Realism, feminism, methodology and law', *International Journal of the Sociology of Law*, 14, 255–267

Cicourel, A. (1964) *Method and Measurement in Sociology*, New York: Free Press

Cicourel, A. (1968) *The Social Organization of Juvenile Justice*, New York: John Wiley

Cicourel, A. and Kitsuse, J. (1963) *The Educational Decision-Makers*, New York: Bobbs-Merrill

Cuff, E.C. and Payne, G.C. (eds) (1979) *Perspectives in Sociology*, London: Allen & Unwin

Culler, J. (1976) *Saussure*, London: Fontana

Cyert, R.M. and March, J.G. (1963) *A Behavioural Theory of the Firm*, New York: John Wiley

Dalton, M. (1959) *Men Who Manage*, New York: John Wiley

Denzin, N. (1970) *The Research Act in Sociology*, London: Butterworth

Dingwall, R. (1980) 'Ethics and ethnography', *Sociological Review*, 28, 4, 871–891.

Dingwall, R. (1981) 'The ethnomethodological movement'. In G. Payne, R. Dingwall, J. Payne and M. Carter (eds), *Sociology and Social Research*, London: Croom Helm

Dingwall, R. (1992) 'Don't mind him – he's from Barcelona: qualitative methods in health studies'. In J. Daly, I. MacDonald and E. Willis (eds), *Researching Health Care: Designs, Dilemmas, Disciplines*, London: Routledge

Dingwall, R. and Murray, T. (1983) 'Categorisation in accident departments: "good" patients, "bad" patients and children', *Sociology of Health and Illness*, 5, 12, 121–148

Dingwall, R., Tanaka, H. and Minamikata, S. (1991) 'Images of parenthood in the United Kingdom and Japan', *Sociology*, 25, 3, 423–446

Douglas, M. (1975) 'Self-evidence'. In M. Douglas *Implicit Meanings*, London: Routledge

Drew, P. and Heritage, J.C. (eds) (1992) *Talk at Work*, Cambridge: Cambridge University Press

Durkheim, E. (1974) *Sociology and Philosophy*, New York: Free Press

Edwards, D. and Mercer, N.M. (1987) *Common Knowledge: The Development of Understanding in the Classroom*, London: Methuen

Eglin, P. and Hester, S. (1992), 'Category, predicate and task: the pragmatics of practical action', *Semiotica*, 8–3/4, 243–268

Emmison, M. (1983) ' "The economy": its emergence in media discourse'. In H. Davis and P. Walton (eds), *Language, Image, Media*, Oxford: Basil Blackwell

Emmison, M. (1988) 'On the interactional management of defeat', *Sociology*, 22, 233–251

Fielding, N.G. (ed.) (1988) *Actions and Structure*, London: Sage

Fielding, N.G. and Fielding, J.L. (1986) *Linking Data*, Qualitative Research Methods Series No. 4, London: Sage

Filmer, P., Phillipson, M., Silverman, D. and Walsh, D. (1972) *New Directions in Sociological Theory*, London: Collier Macmillan

Finch, J. (1984) ' "It's great to have someone to talk to": the ethics and politics of interviewing women'. In C. Bell and H. Roberts (eds), *Social Researching*, London: Routledge

Foucault, M. (1977) *Discipline and Punish*, Harmondsworth: Penguin

Foucault, M. (1979) *The History of Sexuality Volume 1*, Harmondsworth: Penguin

Frake, C. (1964) 'Notes on queries in ethnography', *American Anthropologist*, 66, 132–145

Frake, C. (1972) 'How to ask for a drink in Subanun'. In Giglioli (ed.), *op. cit.*

Garfinkel, E. (1967) *Studies in Ethnomethodology*, Englewood Cliffs, N.J.: Prentice-Hall

Giglioli, P.-P. (ed.) (1972) *Language and Social Context*, Harmondsworth: Penguin

Gilbert, G. N. and Mulkay, M. (1983) 'In search of the action'. In N. Gilbert and P. Abell (eds), *Accounts and Action*, Aldershot: Gower

Glaser, B. and Strauss, A. (1967) *The Discovery of Grounded Theory*, Chicago: Aldine

Glassner, B. and Loughlin, J. (1987) *Drugs in Adolescent Worlds: Burnouts to Straights*, New York: St. Martin's Press

Goffman, E. (1959) *The Presentation of Self in Everyday Life*, New York: Doubleday Anchor

Goffman, E. (1961a) *Asylums*, New York: Doubleday Anchor

Goffman, E. (1961b) *Encounters: Two Studies in the Sociology of Interaction*, Indianapolis: Bobbs-Merrill

Goffman, E. (1964) *Stigma: Notes on the Management of Spoiled Identity*, Englewood Cliffs, N.J.: Prentice-Hall

Goffman, E. (1974) *Frame Analysis*, New York: Harper & Row

Goffman, E. (1981) *Forms of Talk*, Oxford: Basil Blackwell

Goodwin, C. (1981) *Conversational Organization: Interaction between Speakers and Hearers*, New York: Academic Press

Gouldner, A. (1962) ' "Anti-minotaur": the myth of a value-free sociology', *Social Problems*, 9, 199–213

Greimas, A.J. (1966) *Semantique Structurale*, Paris: Larousse

Gubrium, J. (1988) *Analysing Field Reality*, Qualitative Research Methods Series No. 8, Newbury Park: Sage

Gubrium, J. (1992) *Out of Control: Family Therapy and Domestic Disorder*, London: Sage

Gubrium, J. and Buckholdt, D. (1982) *Describing Care: Image and Practice in Rehabilitation*, Cambridge, Mass.: Oelschlager, Gunn & Hain

Gubrium J. and Holstein, J. (1987) 'The private image: experiential location and method in family studies', *Journal of Marriage and the Family*, 49, 773–786

Gubrium, J. and Silverman, D. (eds), (1989) *The Politics of Field Research: Sociology beyond Enlightenment*, London: Sage

Halfpenny, P. (1979) 'The analysis of qualitative data', *Sociological Review*, 27, 4, 799–825

Hall, E. (1969) *The Hidden Dimension*, London: Bodley Head

Hammersley, M. (1989) *The Dilemma of Qualitative Method: Herbert Blumer and the Chicago Tradition*, London: Routledge

Hammersley, M. (1990) *Reading Ethnographic Research: A Critical Guide*, London: Longmans

Hammersley, M. (1992a) *What's Wrong with Ethnography: Methodological Explorations*, London: Routledge

Hammersley, M. (1992b) 'On feminist methodology', *Sociology*, 26, 2, 187–206

Hammersley, M. and Atkinson, P. (1983) *Ethnography: Principles in Practice*, London: Tavistock

Hawkes, T. (1977) *Structuralism and Semiotics*, London: Methuen

Heath, C. (1981) 'The opening sequence in doctor–patient interaction'. In P. Atkinson and C. Heath (eds), *Medical Work: Realities and Routines*, Farnborough: Gower

Heath, C. (1988) 'Embarrassment and interactional organisation'. In P. Drew and A. Wootton (eds), *Erving Goffman: Exploring the Interaction Order*, Cambridge: Polity

Heritage, J. (1984) *Garfinkel and Ethnomethodology*, Cambridge: Polity

Heritage, J. and Greatbatch, D. (1989) 'On the institutional character of institutional talk'. In P.-A. Forstrop (ed.), *Discourse in Professional and Everyday Culture*, University of Linkoping Studies in Communication, SIC 28; reprinted in Drew and Heritage (eds), *op. cit.*

Heritage, J. and Sefi, S. (1992) 'Dilemmas of advice: aspects of the delivery and reception of advice in interactions between health visitors and first time mothers'. In Drew and Heritage (eds), *op. cit.*

Hindess, B. (1973) *The Use of Official Statistics in Sociology*, London: Macmillan

Horowitz, I.L. (1965) 'The life and death of Project Camelot', *Transaction*, 3, 44–47

Hughes, D. (1982) 'Control in the medical consultation', *Sociology*, 16, 3, 359–376

Humphrey, J. (1970) *Tea Room Trade*, London: Duckworth

Hyman, H. (1954) *Interviewing in Social Research*, Chicago: University of Chicago Press

Jacques, M. and Mulhern, F. (eds) (1981) *The Forward March of Labour Halted*, London: Verso

Jeffery, R. (1979) 'Normal rubbish: deviant patients in casualty departments', *Sociology of Health and Illness*, 1, 1, 90–107.

Kirk, J. and Miller, M. (1986) *Reliability and Validity in Qualitative Research*, Qualitative Research Methods Series, No. 1, London: Sage

Kitzinger, J. and Miller, D. (1992) ' "African AIDS": the media and audience beliefs'. In P. Aggleton, P. Davies and G. Hart (eds), *AIDS: Rights, Risk and Reason*, London: Falmer Press

Kuhn, T.S. (1970) *The Structure of Scientific Revolutions*, 2nd edition, Chicago: University of Chicago Press

Laclau, E. (1977) *Politics and Ideology in Marxist Theory*, London: New Left Books

Laclau, E. (1981) 'Politics as the construction of the unthinkable', unpublished paper, translated from the French by D. Silverman, mimeo: Department of Sociology, Goldsmiths' College

Landsberger, H. (1958) *Hawthorne Revisited*, New York: Cornell University Press

Lipset, S.M., Trow, M. and Coleman, J. (1962) *Union Democracy*, Garden City, N.Y.: Doubleday Anchor

Lodge, D. (1989) *Nice Work*, London: Penguin.

Lynch, M. (1984) *Art and Artifact in Laboratory Science*, London: Routledge

McHoul, A. (1987) 'An initial investigation of the usability of fictional conversation for doing conversation analysis', *Semiotica*, 67–1/2, 83–104

McHugh, P. (1970) 'A common-sense conception of deviance'. In H.P. Dreitzel, (ed.), *Recent Sociology, No. 2*, New York: Macmillan

McKeganey, N. and Bloor, M. (1991) 'Spotting the invisible man: the influence of male gender on fieldwork relations', *British Journal of Sociology*, 42, 2, 195–210

Malinowski, B. (1922) *Argonauts of the Western Pacific*, London: Routledge

Manning, P. (1987) *Semiotics and Fieldwork*, Newbury Park: Sage

Marshall, C. and Rossman, G. (1989) *Designing Qualitative Research*, London: Sage

Mäseide, P. (1990) 'The social construction of research information', *Acta Sociologica*, 33, 1, 3–13

Maynard, D. (1985) 'On the functions of social conflict among children', *American Sociological Review*, 50, 207–223

Maynard, D. (1989) 'On the ethnography and analysis of discourse in institutional settings', *Perspectives on Social Problems*, 1, 127–146

Maynard, D.W. (1991) 'Interaction and asymmetry in clinical discourse', *American Journal of Sociology*, 97, 2, 448–495

Maynard, D. and Clayman, S. (1991) 'The diversity of ethnomethodology', *Annual Review of Sociology*, 17, 385–418

Mehan, H. (1979) *Learning Lessons: Social Organization in the Classroom*, Cambridge, Mass.: Harvard University Press

Mills, C.W. (1940) 'Situated actions and vocabularies of motive', *American Sociological Review*, 5, 904–913

Mills, C.W. (1953) *The Sociological Imagination*, New York: Oxford University Press

Mishler, E.G. (1986) *Research Interviewing: Context and Narrative*, London: Harvard University Press

Mitchell, J.C. (1983) 'Case and situational analysis', *Sociological Review*, 31, 2, 187–211

Moerman, M. (1974) 'Accomplishing ethnicity'. In R. Turner (ed.), *Ethnomethodology*, Harmondsworth: Penguin

Molotch, H. and Boden, D. (1985) 'Talking social structure: discourse, domination and the Watergate Hearings', *American Sociological Review*, 50, 3, 273–288

Mulkay, M. (1984) 'The ultimate compliment: a sociological analysis of ceremonial discourse', *Sociology*, 18, 531–549

Mulkay, M. (1985) *The Word and the World*, London: Allen & Unwin

Nelson, B. (1984) *Making an Issue of Child Abuse: Political Agenda Setting for Social Problems*, Chicago: University of Chicago Press

Oakley, A. (1981) 'Interviewing women: a contradiction in terms'. In H. Roberts (ed.) *Doing Feminist Research*, London: Routledge

Oboler, R. (1986) 'For better or for worse: anthropologists and husbands in the field'. In T. Whitehead and M. Conway (eds), *Self, Sex and Gender in Cross-Cultural Fieldwork*, Urbana: University of Illinois Press, 28–51

Peräkylä, A. (1989) 'Appealing to the experience of the patient in the care of the dying', *Sociology of Health & Illness*, 11, 2, 117–134

Peräkylä, A. and Silverman, D. (1991a) 'Reinterpreting speech-exchange systems: communication formats in AIDS counselling', *Sociology* 25, 4, 627–651　　.

Peräkylä, A. and Silverman, D. (1991b) 'Owning experience: describing the experience of other persons', *Text*, 11, 3, 441–480

Popper, K. (1959) *The Logic of Scientific Discovery*, New York: Basic Books

Prior, L. (1987) 'Policing the dead: a sociology of the mortuary', *Sociology*, 21, 3, 355–376

Prior, L. (1988) 'The architecture of the hospital: a study of spatial organization and medical knowledge', *British Journal of Sociology*, 34, 1, 86–113

Propp, V.I. (1968) *The Morphology of the Folktale*, 2nd revised edition, ed. L.A. Wagner, Austin and London: University of Texas Press

Radcliffe-Brown, A.R. (1948) *The Andaman Islanders*, Glencoe, Ill.: Free Press

Rayner, G. and Stimson, G. (1979) 'Medicine, superstructure and micropolitics: a response', *Social Science and Medicine*, 13A, 611–612

Reason, P. and Rowan, J. (1981) *Human Inquiry: A Sourcebook of New Paradigm Research*, Chichester: John Wiley

Richards, L. and Richards, T. (1987) 'Qualitative data analysis: can computers do it?', *Australia and New Zealand Journal of Sociology*, 23, 23–35

Sacks, H. (1972) 'On the analysability of stories by children'. In J. Gumperz and D. Hymes (eds), *Directions in Sociolinguistics*, New York: Holt, Rinehart & Winston

Sacks, H. (1974) 'On the analysability of stories by children'. In R. Turner (ed.), *Ethnomethodology*, Harmondsworth: Penguin

Sacks, H. (1989) 'Lecture four: an impromptu survey of the literature', *Human Studies*, 12, 253–259

Sacks, H. (1992) *Lectures on Conversation*, ed. G. Jefferson, introduction by E. Schegloff, Oxford: Basil Blackwell, 2 volumes (note: page references in the text refer to each volume in the following format: Volume 1 (1992a); Volume 2 (1992b))

Sacks, H., Schegloff, E.A. and Jefferson, G. (1974) 'A simplest systematics for the organization of turn-taking in conversation', *Language*, 50, 4, 696–735

Saussure, F. de (1974) *Course in General Linguistics*, London: Fontana

Schegloff, E.A. (1968) 'Sequencings in conversational openings'. *American Anthropologist*, 70, 1075–1095

Schegloff, E.A. (1980) 'Preliminaries to preliminaries: "can I ask you a question?"', *Sociological Inquiry*, 50, 3/4, 104–152

Schegloff, E.A. (1991) 'Reflections on talk and social structure'. In D. Boden and D. Zimmerman (eds), *Talk and Social Structure: Studies in Ethnomethodology and Conversation Analysis*, Cambridge: Polity

Schegloff, E.A. and Sacks, H. (1974) 'Opening up closings'. In R. Turner (ed.), *Ethnomethodology*, Harmondsworth: Penguin

Schwartz, H. and Jacobs, J. (1979) *Qualitative Sociology: A Method to the Madness*, New York: Free Press

Selltiz, C., Jahoda, M., Deutsch, M. and Cook, S. (1964) *Research Methods in Social Relations*, New York: Holt, Rinehart & Winston

Sharrock, W. and Watson, R. (1988) 'Autonomy in social theories: the incarnation of social structures'. In N. Fielding (ed.), *Actions and Structure*, Sage: London

Silverman, D. (1973) 'Interview talk: bringing off a research instrument', *Sociology*, 7, 1, 31–48

Silverman, D. (1975a) 'Accounts of organizations: organizational structures and the accounting process'. In J. McKinlay (ed.), *Processing People: Cases in Organizational Behaviour*, London: Holt, Rinehart, Winston

Silverman, D. (1975b) 'Speaking seriously: part 1', *Theory and Society*, 1, 1, 1–15

Silverman, D. (1981) 'The child as a social object: Down's Syndrome children in a paediatric cardiology clinic', *Sociology of Health and Illness*, 3, 3, 254–274

Silverman, D. (1982) 'Labour's marches: the discursive politics of a current debate', mimeo: Department of Sociology, Goldsmiths' College

Silverman, D. (1984) 'Going private: ceremonial forms in a private oncology clinic', *Sociology*, 18, 191–202

Silverman, D. (1985) *Qualitative Methodology and Sociology*, Aldershot: Gower

Silverman, D. (1987) *Communication and Medical Practice*, London: Sage

Silverman, D. (1989a) 'Telling convincing stories: a plea for cautious positivism in case-studies'. In B. Glassner and J. Moreno (eds), *The Qualitative–Quantitative Distinction in the Social Sciences*, Dordrecht: Kluwer

Silverman, D. (1989b) 'The impossible dreams of reformism and romanticism'. In J. Gubrium and D. Silverman (eds), *The Politics of Field Research: Sociology beyond Enlightenment*, London: Sage

Silverman, D. (1989c) 'Making sense of a precipice: constituting identity in an HIV clinic'. In P. Aggleton, G. Hart and P. Davies (eds), *AIDS: Social Representations, Social Practices*, Lewes: Falmer Press

Silverman, D. (1993) 'Unfixing the subject: viewing "Bad Timing"'. In C. Jenks (ed.), *Cultural Reproduction*, London: Routledge

Silverman, D. and Jones, J. (1976) *Organizational Work: The Language of Grading/the Grading of Language*, London: Collier Macmillan

Silverman, D. and Peräkylä, A. (1990) 'AIDS counselling: the interactional organization of talk about "delicate" issues', *Sociology of Health and Illness*, 12, 3, 293–318

Silverman, D., Bor, R., Miller, R. and Goldman, E. (1992) 'Advice-giving and advice-reception in AIDS counselling'. In P. Aggleton, P. Davies and G. Hart (eds), *AIDS: Rights, Risk and Reason*, London: Falmer Press

Simmel, G. (1950) *Sociology*, Glencoe, Ill.: Free Press

Singleton, R., Straits, B., Straits, M. and McAllister, R. (1988) *Approaches to Social Research*, Oxford: Oxford University Press

Slater, D. (1989) 'Corridors of power'. In Gubrium and Silverman (eds), *op. cit.*

Sontag, S. (1979) *Illness as Metaphor*, Harmondsworth: Penguin

Spradley, J.P. (1979) *The Ethnographic Interview*, New York: Holt, Rinehart & Winston

Stanley, L. and Wise, S. (1983) *Breaking Out: Feminist Consciousness and Feminist Research*, London: Routledge

Stimson, G. (1986) 'Place and space in sociological fieldwork', *Sociological Review*, 34, 3, 641–656

Strauss, A. (1987) *Qualitative Analysis for Social Scientists*, Cambridge: Cambridge University Press

Strong, P. (1979a) *The Ceremonial Order of the Clinic*, London: Routledge

Strong, P. (1979b) 'Sociological imperialism and the profession of medicine', *Social Science and Medicine*, 13A, 199–215

Strong, P. (1988) 'Minor courtesies and macro structures'. In P. Drew and A. Wootton (eds), *Erving Goffman: Exploring the Interaction Order*, Cambridge: Polity

Stubbs, M. (1981) 'Scratching the surface'. In C. Adelman (ed.), *Uttering, Muttering: Collecting, Using and Reporting Talk for Educational Research*, London: Grant McIntyre

Sudnow, D. (1968a) *Passing On: The Social Organization of Dying*, Englewood Cliffs, N.J.: Prentice-Hall

Sudnow, D. (1968b) 'Normal crimes'. In E. Rubington and M. Weinberg (eds), *Deviance: The Interactionist Perspective*, New York: Macmillan

Tesch, R. (1991) *Qualitative Research: Analysis Types and Software Tools*, Basingstoke: Falmer Press

Thomas, W. and Znaniecki, F. (1927) *The Polish Peasant in Europe and America*, New York: Alfred Knopf

Turner, R. (1989) 'Deconstructing the field'. In Gubrium and Silverman (eds), *op. cit.*

Voysey, M. (1975) *A Constant Burden*, London: Routledge

Waitzkin, H. (1979) 'Medicine, superstructure and micropolitics', *Social Science and Medicine*, 13A, 601–609

Warren, A. (1988) *Gender Issues in Field Research*, Qualitative Research Methods Series No. 9, Newbury Park: Sage

Warren, A. and Rasmussen, P. (1977) 'Sex and gender in fieldwork research', *Urban Life*, 6, 359–369

Weatherburn, P. and Project SIGMA (1992) 'Alcohol use and unsafe sexual behaviour: any connection?'. In P. Aggleton, *et al*, (eds) *AIDS: Rights, Risk and Reason*. London: Falmer Press

Webb, B. and Stimson, G. (1976) 'People's accounts of medical encounters'. In M. Wadsworth (ed.), *Everyday Medical Life*, London: Martin Robertson

Weber, M. (1946) 'Science as a vocation'. In H. Gerth and C.W. Mills (eds), *From Max Weber*, New York: Oxford University Press

Weber, M. (1949) *Methodology of the Social Sciences*, New York: Free Press

Whyte, W.F. (1949) 'The social structure of the restaurant', *American Journal of Sociology*, 54, 302–310

Whyte, W.F. (1980) 'Interviewing in field research'. In Burgess (ed.), *op. cit.*

Wittgenstein, L. (1968) *Philosophical Investigations*, Oxford: Basil Blackwell

Wittgenstein, L. (1971) *Tractatus Logico-Philosophicus*, London: Routledge

Wolcott, H. (1990) *Writing Up Qualitative Research*, Qualitative Research Methods Series No. 20, Newbury Park: Sage

Woolgar, S. (1985) 'Why not a sociology of machines: the case of sociology and artificial intelligence', *Sociology*, 19, 4, 557–572

Zimmerman, D. (1974) 'People work and paper work'. In R. Turner (ed.), *Ethnomethodology*, Harmondsworth: Penguin

Name Index

Subject Index